SCHOLASTIC

Children's
Thesaurus

John K. Bollard

Illustrated by Mike Reed

SCHOLASTIC REFERENCE
An imprint of
SCHOLASTIC

Art Direction: Tatiana Sperhacke
Book Design: Kay Petronio
Composition: Brad Walrod and Tatiana Sperhacke

Library of Congress Cataloging-in-Publication Data

Bollard, John K.
    Scholastic children's thesaurus / John K. Bollard ; illustrated by Mike Reed.
        p. cm.
    Includes index.
    ISBN 978-0-439-79831-0
1. English language—Synonyms and antonyms—Dictionaries, Juvenile.
I. Title: Children's thesaurus. II. Reed, Mike, 1951– III. Title.

    PE1591.B585 2006
    423'.12—dc22

10 9 8 7 6 5 4 3   07 08 09 10

Printed in the U.S.A.
This edition first printing, July 2006

Contents

Introduction

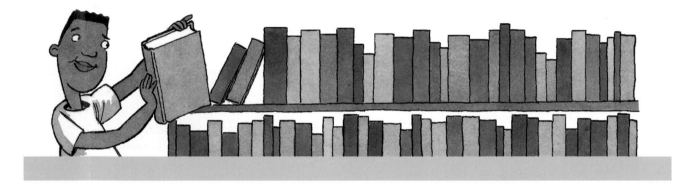

The **Scholastic Children's Thesaurus** is a thesaurus designed for young writers ranging in age from nine to thirteen years. It contains more than 500 alphabetic entries and 2,700 words. Synonyms have been carefully selected, defined, and illustrated in sentence context to give the users of this thesaurus enough information to determine the differences in meaning and use among the words in each entry.

An **entry** is made up of a group of synonyms that cluster around a common general sense or meaning. The headword under which an entry is alphabetized is a simple and familiar word that lies close to the core of this sense. Each synonym in an entry has its own definition. In general, the synonyms in an entry progress from the more common or familiar terms to the less common or more sophisticated vocabulary. In many cases, of course, synonyms may be equally common.

Another important principle of order is provided by the **definitions**. The definitions are the feature that most readily distinguishes the *Scholastic Children's Thesaurus* from other thesauruses. Each synonym is defined in contrast to, or as an expansion of, the headword and its definition. The progression of senses from one synonym to the next can be followed as you read through the entry. This allows the thesaurus user to see more clearly the differences among the synonyms and to make an informed selection.

The defining has been done very carefully to avoid circularity. In virtually all current dictionaries, synonyms are frequently defined in terms of one another. In the *Scholastic Children's Thesaurus,* only the headword is used with any regularity in the definitions of the subsequent synonyms to show how a synonym varies from it in sense.

Synonyms other than the headword are used in definitions only when it is necessary to express a particularly close or direct relationship. No synonym is ever used in a definition that precedes it in an entry. Thus the reader always has all the information necessary for understanding how a synonym relates to the entry.

Example sentences for each synonym illustrate the ways in which the word is typically used. Frequently, synonyms that are closely related in meaning are used in different contexts or grammatical situations. The example sentences illustrate these differences in usage without the necessity of lengthy (or overly dry) explanations. Naturally, not all possible contexts or constructions can be included, but the examples steer the reader toward the type of sentence or usage in which the synonyms fit smoothly and idiomatically.

Tip boxes below the main body of the entry give additional information about the words treated in the entry. This feature allows for the inclusion of a wide range of information that cannot be easily included in the definitions of individual words. In some cases tip boxes list additional terms more specific in nature than the defined synonyms. Some tip boxes point out that the synonyms in the entry are also used as a different part of speech. Others explain differences in grammatical usage, as in the entries for **BROAD**, **ENOUGH**, and **NUMBER**.

Cross-references at the end of many entries direct the reader to a group of related synonyms. This greatly expands the number of synonyms easily available to the thesaurus user.

A complete **index** of all headwords and synonyms in a single alphabetical list makes it easy for the reader to find an entry of synonyms for the word the reader has in mind. The index also includes the cross-references shown at many headwords. These indexed cross-references will help the user to get to the proper entry without having to look up two or three other entries before finding the right word. Also included in the index entries for many of the headwords (listed in capital letters) are **antonyms** that are themselves headwords to entries. This allows the user to expand a search for an elusive synonym by taking an opposite approach to the problem.

These features in the *Scholastic Children's Thesaurus* combine to create a thesaurus that makes available a great deal of information about individual words and their synonyms. The developing writer can draw upon this information not only to learn how to make well-informed decisions about word choice; the information and distinctions in this thesaurus will help to foster an appreciation of the complex richness of the English language. Such an appreciation turns young students into discriminating writers and critical thinkers able to express themselves clearly and with precision.

Using Your Thesaurus

Finding the Entry You Want

Using the headwords: Your thesaurus is arranged in word groups called **entries**. The entries are in alphabetical order according to the first word in the entry, called the **headword**. The simplest way to find synonyms for a word you have in mind is to look for it as the headword of an entry. The headwords are printed in **BOLD RED CAPITALS**. Most entries in the *Scholastic Children's Thesaurus* use one of the most common or familiar synonyms as a headword. For example, if you want to find some synonyms for **nice**, you will find them listed in the entry with the headword **NICE**.

Using the cross-references: Some of the entries in your thesaurus end with a cross-reference to another entry.

These cross-references are printed in **ORANGE CAPITALS** after the word *see*. If none of the synonyms in an entry is the word you want, look up the cross-reference entry for another set of synonyms related in meaning. The entry for **NICE**, for example, includes cross-references to the entries for **FRIENDLY**, **GOOD**, and **GREAT**. This leads you to a total of 23 synonyms. At least one of these will be a more specific or precise word suitable for your writing than the overused word **nice**.

Using the index: In many cases the word you start out with will not be the headword to an entry. If you don't find an entry with your starting word as the headword, you should look in the alphabetical **index** at the end of the book. All of the words in the *Scholastic Children's Thesaurus* are included in this index. Headwords are printed in capital letters.

Let's say you have thought of the word **positive**, but it is not quite the word you want. There is no entry with the headword **positive**, so you look it up in the index. There you will find a reference to the entry **SURE**. When you go to the entry for **SURE**, you see that it includes the synonyms **CERTAIN**, **POSITIVE**, **CONFIDENT**, and **DEFINITE**.

Sometimes you will find more than one reference for a word in the index. If you look up the word **struggle**, you will find references to **FIGHT** and to **TRY**. Choose the reference that is closest to the idea you want to convey and look for synonyms under that entry. Sometimes these references may be closely related in meaning. In this case it is a good idea to check both entries for the best synonym to fit your own sentence. For instance, if you look up **disclose** in the index, you will find references to **REVEAL** and **TELL**. One of the nine synonyms of **disclose** in these two entries should be just what you are looking for.

Some of the headwords in the index are followed by cross-references to other entries with related meanings. These cross-references are printed in CAPITALS after the words *see also*. These are the same as the cross-references listed at the end of the entries and will help you to get to the proper entry without looking in too many places.

SAY . . . . *see* SAY *see also* TALK, TELL

Also included after some headwords in the index are **antonyms**, words meaning the opposite of the headword. The antonyms are listed in *ITALIC CAPITALS*. These antonyms are also headwords for entries in the thesaurus.

MANY . . . . *see* MANY *FEW*

These antonyms can help you to express your idea by finding a word that means the opposite of the word or idea you started with.

Choosing the Right Synonym

Once you have found the right entry, you will want to choose the best synonym for your own writing. Most thesauruses simply list a number of synonyms and expect you to know the differences between them or to find them out by looking in a dictionary. The *Scholastic Children's Thesaurus* gives you much more help than this.

A **synonym** is a word that means the same thing or nearly the same thing as another word. Most synonyms are closely related in meaning, but there are very few synonyms in English that mean *exactly* the same thing or that could be used in all of the same sentences without making a difference to the meaning, tone, or feeling of the sentences. A few examples should help to make this clear:

> **RUN**, **JOG**, **TROT**, **DASH**, **RACE**, and **SPRINT** are all synonyms related to moving quickly on your feet. Each of these words, however, suggests either a different rate of speed or a different sort of running. **RUN** is the most common and most general of these synonyms. Thus you can say *I **ran** all the way home* or *Will you **run** to the store and get some milk?* Neither sentence says anything about how fast or slow the running was or should be. But notice how the meaning changes if you substitute any of the more specific synonyms. *I **jogged** all the way home* suggests that you didn't run very fast; rather, you paced yourself so that you could run the entire way

without stopping. *I **sprinted** all the way home* tells us that you ran as fast as you could and it also implies that the distance was not very great. If someone asks *Will you **trot** to the store and get some milk?*, you wouldn't be in a great hurry, but if they ask *Will you **dash** to the store and get some milk?*, you would put on a little more speed. And if they said *Will you **race** to the store and get some milk?*, you would realize that they need the milk as soon as possible. You can see that the careful choice of just the right synonym can help you to say or write precisely what you mean.

TEACH, **INSTRUCT**, and **EDUCATE** are synonyms that are not always interchangeable. **TEACH** is the most general in meaning: *I would like you to **teach** me French. I **taught** her everything I know about hockey.* **INSTRUCT** refers to a more formal situation and often implies regular lessons: *She **instructs** me in spelling and grammar three times a week.* **EDUCATE** refers to the teaching of a broad range of knowledge: *I was **educated** in the Houston public school system. She lived far from the nearest town and had to **educate** herself.* Notice that you cannot switch these synonyms

without changing other parts of the sentence. For example, *I would like you to **educate** me French* and *I **instructed** her everything I know about hockey* are not meaningful or grammatical English sentences. So as you move from one synonym to another, you may find that you will also have to change other parts of your sentence and perhaps even express your thoughts quite differently. In the first sentence, for instance, you could use **EDUCATE** if you want to suggest the broader range of knowledge you want to acquire: *I would like to be **educated** in French language and literature.*

Using the definitions: Even though two words may mean very nearly the same thing, there are usually some differences that make one synonym work better than another in a particular sentence. Each synonym in this thesaurus has its own definition. If you read through the definitions carefully, you will see that each one is different. In order to decide which synonym to select, you should think carefully about the differences in meaning in these definitions. One good way to decide is to see how each definition would fit into your sentence in place of the synonym itself.

After the headword is defined, it may be used in the definitions of the synonyms. In a few cases, one of the other synonyms may be used in a definition to make clear the meaning of two closely related words. Every synonym used in a definition has already been defined in an earlier part of the entry. Thus if you read an entry from the beginning, you will have all the information you need to understand the differences between the words.

Using the example sentences:

Each headword and synonym is used in at least one sentence that shows the word in a typical use. You will find an example sentence after the ▶ symbol in each entry. These sentences will help you to see how the word is normally used, and they also illustrate the grammatical constructions that they are often used in. Of course, there is an infinite number of possible sentences, and your own sentence may not be like the example sentences at all; but the examples will give you a guide as to how each synonym fits into a sentence.

Using the tip boxes: Some entries include a colored box that contains additional information about the words in the entry. Many of these tip boxes include more specific terms than the synonyms defined in the entry. For example, at the entry for **BOAT**, you will find a list of specific kinds of boats and ships. It is often better to use one of these terms in order to make your writing more precise.

The boxes are marked:

Some of the tip boxes tell you about the grammatical usage of the words in the entry. For instance, the tip box at the entry **FEW** explains how the words **few**, **several**, and **couple** are used in different grammatical constructions.

Other tip boxes point out that some sets of synonyms may be used as different parts of speech, as in the entries for **FIGHT** and **LAUGH**. Some of the tip boxes also give you additional interesting information about the words in the entry.

Using your own judgment: Remember that one of the best guides in choosing a synonym is your own knowledge and sense of the language. First, pick the synonym that seems to you to be the right one. You may change your mind after thinking it over, but in many cases you will have made a good choice. Read your sentence aloud with the new synonym in it. Does the sentence sound correct and does it express your idea well? If you do not think the words sound just right or say just what you want to say, trust your judgment. Check your thesaurus again and you may come up with a better choice.

▶ **ABLE** adj having the power, skill, or ability to do something; skillful or talented ▶ *I was not **able** to lift that big box of books. Are you **able** to read this? We picked the most **able** players for the team.*

CAPABLE able to do something well; skillful or talented but not outstanding ▶ *Of course he is **capable** of cooking a complete dinner. Chris is a **capable** basketball player.*

COMPETENT having the ability or skill to do something well ▶ *Dr. Morris is a **competent** doctor who has worked in this hospital for ten years.*

QUALIFIED having met the requirements or conditions necessary for doing something ▶ *Martin has become a **qualified** welder. If we win the next game we will be **qualified** to play in the state finals.*

▶ **ABOUT** adv almost; fairly close to ▶ *My dad is **about** forty years old.*

APPROXIMATELY in a manner, number, amount, or degree that is nearly the same as what is stated ▶ *She is coming to visit in **approximately** three weeks. The whale was **approximately** the size of a school bus.*

AROUND more or less ▶ *There were **around** thirty of us at the party.*

ROUGHLY without exactness; in a general way ▶ *The builder **roughly** outlined the plan for us before beginning the work.*

The whale was **approximately** the size of a school bus.

n = noun   vb = verb   adj = adjective   adv = adverb   prep = preposition   conj = conjunction   **11**

▶ **ABOUT** prep on the subject of
▶ *Tell me **about** your vacation.*

CONCERNING having to do with
▶ *Have you heard any news **concerning** your lost dog?*

REGARDING in connection with
▶ *I would like some information **regarding** flights to Dallas.*

▶ **ACT** vb to do something in a certain way
▶ *My friend **acted** quickly and rescued me from the icy water.*

PERFORM to carry out an action or a task
▶ *The whole class **performed** well on the test. He loves to **perform** magic tricks.*

WORK to do a task as expected; to do a job ▶ *My solar-powered calculator **works** without batteries. Amie's sister **works** for a boat builder in Maine.*

FUNCTION to act properly or do a task as expected ▶ *I can't **function** when I'm tired. Maria fixed the lawn mower and now it **functions** perfectly.*

OPERATE to function or work, especially referring to a machine or device
▶ *The machine **operates** automatically when you push this button. You can **operate** the controls while I watch.*

see **DO**

Maria fixed the lawn mower and now it **functions** perfectly.

▶ **ADMIT** vb to state or agree that something is true, often reluctantly ▶ *Sonia* ***admitted*** *that she had eaten seven cookies. You have to* ***admit*** *that the view was worth the climb, don't you?*

ACKNOWLEDGE to admit to something, especially something you might have kept secret ▶ *I* ***acknowledge*** *that I could have run faster. Eddie* ***acknowledged*** *that he was scared during the movie.*

CONFESS to admit that you have done something wrong ▶ *I* ***confess*** *to stealing the money from the drawer.*

▶ **ADULT** adj fully developed ▶ *An* ***adult*** *male gorilla weighs more than 300 pounds.*

GROWN-UP like or for adults; not childish ▶ *His* ***grown-up*** *manners make him seem older than he really is.*

MATURE having reached full growth; like an adult ▶ ***Mature*** *sequoias can reach more than 300 feet. I would like him better if he would only act more* ***mature***.

FULL-GROWN grown to full size ▶ *You should train your dog before it is* ***full-grown***.

RIPE ready to be picked or eaten; advanced in years ▶ *Don't pick the tomatoes until they are* ***ripe***. *Uncle Harry lived to the* ***ripe*** *old age of ninety-seven.*

All of these words except **ripe** can be used before a noun referring to a person or an animal: *an* ***adult*** *member of the audience; a* ***grown-up*** *man; a* ***mature*** *woman; a* ***full-grown*** *camel.* **Ripe** is usually used before nouns only when it means "ready to eat": ***ripe*** *bananas;* ***ripe*** *fruits and vegetables.*

▶ **AFFECT** vb to have an effect on, or to produce a reaction in, someone or something ▶ *Jason's accident* ***affected*** *him so badly he was unable to walk for months. How has all this rain* ***affected*** *the tourist industry?*

INFLUENCE to have an effect on someone or something so as to produce a change ▶ *I am not going to let the rain* ***influence*** *my decision to go camping this weekend.*

IMPRESS to have an effect on someone's mind, especially to make people think highly of someone or something ▶ *Charlie's work greatly* ***impressed*** *his teachers. The whole group was* ***impressed*** *by the Statue of Liberty.*

In the most common or frequent uses of **affect** and **effect**, **affect** is a verb and **effect** is a noun. There is also a verb **effect**, which you should not confuse with **affect**. *See the note at* **EFFECT** n.

▶ **AFRAID** adj filled with or feeling fear
▶ *We are both **afraid** of the dark. Don't be **afraid** to tell the truth.*

SCARED filled with fear; afraid
▶ *I was **scared** to tell my mother that I broke her watch.*

FRIGHTENED suddenly filled with fear
▶ *Andrea was **frightened** by a loud crash in the kitchen.*

TERRIFIED filled with terror or great fear; very afraid ▶ *She is so **terrified** of snakes that she doesn't even like to hear the word.*

PETRIFIED so frightened that it is hard to move or do anything ▶ *I was **petrified** when I saw the tornado coming this way.*

▶ **AGREE** vb to say yes to something; to share the same opinion or opinions, especially after settling any differences ▶ *I **agreed** to his plan. Dan and I always **agree** on politics. After a long discussion, we finally **agreed** to sell the car.*

CONSENT to agree to do something; to give permission or approval ▶ *I will **consent** to drive you to the movies if you clean your room.*

ASSENT to say that you agree to a suggestion or request or with an opinion ▶ *Robert **assented** to our proposal that we leave at dawn.*

> **Consent** and **assent** are often used as nouns: *You cannot go on the field trip without the **consent** of a parent or guardian. Phil gave his **assent** with a nod of his head.*

▶ **AGREEMENT** n an understanding between two people or groups ▶ *We have an **agreement** that when I cook, you will do the dishes.*

BARGAIN an agreement in which each side agrees on what they should do or pay ▶ *We made a **bargain** that if I did his chores, he would fix my bike.*

DEAL an agreement, especially one that benefits all sides or that involves a trade ▶ *We made a **deal** to share both the work and the profits. Phyllis got a good **deal** when she traded in her old car for a new one.*

CONTRACT a written agreement between people ▶ *She signed a **contract** with a recording company to produce three CDs in the next three years.*

PACT an agreement to do something ▶ *The two friends made a **pact** to tell each other all their secrets.*

▶ **AIRPLANE** n a vehicle with wings for traveling through the air ▶ *I like to build model **airplanes**. Is that a bird or an **airplane** in the sky?*

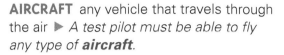

AIRCRAFT any vehicle that travels through the air ▶ *A test pilot must be able to fly any type of* ***aircraft***.

FLYING MACHINE an old-fashioned term for airplane or other aircraft ▶ *The Wright brothers built the first successful* ***flying machine***. *Leonardo da Vinci designed several* ***flying machines*** *that never worked.*

> **tip**
>
> Types of **aircraft** include: **airliner, airship, biplane, cargo plane, executive jet, fighter, glider, hang glider, helicopter, hot-air balloon, jet, jumbo jet, reconnaissance plane, seaplane, supersonic transport, tanker, ultralight.**

▶ **ALERT** adj quick to see things and to act; watchful and ready ▶ *A pilot has to stay* ***alert***, *particularly when flying at night. Because he was careful and* ***alert***, *the nurse spotted the doctor's mistake.*

ATTENTIVE observant and paying attention ▶ *It is hard to be* ***attentive*** *in class on a hot afternoon.*

WIDE-AWAKE alert for opportunities ▶ *The security guard needs to stay* ***wide-awake*** *to make sure nobody breaks in.*

WATCHFUL observant and prepared for action ▶ *Under the* ***watchful*** *eye of my instructor, I learned to ride a horse without ever falling off.*

VIGILANT constantly alert, especially against danger ▶ *The townspeople remained* ***vigilant*** *as the two armies came nearer.*

The security guard needs to stay **wide-awake** to make sure nobody breaks in.

n = noun   vb = verb   adj = adjective   adv = adverb   prep = preposition   conj = conjunction

▶ **ALIVE** adj having life; not dead
▶ *This tree is still **alive**. All of my grandparents are **alive**.*

LIVING alive now; not dead
▶ *Almost all **living** things need oxygen.*

ANIMATE having life, especially animal life as opposed to plant life or to the complete absence of life ▶ *People, mice, and worms are **animate**, while rocks and minerals are inanimate.*

ANIMATED living or seeming alive; lively
▶ ***Animated** cartoons are really a series of rapidly changing pictures. We had an **animated** conversation about money.*

VITAL energetic or full of life; necessary for life ▶ *She has a **vital** personality and is enjoyable to be with. The heart and lungs are **vital** organs.*

> **tip**
>
> **Alive** and **living** are both general terms meaning "having life," but they are used differently in sentences. **Alive** usually comes after the noun it refers to and after a form of the verb *be,* such as *is, are, was,* and *were*: *"This fish is alive."* The adjective **living** is usually used before the noun it refers to: *"This is a living fish."*

▶ **ALONE** adj not with anyone else or anything else ▶ *I like to do my homework when I'm all **alone**. The house stood **alone** on the side of the mountain.*

LONE apart from others of the same kind
▶ *A **lone** tree stood in the middle of the prairie far away from the forest.*

SOLITARY without any companions; single
▶ *She lives a **solitary** but contented life. I took a **solitary** walk along the river. On the bush was a **solitary** rose.*

ISOLATED separated from others; distant or hard to reach ▶ *Polly was kept **isolated** because she had a highly contagious disease. We landed on an **isolated** island in the South Pacific.*

UNACCOMPANIED going without anyone else; without any other instrument playing
▶ *This is the first time I ever walked to school **unaccompanied** by my friends. She wrote a sonata for **unaccompanied** violin.*

SOLO done by one person ▶ *After playing a duet with Bob, Bryn played a **solo** piece. Lindbergh made the first nonstop **solo** flight across the Atlantic.*

see **LONELY**

▶ **ANGER** n the strong feeling of being very annoyed or wanting to argue or fight
▶ *Rachel tried to hide her **anger** from her friends.*

RAGE strong or violent anger, often out of control ▶ *Tom lashed out in **rage** at anyone who spoke to him.*

FURY extreme anger or force ▶ *The boxer attacked with such **fury** that his opponent was taken completely by surprise.*

WRATH very strong anger, especially when accompanied by a desire to punish or get revenge for some wrong ▶ *I could not hide my **wrath** after hearing that the factory was closing, leaving 2,500 people out of work.*

INDIGNATION strong anger, especially when caused by something you believe is mean or shameful ▶ *We were filled with **indignation** when the mayor refused to meet with us.*

▶ **ANGRY** adj feeling that you want to argue or fight with someone ▶ *Eva grew **angry** when the boys started throwing snowballs at her dog.*

MAD very angry (often used with at) ▶ *Phyllis was **mad** when I arrived an hour late. Richard got **mad** at me when I spilled grape juice on his new shirt.*

FURIOUS extremely or violently angry ▶ *Mother became **furious** when someone smashed into her new car.*

UPSET nervous and worried, or slightly angry ▶ *Jill was **upset** because her mother was very late getting home. I am **upset** at you for interrupting me several times.*

ANNOYED feeling slightly angry, especially because of something bothering you repeatedly ▶ *You are making too much noise and I am getting **annoyed**.*

IRRITATED feeling slightly angry or impatient ▶ *I became **irritated** when the phone rang for the sixth time in an hour.*

AGGRAVATED displeased, especially because of some petty or trivial thing ▶ *I became more and more **aggravated** as the water continued to drip all night long*

EXASPERATED angry and out of patience ▶ *I've been working on this math problem all day and I am completely **exasperated**.*

see **CROSS**

▶ **ANIMAL** n any living thing that can breathe and move about ▶ *Worms, insects, fish, birds, and people are all **animals**.*

CREATURE all living beings, but especially all animals and humans ▶ *He loved to study the **creatures** of the sea. The praying mantis is a strange-looking **creature**.*

BEAST any large, four-footed animal; a wild animal ▶ *The prizewinning bull was a large **beast** with long horns. Are there many dangerous wild **beasts** in the rain forest?*

▶ **ANSWER** n 1 something said or written in return to a question or statement ▶ *If you want to come to the play with us, give me your **answer** by tomorrow.*

REPLY an answer to a question, letter, or message ▶ *I sent a **reply** as soon as I got your letter.*

RESPONSE something said or done in answer to something ▶ *When I asked for $100, her **response** was a loud laugh. The fire department's **response** to the alarm was immediate.*

▶ **ANSWER** n 2 the correct number, statement, or action that solves a problem ▶ *I gave the wrong **answer** on three of my math problems.*

SOLUTION the answer to a problem; an explanation ▶ *The detective found the **solution** to the mystery when she read the old man's will.*

KEY a thing that explains or solves something ▶ *The **key** to getting through the maze is to turn right every time.*

▶ **ANSWER** vb to say or write something in return to a question or statement ▶ *When he asked if we wanted ice cream, we all **answered**, "Yes!" I will **answer** your question tomorrow.*

REPLY to give an answer to a question, letter, or message ▶ *Will you please **reply** to her request before Monday?*

RESPOND to say or do something in answer to something ▶ *When my grandmother asks a question, I always **respond** right away.*

RETORT to make an answer, especially a sharp, humorous, or angry one ▶ *"You're so lazy I'll just do it myself!" she **retorted**.*

▶ **APPRECIATE** vb to think well of someone or something; to understand and be grateful for something ▶ *Laurie really **appreciates** ancient Chinese painting. I **appreciate** very much the help you gave me yesterday.*

VALUE to think that something is important ▶ *I **value** Anna's friendship greatly.*

PRIZE to appreciate something very highly ▶ *Juan **prizes** the time he spends with his children.*

CHERISH to care for someone or something in a kind and loving way ▶ *Bradley **cherishes** the time he spent with his great-grandfather last year. Sally **cherishes** her parakeet Sam.*

TREASURE to love something that you have or own ▶ *I **treasure** my independence. Kate **treasures** her memories of living on the island.*

see **RESPECT**

▶ **ARGUE** vb to have a disagreement; to give reasons for or against something ▶ *He is always **arguing** with his sister. Wilson **argues** that air pollution is getting worse in this city.*

QUARREL to argue angrily ▶ *I am tired of listening to them **quarrel** about whose turn it is.*

DEBATE to discuss something by giving reasons for and against it ▶ *Anne and Tom **debated** whether to buy a new car or take a vacation.*

DISPUTE to argue against something, especially in an angry or excited way ▶ *Walter annoyed me by disputing everything I said. Carol called the manager to dispute the amount of her bill.*

tip

Some synonyms of **argue** suggest that an argument is silly or unnecessary: **squabble, bicker, quibble, wrangle.**

see **FIGHT**

▶ **ARGUMENT** n a discussion during which there is some disagreement, often resolved by using logic, facts, and evidence ▶ *The lawyers presented their opening arguments at the beginning of the trial. Carlos and Mike had a brief argument.*

QUARREL a disagreement marked by anger or resentment ▶ *We ruined the game by getting into a quarrel about who should go first.*

DISPUTE a disagreement that involves a clash of opinions ▶ *The two countries have had a dispute over the boundary for many years.*

DEBATE an argument in which opposing views are discussed, often according to a set of rules about how to proceed ▶ *We held a debate about whether or not to adopt school uniforms.*

CONTROVERSY an argument or dispute that has been going on for a long time and that cannot be settled easily ▶ *There has been a lot of controversy about the origins of language in humans.*

tip

Some informal synonyms of **argument** and **quarrel** are **wrangle, squabble, spat, falling-out,** and **fuss.**

He is always **arguing** with his sister.

I **arranged** my books in alphabetical order by author.

▶ **ARRANGE** vb to put things into a proper, suitable, or attractive order
▶ *I **arranged** my books in alphabetical order by author. Michael is learning the art of **arranging** flowers.*

ORGANIZE to arrange things neatly and in order ▶ *Rita **organized** the clothes in her bureau so that she could find things more easily. I need time to **organize** my thoughts.*

SORT to separate things into groups
▶ *Before doing the washing, **sort** the laundry into white clothes and colored clothes. The eggs are **sorted** by size.*

CLASSIFY to put things into groups according to their characteristics
▶ *The librarian **classifies** new books as fiction, nonfiction, or reference.*

▶ **ART** n the ability to make or do something, especially of creating something beautiful
▶ *She studied the **art** of painting for many years. Megan has mastered the **art** of making friends.*

SKILL the ability to do something well, especially something that takes great care and special knowledge ▶ *Ian has developed considerable **skill** in repairing bicycles.*

CRAFT the ability to do a certain kind of work; work or a hobby in which you make things with your hands ▶ *It takes years to master the **craft** of carpentry. Woodwork, pottery, and needlework are all **crafts**.*

▶ **ASCEND** vb to move or go up
▶ *The hot-air balloons slowly **ascended** toward the clouds.*

CLIMB to move or go up; to move up or down by using the hands and feet
▶ *The car slowly **climbed** the steep mountainside. We had to **climb** down a ladder to get out of the attic.*

RISE to ascend; to reach a higher level; to be higher than something else
▶ *We watched the cake **rise** in the oven and grew hungry. The water tower **rises** above the trees.*

MOUNT to get onto something above ground level ▶ *The mayor **mounted** the platform to give a speech. She **mounted** her horse.*

SCALE to climb up or over
▶ *It took the climbers all day to **scale** the cliff.*

▶ **ASK** vb to use words to try to get an answer, information, or something else ▶ *May I **ask** you a question? He **asked** his brother what to do next. She doesn't like to **ask** for money.*

INQUIRE to seek information by asking questions ▶ *We can **inquire** about directions at the post office.*

REQUEST to ask for, especially in a polite way ▶ *May we **request** your presence at our party? I would like to **request** that you remain completely quiet for a moment.*

QUESTION to ask a question or questions of ▶ *Her father **questioned** her about the concert when she got home.*

INTERROGATE to ask questions of, especially in a formal situation ▶ *The lawyers both **interrogated** the witnesses very carefully.*

▶ **ATOM** n 1 the tiniest part of an element that has all the properties of that element; atoms combine to form molecules. ▶ *Everything is made of **atoms**.*

MOLECULE the smallest part of a substance that contains all the chemical properties of that substance ▶ *A **molecule** of water is made of two hydrogen atoms and one oxygen atom.*

▶ **ATOM** n 2 a tiny amount of anything ▶ *There is not an **atom** of unkindness in anything she says.*

BIT a small piece or amount of something ▶ *There are **bits** of bacon in this salad dressing. Could I have a **bit** of help, please?*

PARTICLE an extremely small piece or fragment of something ▶ *We could see dust **particles** floating in the sunbeams coming through the attic window.*

GRAIN a tiny solid piece of something; the slightest amount of something ▶ *I got a **grain** of sand in my eye. There isn't a single **grain** of truth in anything he said!*

see **SPOT**

▶ **ATTACK** vb to use force to harm someone or something; to criticize someone strongly ▶ *The rebels **attacked** the fort at dawn. The newspaper editorial strongly **attacked** the plan to close the city park.*

INVADE to enter with force or as an enemy; to interrupt or intrude upon ▶ *Julius Caesar first **invaded** Britain in 55 BC. Don't **invade** your brother's privacy.*

ASSAULT to make a violent attack with physical force or with words ▶ *A man was **assaulted** last night by three thieves. The crowd **assaulted** the police with shouts and insults.*

CHARGE to move quickly to attack with force ▶ *The soldiers **charged** up the hill to capture the palace. A bull **charged** us when we climbed the fence.*

AMBUSH to make a surprise attack from a hiding place ▶ *The troops were **ambushed** as they marched into the valley.*

MUG to attack and rob or try to rob someone ▶ *My dog scared away the man who tried to **mug** me.*

see **FIGHT, ARGUE**

▶ **AVOID** vb to stay away from a person or place; to try to prevent something from happening ▶ *I've been **avoiding** Elaine since we had an argument. We must **avoid** making that mistake again.*

DODGE to get out of the way of something quickly ▶ *That bully tried to hit me, but I **dodged** the blow and walked away.*

EVADE to get away from something by being clever or skillful; to avoid something you should do ▶ *The fox **evaded** capture by outsmarting the dogs. Roger always tries to **evade** his chores.*

DUCK to lower your head quickly, so as not to be seen or hit by something; to avoid by getting out of sight ▶ *I **ducked** when I saw the ball coming right at me. The celebrity **ducked** the reporters by getting into her car quickly.*

SIDESTEP to avoid or dodge a problem or decision as if by stepping around it ▶ *The politician **sidestepped** the reporter's question about the budget and talked about his trip to China instead.*

see **ESCAPE**

▶ **AWFUL** adj causing fear or awe; very bad, unpleasant, or disagreeable ▶ *It was **awful** to see the damage done by the hurricane. What's that **awful** smell?*

TERRIBLE causing great fear or terror; extremely bad or awful ▶ *The avalanche made a **terrible** noise. There was a **terrible** accident on the highway last night.*

HORRIBLE causing great fear or horror; extremely bad or awful ▶ *It was such a **horrible** dream that I woke up screaming. Mary had a **horrible** trip because she was seasick most of the time.*

DREADFUL causing great fear, dread, or anxiety, especially about what might happen ▶ *We spent a **dreadful** night waiting to be rescued from the flood. I apologize for making such a **dreadful** mistake.*

Mary had a **horrible** trip because she was seasick most of the time.

▶ **BAD** adj a term of disapproval suggesting that something is of poor quality, ill-behaved, undesirable, or displeasing ▶ *It was a **bad** idea to leave my bike unlocked. That was a very **bad** movie. You've been a **bad** dog!*

WICKED morally bad or wrong
▶ *Lying is a **wicked** habit.*

EVIL extremely bad or wrong
▶ *He turned out to be an **evil** tyrant.*

SINFUL contrary to religious or moral principles ▶ *Most religions consider it **sinful** to kill another person.*

MISCHIEVOUS causing minor trouble or annoyance ▶ *She is very **mischievous** and likes to play practical jokes on people.*

▶ **BAND** n a group of people who play music together ▶ *Amie and Josh started a rock **band**. Sophie plays clarinet in the school **band**.*

ORCHESTRA a large group of musicians including string, wind, and percussion instruments ▶ *Alexa and Jessie play violin in the school **orchestra** and Gabe plays the oboe.*

ENSEMBLE a small group of musicians who play together ▶ *She plays flute in a wind **ensemble**. Catrin and her friends formed an **ensemble** to play chamber music.*

tip

Some words for a group of musicians identify the number of people playing: 2: **duet, duo**; 3: **trio**; 4: **quartet**; 5: **quintet**; 6: **sextet**; 7: **septet**; 8: **octet**

▶ **BEAR** vb to take on the burden of; to put up with ▶ *Do you think we can **bear** the expense of a new roof? I can't **bear** the pain of losing my puppy.*

ENDURE to hold up firmly against suffering, especially over a long time ▶ *If the war doesn't end soon, those people remaining in the city will have to **endure** another winter of extreme cold and illness.*

STAND to bear or put up with without flinching ▶ *I can **stand** their teasing, but I won't allow them to make fun of my brother. I can't **stand** loud noise.*

TOLERATE to put up with something or someone ▶ *I don't mind a little noise, but I won't **tolerate** these constant interruptions.*

▶ **BEGINNING** n the point at which something begins ▶ *We arrived late and missed the very **beginning** of the movie. Start from the **beginning** and tell me the whole story.*

ORIGIN the place that something comes from or its cause ▶ *The **origin** of the story is an adventure that actually happened to me. Does anybody know the **origin** of April Fools' Day?*

SOURCE the place where a stream or river begins; the very beginning or cause of something ▶ *We traced the creek to its **source** in a mountain spring. Coal provided a cheap **source** of energy for early factories.*

START a beginning of motion or of some action ▶ *I was in fourth place right from the **start** of the race. After a couple of false **starts** Mitch was finally able to write his essay.*

ROOT the early or most basic origin of something ▶ *"The love of money is the **root** of all evil." Larissa traced back her family's **roots** to the sixteenth century.*

▶ **BELIEF** n the acceptance that something is true, even though there is no absolute proof ▶ *She has a firm **belief** in the basic goodness of people. His **beliefs** are based on careful thinking and a trust in others.*

FAITH belief that does not require proof, evidence, or logical reason ▶ *I have **faith** in my friends and I know they will help me if I need it.*

CONVICTION a strong belief ▶ *I will stand by my firm **conviction** that there is never a good reason for an adult to hit a child.*

TRUST a firm belief in the strength, honesty, or reliability of someone or something ▶ *If you put your **trust** in me, I will make sure that the money gets delivered to the bank on time.*

OPINION a belief based on the evidence and on what seems likely to be true in your own mind ▶ *Don't form an **opinion** before hearing both sides of the story. We need an expert **opinion** to know if this is an antique.*

VIEW a belief that is influenced by your own feelings or bias ▶ *In my **view** this whole afternoon has been a waste of time. What are your **views** on the election?*

CREED a statement of religious belief; a guiding belief ▶ *A **creed** summarizes what people of a religion believe in. Wendy's personal **creed** is to treat other people with respect.*

see **RELIGION**

▶ **BEND** vb to change directions by turning to one side; to change the shape of something so that it is no longer straight ▶ *You will come to our house right after the road **bends** to the left. My injured finger is in a splint so I can't **bend** it.*

TWIST to bend or turn sharply, especially against resistance ▶ *Andy **twisted** the top off the jar. I **twisted** my ankle. The road **twisted** through the mountains.*

CURVE to change direction gradually and continuously ▶ *The driveway **curves** gracefully from the road to the front of the house.*

WIND to move or go with many turns ▶ *We will **wind** up the mountain along a narrow road. This path **winds** through the park toward the lake.*

see **TURN**

▶ **BETWEEN** prep in the space, time, or amount that separates two things; from one or another of ▶ *The car is parked **between** two trucks. Meet me **between** two and three o'clock. I can't decide **between** the blue hat or the green.*

AMONG in the middle of, surrounded by, or in the presence of; with some for each of ▶ *There is a small park **among** the buildings. Kerry felt safe **among** her friends. The money was shared **among** his relatives.*

AMID in the middle of; among ▶ *It is hard to hear you **amid** all this noise.*

> **tip**
>
> While **among** always refers to more than two people or things, **between** most often refers to two, as in the examples above. However, **between** is often used to express the relationship of several things to one another: *Sarah, Dan, and Marie had only a dollar **between** them. It is sometimes hard to tell the difference **between** several synonyms. French, Spanish, and Italian have many things in common **between** them. Just **between** you, me, and the gatepost, I think Justin is lying.*

▶ **BIG** adj of great size, weight, or volume ▶ *It came in a box that was too **big** to carry.*

LARGE of great size, quantity, or amount ▶ *You will need a **large** basket to hold all those apples. I am lucky to have a **large** number of friends.*

HUGE of very great size or bulk ▶ *He is a strong man with **huge** shoulder muscles.*

ENORMOUS extremely big, especially much bigger than usual ▶ *It will take an **enormous** amount of food to feed everyone in the stadium. I've never seen such an **enormous** mosquito.*

VAST extremely big or broad in size or extent ▶ ***Vast** herds of bison once roamed the plains. The distance between stars is almost too **vast** to imagine.*

▶ **BLAME** vb to say that someone or something is at fault ▶ *Why do you always **blame** me when something gets broken? We **blamed** the storm for ruining our hike.*

CRITICIZE to tell someone what he or she has done wrong; to point out the good and bad parts of a book, play, movie, or other work of art ▶ *Dad is always **criticizing** me for spending my allowance too quickly. Will you **criticize** this draft of my essay, please?*

CONDEMN to say very strongly that you disapprove of something ▶ *Dr. Martin Luther King, Jr., **condemned** the use of all violence.*

DENOUNCE to say in public that someone has done something wrong ▶ *The senator was **denounced** in the paper for not helping the poor.*

▶ **BOAST** vb to talk proudly about yourself or someone or something connected with you; to be proud of ▶ *Bryan loved to boast about his sister, who is a state champion swimmer. The school boasts a new computer lab.*

BRAG to boast too much, especially about yourself ▶ *After a week everyone got tired of Alice's bragging about how the team won the game because of her home run.*

GLOAT to think or talk about in a highly self-satisfied or smug way ▶ *He just sat in his room, gloating over his trophy. Annie was taught not to gloat over another person's loss.*

CROW to boast too much and too loudly ▶ *Henry crowed over his victory in the bicycle race.*

▶ **BOAT** n a hollow structure that floats on, or sometimes moves under, the water and is used for transportation or recreation ▶ *My mother always wanted a small boat to sail in on weekends. Many products are sent by boat from China to the U.S.*

SHIP a large boat that sails in deep waters ▶ *The whole family came on a ship from England to New York.*

VESSEL a large boat or ship ▶ *The Calypso is a vessel equipped to study life in the depths of the sea.*

CRAFT a small boat ▶ *Hundreds of small craft sailed out to watch the yacht races.*

tip

There are many different kinds of boats and ships: **canoe, kayak, rowboat, dinghy, racing shell; sailboat, catamaran, schooner, square rigger, clipper; motorboat, speedboat, cabin cruiser, yacht, cruise ship, liner; fishing boat, lobster boat, shrimp boat, trawler; tugboat, ferry, hovercraft, freighter, tanker, supertanker, icebreaker; PT boat, submarine, destroyer, cruiser, battleship, aircraft carrier.**

He just sat in his room, **gloating** over his trophy.

▶ **BODY** n all the parts that a person or an animal is made of; a dead person
▶ *The human **body** needs proper food and exercise to stay healthy. The detectives have found another **body**.*

CORPSE a dead body, especially of a human
▶ *Hikers found the frozen **corpse** of a man who died more than four thousand years ago.*

CARCASS the dead body of an animal
▶ *After the flood, the **carcasses** of many cattle and sheep were found near the river.*

CADAVER a dead body, especially a human body used for medical study
▶ *Students at a medical college must study an actual **cadaver**.*

REMAINS a polite or euphemistic term for a dead human body ▶ *Her **remains** were laid to rest Thursday in Forest Lawn Cemetery.*

▶ **BOSS** n someone in charge of a company; someone for whom people work
▶ *Alice has been the **boss** here since she started the business thirty years ago. I will have to ask the **boss** for the afternoon off.*

CHIEF a person in the highest position or authority over a group of people
▶ *The mayor has appointed a new **chief** of police. Dr. Yoss is **chief** of the surgical staff at the hospital.*

LEADER a person or animal leading, guiding, or commanding a group or an activity
▶ *Tom is the **leader** of the school marching band. The strongest of the hyenas will become **leader** of the pack.*

HEAD the person in charge; a position of honor or leadership ▶ *The president is **head** of the executive branch of the government. Katie is always at the **head** of her class.*

EMPLOYER a person or business that hires others to work for pay ▶ *My **employer** is a very fair man. The paper mill is the largest **employer** in town.*

The human **body** needs proper food and exercise to stay healthy.

▶ **BOTHER** vb to disturb, interrupt, or worry someone, especially with unimportant things ▸ *Please don't **bother** me while I am working. Are the mosquitoes **bothering** you?*

ANNOY to make someone lose patience or feel angry ▸ *The sound of the traffic **annoyed** her for most of the night. I am getting **annoyed** by your constant interruptions!*

IRRITATE to make someone angry or impatient ▸ *It really **irritates** me that he never said "Thank you" for the help I gave him. She was **irritated** by the loss of her glasses.*

TEASE to mock someone by saying unkind or hurtful things ▸ *Shana was always being **teased** by her older sister.*

▶ **BRAVE** adj not afraid; willing to face pain or danger ▸ *It was very **brave** of you to stand up to those boys to stop them from teasing your brother.*

COURAGEOUS having courage; very brave in the face of danger ▸ *Keri was very **courageous** to complete her performance even though she was injured.*

HEROIC like a hero or heroine; strong, brave, or powerful ▸ *The firefighter was given an award by the mayor for his **heroic** rescue of two children.*

FEARLESS without fear ▸ *Elaine seemed **fearless** as she climbed the sheer cliff.*

DARING willing to take chances ▸ *The coast guard made a **daring** rescue of six people from a sinking boat during the storm.*

▶ **BREAK** vb to come apart suddenly; to cause to come apart ▸ *If you drop an egg it will certainly **break** when it hits the floor. I **broke** the handle of the hoe when I hit a rock.*

CRACK to break with a sharp sound, especially without coming completely apart ▸ *The window **cracked** when I knocked it with the ladder, but at least it didn't shatter.*

SHATTER to break into many pieces all at once ▸ *The glass **shattered** on the floor when it slipped out of my hand.*

SMASH to break or crush violently or with a loud noise ▸ *I tried to crack open a walnut with a hammer, but I hit it too hard and **smashed** it.*

FRACTURE to break or crack ▸ *Margaret **fractured** her wrist when she fell on the ice.*

SPLIT to divide or break apart, especially lengthwise ▸ *After cutting down the trees we had to **split** the logs for firewood.*

► **BRIGHT** adj giving off or reflecting a lot of light ► *We could see the **bright** lights of the city from many miles away as we flew into the airport.*

BRILLIANT very bright; sparkling ► *That is the most **brilliant** diamond I have ever seen.*

GLOWING giving off a steady light or heat ► *I like to watch the embers of the campfire **glowing** in the darkness.*

SHINY polished and smooth enough to reflect light ► *She found a **shiny** new penny in the grass. I like wearing **shiny** new shoes.*

RADIANT giving off or seeming to give off its own light ► *The artist captured the effect of a **radiant** sunset across the harbor. I was struck by her **radiant** smile.*

SUNNY full of sunshine ► *I love the hot, **sunny** afternoons in July.*

GLARING shining with a light that is too bright to be looked at comfortably ► *The cat stood motionless in the **glaring** headlights of the car.*

► **BRING** vb to carry, move, or lead something toward the speaker or along with you ► ***Bring** your bike here and I'll try to fix it. Let's **bring** some games to play in the evenings during vacation.*

TAKE to carry, move, or lead something away from the speaker or along with you ► ***Take** your dishes into the kitchen. Will you **take** these letters to the post office for me?*

FETCH to go after and bring back something or someone ► *I taught my dog to **fetch** a stick when I throw one into the water. Will you **fetch** my glasses from the desk?*

► **BROAD** adj extending a great distance from side to side ► *Richard is six feet tall and has **broad** shoulders. The current is not very swift in this **broad** stretch of the river.*

WIDE having a certain distance from one side to the other; large from side to side ► *The lake is twelve miles long and two miles **wide**. Use a jar with a **wide** mouth.*

tip

Broad and **wide** are close synonyms that both refer to the distance across something, as in *a broad street* or *a wide street*. However, **broad** suggests the whole area or expanse of the surface itself and **wide** stresses more the distance from one side to the other. If you want to give the actual distance, use **wide**: *three feet **wide**.*

▶ **BUG** n any small creeping or crawling creature with no backbone ▶ *The cabin had been empty for three years and was full of **bugs**. Dozens of **bugs** and moths were flying around the light.*

INSECT a small creature with three pairs of legs, one or two pairs of wings, three main sections to its body, and no backbone ▶ *There are thousands of different species of **insects**.*

BEETLE an insect with a pair of hard front wings that protect the soft flying wings folded underneath ▶ *You will have to work hard to keep the **beetles** from destroying the vegetables in your garden.*

SPIDER a small animal with eight legs, no wings, and a body divided into two parts. ▶ *Many **spiders** spin webs to trap food. We watched a tiny **spider** build a large web among the flowers.*

▶ **BUILD** vb to make by putting together materials or parts ▶ *Henry **builds** canoes by hand with real birch bark. A lawyer tries to **build** a case from the known evidence.*

CONSTRUCT to build by putting parts together in the proper order ▶ *Hornets **construct** their nests gradually, layer by layer.*

ERECT to raise or build something, such as a building, from the bottom up ▶ *The Empire State Building was **erected** in 1931. The town decided to **erect** a statue of Sojourner Truth.*

There are thousands of different species of **insects**.

▶ = example

ASSEMBLE to gather and put together the parts ▶ *I **assembled** this bicycle myself, without any help.*

see FORM, INVENT, MAKE

▶ **BULK** n the great size or weight of something; the largest part or portion of something ▶ *We were surprised by the **bulk** of the dresser. The **bulk** of her money is in the bank.*

MASS a large quantity of matter, often with no particular shape; a large number of people or things together ▶ *An immense **mass** of snow had blocked the road over the mountain. A great **mass** of people gathered in the street.*

VOLUME the amount of space taken up by a three-dimensional object; a moving or flowing quantity ▶ *To figure out the **volume** of a cube, multiply the height by its width and then by its length. A **volume** of smoke drifted by.*

▶ **BURN** vb to be on fire; to damage or be damaged by fire ▶ *The logs **burned** brightly in the fireplace. The lightning started a fire that **burned** down one hundred acres of forest.*

BLAZE to burn fiercely ▶ *The bonfire **blazed** brightly in the darkness.*

FLARE to burn with sudden brightness ▶ *The campfire **flared** up when I spilled grease on it.*

INCINERATE to burn completely ▶ *All of his books were **incinerated** in the fire, and not one was saved.*

SCORCH to burn slightly on the surface ▶ *I **scorched** my new shirt while I was ironing it.*

SINGE to burn slightly, without flames ▶ *Her hair was **singed** when she got too near the stove.*

We were surprised by the **bulk** of the dresser.

n = noun vb = verb adj = adjective adv = adverb prep = preposition conj = conjunction

GLOW to give a steady light without flames ▶ *The hot coals **glowed** as the fire died down.*

▶ **BUSINESS** n 1 the buying and selling of goods and services ▶ ***Business** was very good in September. The two friends quit their jobs and went into **business** for themselves.*

INDUSTRY the companies and activities involved in making things for sale ▶ *The typewriter **industry** has lost its business to the computer **industry**.*

COMMERCE all the activities connected with business ▶ *The ancient Romans engaged in **commerce** with neighboring peoples.*

▶ **BUSINESS** n 2 a type of work ▶ *Alison is in the music **business**.*

OCCUPATION a person's job ▶ *When I asked her **occupation**, she said she was a police officer.*

CAREER the work or series of jobs that a person has over a long period of time ▶ *Ms. Anderson has had a long **career** in teaching.*

PROFESSION a type of work that needs special training or education ▶ *Alicia is studying in college to prepare herself for the medical **profession**.*

▶ **BUSINESS** n 3 a person or group of people who make and sell products or perform services ▶ *Dad runs his own car repair **business**.*

FIRM a partnership of two or more people in business together ▶ *He started working in a large law **firm**.*

COMPANY a group associated in a business or for some other purpose ▶ *They started a restaurant supply **company**. I'm a member of a theater **company**.*

▶ **BUT** conj on the other hand; on the contrary ▶ *He may be handsome, **but** he's not very friendly. I am old, **but** you are young.*

HOWEVER even so; in spite of that ▶ *It's very cold; **however**, we still plan to go.*

ALTHOUGH in spite of the fact that ▶ ***Although** it was raining, we all enjoyed ourselves. Lulu is only nine, **although** she seems older.*

THOUGH in spite of the fact that ▶ *I'm still hungry even **though** I just had breakfast. You wrote a good report, **though** you could have put in more details.*

YET but or however ▶ *Celia studied hard **yet** didn't pass the exam.*

EXCEPT but for the fact that ▶ *I would have won the race **except** I tripped and fell down.*

▶ **BUT** prep with the exception of; other than ▶ *We've chosen everyone **but** him. There is no road to riches **but** hard work.*

EXCEPT apart from ▶ *Everyone **except** Hannah went home.*

▶ **CALL** vb to speak or shout loudly; to order or ask a person or an animal to come ▶ *We each answered "Here" as the teacher **called** our names. Will you **call** your brother in for dinner, please? **Call** the cat!*

SUMMON to formally call or request someone to come ▶ ***Summon** the next witness, please. They were **summoned** to the principal's office.*

INVITE to courteously request someone to do something or go somewhere, leaving them to decide whether or not to do it ▶ *I would like to **invite** you to a party next weekend. May I **invite** her to join our game?*

▶ **CALM** adj quiet and not troubled or excited ▶ *The passengers remained **calm** when the train stopped in the tunnel.*

PEACEFUL calm, quiet, and free from trouble or war ▶ *We spent a **peaceful** afternoon canoeing on the lake. The city is **peaceful** now that a treaty has been signed.*

SERENE calm and at peace ▶ *She remained **serene** while the reporters shouted questions at her.*

TRANQUIL quiet, still, and undisturbed ▶ *The lake became **tranquil** as the storm passed and evening fell.*

PLACID calm in nature or appearance ▶ *He was a **placid** child who never caused trouble.*

see QUIET

She remained **serene** while the reporters shouted questions at her.

n = noun   vb = verb   adj = adjective   adv = adverb   prep = preposition   conj = conjunction

▶ **CAREFUL** adj paying close attention when you are doing something, so that you avoid mistakes or injuries ▶ *I tried to be* **careful** *during the math test. I was very* **careful** *as I walked down the icy steps.*

PAINSTAKING taking great care while you are doing something ▶ *Scientists conduct* **painstaking** *research to make sure their findings are accurate.*

THOROUGH doing something carefully and completely without missing anything ▶ *After the smoke cleared, the firefighters made a* **thorough** *search to make sure nothing was left burning.*

EXACT doing something correctly and accurately, with great attention to detail ▶ *The carpenter made* **exact** *measurements of the space where the bookshelves will go.*

ACCURATE truthful and detailed, without any mistake ▶ *Make sure you give an* **accurate** *description of the accident.*

▶ **CARRY** vb to hold something and move it ▶ *Will you please* **carry** *these groceries for your grandmother?*

BEAR to hold up or support whether moving or not; to carry ▶ *The roof can't* **bear** *the weight of all this snow. Can you* **bear** *this load up the mountain in your backpack?*

TRANSPORT to carry from one place to another over a long distance ▶ *New cars are* **transported** *by train and ship from the factory to dealers all around the country.*

CONVEY to carry from one place to another in a continuous flow; to deliver or communicate ▶ *Telephone signals are* **conveyed** *by wires, cables, and satellite. Devon* **conveyed** *the message to her parents.*

PACK to carry on foot, especially on your back, or on an animal's back ▶ *We* **packed** *our equipment by donkey to the camp at the base of the mountain.*

HAUL to carry or transport in a vehicle; to pull a heavy load ▶ *Fresh produce is* **hauled** *to the supermarket by truck every day. We* **hauled** *the sack of potatoes into the shed.*

TAKE to move, carry, or remove something ▶ ***Take*** *your plate into the kitchen. Will you* **take** *these letters to the post office, please?*

▶ **CASTLE** n a large building, often surrounded by a thick wall and a moat ▶ *The earl built a* **castle** *to protect his lands.*

FORT a strong building or buildings used for military defense ▶ *The army built a series of* **forts** *along the river.*

STRONGHOLD a place with strong defenses ▶ *The rebels had a* **stronghold** *in the mountains.*

PALACE a large, splendid house for a king, queen, ruler, or other important person ▶ *The presidential* **palace** *contains many fine works of art.*

▶ **CATCH** vb to take hold or get hold of something, especially if it is moving ▶ *Megan* **caught** *the ball and threw it to first base.*

CAPTURE to take hold or get hold of something by force or skill
▶ *The thieves were* **captured** *after a long search. This painting* **captures** *the effect of sunlight on water.*

TRAP to catch by using a device or a trick
▶ *We had to* **trap** *the skunk and let it loose in the woods. Sharon told so many lies that she finally* **trapped** *herself.*

SNATCH to grab hold of something suddenly
▶ *Phyllis* **snatched** *the book right out of my hand as I was reading it.*

ARREST to take into official custody; to bring to a stop ▶ *The police will* **arrest** *anyone caught stealing. Polio was* **arrested** *by the discovery of a vaccine.*

see **SEIZE**

▶ **CAVE** n a large hole underground or in the side of a hill or cliff ▶ *This is a picture of prehistoric paintings in a* **cave** *in Spain. A spelunker is a person who likes to explore* **caves**.

CAVERN a large cave ▶ *The narrow passageway opened into a large* **cavern**.

TUNNEL a passage built beneath the ground or water or through a mountain for use by vehicles ▶ *There are several* **tunnels** *from New York City to New Jersey.*

BURROW a tunnel or hole in the ground made or used by an animal ▶ *We discovered a woodchuck* **burrow** *on the side of the hill.*

▶ **CELEBRATE** vb to do something enjoyable on a special occasion; to honor or remember by doing something special
▶ *We* **celebrated** *her birthday with a surprise party. Susie and Chris are* **celebrating** *their fifth anniversary.*

OBSERVE to celebrate an occasion or holiday in a customary way ▶ *A Seder is a feast during which Jews around the world* **observe** *the beginning of Passover.*

COMMEMORATE to do something special to honor and remember a person or event
▶ *This statue* **commemorates** *the end of the war. On July 4th we* **commemorate** *the country's independence.*

KEEP to celebrate with the proper ceremonies or behavior ▶ *They* **keep** *the Sabbath with family prayers and by going to services.*

▶ **CEREMONY** n formal actions performed in order to mark an important occasion
▶ *The wedding* **ceremony** *was held in a beautiful garden.*

SERVICE a religious ceremony or meeting
▶ *Church* **services** *are held every Sunday at eight and ten.*

RITUAL a set of actions that is always performed in the same way as part of a religious ceremony or social custom
▶ *A bar mitzvah is an important Jewish* **ritual**.

RITE a formal act or set of actions performed according to certain rules or custom
▶ *He was buried according to the usual burial* **rites** *of his religion.*

CHANGE vb to make different
▸ *A chameleon **changes** color according to its background. I **changed** my mind about him.*

VARY to give variety to; to make different from something else ▸ *I like to **vary** my routine so that I don't have to do the same things at the same time every day.*

ALTER to change part of
▸ *Can you **alter** this coat so that it will fit?*

TRANSFORM to change the form or appearance of ▸ *Edison invented a way to **transform** electricity into light. That new hairdo completely **transforms** her appearance.*

CONVERT to change from one belief or function to another ▸ *After careful thought she **converted** to Judaism. We want to **convert** the attic into a bedroom.*

CHATTER vb to talk about unimportant things ▸ *The three boys **chattered** endlessly during the entire trip.*

BABBLE to talk in an excited way, without making any sense
▸ *She was **babbling** in her sleep something about crickets and ice cream.*

GIBBER to speak rapidly, without making any sense ▸ *With all four of you **gibbering** at once, I can't make out a word you are saying.*

JABBER to talk in a fast, confused, or foolish way that is hard to understand ▸ *Julie was distracted from the video game she was playing because Stan kept **jabbering** to her.*

PRATTLE to chatter or babble in a childish way ▸ *Moira just **prattled** on happily about whatever came into her mind.*

see **TALK**

CHEAP adj 1 not costing or worth very much, and often of poor quality ▸ *I bought some **cheap** earrings from a street vendor in the city, and they fell apart two days later.*

INEXPENSIVE not costing a lot of money ▸ *We bought an **inexpensive** used car, and it ran well for nine years.*

He made me a **reasonable** offer for the lawn mower, so I sold it to him.

REASONABLE costing a fair price
▶ *He made me a **reasonable** offer for the lawn mower, so I sold it to him.*

AFFORDABLE having a cost low enough that you can pay it ▶ *We will move to the city as soon as my parents can find an **affordable** apartment that they like.*

▶ **CHEAP** adj 2 not liking to spend money
▶ *He was too **cheap** to buy ice cream for the three of us. That was a **cheap** trick you played on me.*

THRIFTY not wasteful ▶ *James was very **thrifty** last year and saved $400.*

FRUGAL very careful not to waste anything or to spend money unnecessarily ▶ *If we are **frugal**, we will be able to pay all our bills this month.*

STINGY not generous; not willing to give or spend money ▶ *Michael is too **stingy** to share his toys with me! The **stingy** old man refused to give any money to help the poor.*

MISERLY spending as little money as possible in order to hoard it ▶ *His **miserly** behavior lost him all his friends.*

▶ **CHEAT** vb to get dishonestly; to behave dishonestly ▶ *That salesperson **cheated** me out of a dollar. Chris was caught **cheating** on the exam.*

TRICK to cheat or outwit by using a clever or misleading action ▶ *The magician **tricked** us into thinking the egg had turned into a rabbit.*

DECEIVE to make someone believe something that is not true ▶ *Roy thought he could **deceive** his teacher by writing a note himself and signing it with his mother's name.*

FOOL to make someone feel foolish by doing something he or she doesn't expect or know about ▶ *The twins liked to try to **fool** their friends by changing places with each other.*

SWINDLE to cheat or steal using a dishonest scheme or plan ▶ *A gang of crooks **swindled** people out of thousands of dollars by selling them worthless swampland.*

HOODWINK to prevent someone from seeing the truth, as if the person were blindfolded ▶ *The used-car dealer tried to **hoodwink** her customers by painting over any rust on the old cars.*

The twins liked to try to **fool** their friends by changing places with each other.

▶ **CHILD** n a girl or boy not yet adult
▸ *Rosie is a very bright child who loves to read.*

BABY a newly born or very young child or animal ▸ *We bought a little present for Aunt Sylvia's baby.*

INFANT a newborn child; a baby that has not yet learned to walk ▸ *Brian is still an infant and needs someone to take care of him during the day.*

TODDLER a young child who has just learned to walk ▸ *Now that Jamie is a toddler, we have had to put everything breakable out of his reach.*

YOUNGSTER a young girl or boy
▸ *Stephen had bright red hair when he was a youngster.*

▶ **CHILDISH** adj like a child, often in an unfavorable way; immature and silly; not suitable for an adult ▸ *We heard peals of childish laughter. Her childish behavior annoyed everyone. It was childish of you to make faces at him.*

CHILDLIKE like a child in a favorable way; innocent and trusting ▸ *The story was written with a childlike simplicity. His smiling, open response struck us as childlike and charming.*

see YOUNG

▶ **CHOICE** n the chance to choose; all the things that you can choose from; the person or thing that has been chosen
▸ *I had the choice of studying either Spanish or Latin. This menu offers a wide choice. Sarah was a good choice as team captain.*

ALTERNATIVE something you can choose to have or do instead of something else
▸ *You have two alternatives—either stay here or come along with me.*

OPTION something you can choose to do
▸ *You have the option of staying home if you wish to.*

SELECTION the act of selecting something; all the things you can select from; a person or thing that has been selected
▸ *It was hard to make a selection from so many books. They sell a wide selection of chairs. Jim is my selection for captain.*

▶ **CHOOSE** vb to take or prefer something out of a larger number
▸ *We had a hard time choosing the right colors to paint my room. It is important to choose a career you will enjoy.*

SELECT to choose carefully and thoughtfully
▸ *The members of the all-star team were selected from all the players in the league.*

PICK to choose carefully using your own preference ▸ *I picked my favorite CDs to listen to during the trip.*

ELECT to choose by vote
▸ *The class elected a president, secretary, and treasurer.*

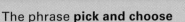

tip

The phrase **pick and choose** means "to choose very carefully from a number of possibilities": *There are some subjects you must study in school; you can't just* **pick and choose** *the things you like. Beth must have a dozen outfits she can* **pick and choose** *from!*

see **DECIDE**

▶ **CHURCH** n a building used by Christians for worship; Christian religious services; a group of Christians ▶ *It was a small* **church** *built in 1872. Their family usually goes to* **church** *on Sunday. She is a member of the Baptist* **church***.*

CATHEDRAL a large and important church with a bishop or archbishop as its main priest ▶ *Medieval* **cathedrals** *in Europe attract many tourists as well as worshippers.*

TEMPLE a building used for worship ▶ *The Parthenon is an ancient Greek* **temple** *built for the worship of the goddess Athena.*

SYNAGOGUE a building used by Jewish people for worship and religious study ▶ *Alexa and Jake study at the* **synagogue** *on Tuesday and Friday and go to services on Saturday.*

MOSQUE a building used by Muslims for worship ▶ *Mats or carpets covered the floor of the* **mosque** *for worshippers to pray.*

▶ **CIRCUMFERENCE** n the outer edge of a circle or the length of this edge; the distance around something ▶ *The* **circumference** *of a circle is the diameter times 3.1416. We walked around the whole* **circumference** *of the ranch.*

PERIMETER the outside edge of an area; the distance around the edge of a shape or an area ▶ *We put up a fence around the* **perimeter** *of the field. The* **perimeter** *of our lot is 454 feet.*

see **EDGE**

▶ **CITIZEN** n a member of a particular country who has a right to live there; a resident of a particular town or city ▶ *U.S.* **citizens** *do not need a passport to travel in Canada. The* **citizens** *of San Francisco have elected a new mayor.*

SUBJECT a person who lives in a kingdom or under the authority of a king or queen ▶ *The coronation of the queen was cheered by thousands of her loyal* **subjects***.*

NATIVE someone born in a particular place; a person, plant, or animal that originally lived or grew in a particular place ▶ *Warren is a* **native** *of New Hampshire. The kangaroo is a* **native** *of Australia.*

▶ **CLEAN** vb to remove the dirt from something; to make something neat ▶ *I had to **clean** my boots after hiking through the mud all afternoon. I try to **clean** my room every week.*

CLEANSE to make something clean or pure ▶ *Distilled water has been **cleansed** of all impurities. I tried to **cleanse** my mind and heart of any jealousy.*

WASH to clean with water or soap and water ▶ *Employees must **wash** their hands before returning to work. I think I will **wash** the car today.*

SCOUR to clean or polish something by rubbing it hard ▶ *Neil **scoured** the bathtub. If you wash the dishes, I will **scour** the pots and pans.*

▶ **CLOSE** vb to move a door or lid to cover or block an opening ▶ *She **closed** the door*

behind her. Please **close** your mouth when you chew!*

SHUT to close, especially to close tightly or in order to block the passage of someone or something ▶ *We **shut** all the doors and windows before the storm hit. **Shut** your eyes and count to fifty.*

FASTEN to lock, latch, or button in order to keep something closed ▶ *Be sure to **fasten** the gate so the dog can't get out.*

tip

In general, **shut** is a stronger or more forceful word than **close** and it suggests the action of moving the door, lid, or cover to a closed and fastened position.

I think I will **wash** the car today.

▶ **CLOTHES** n the various things that you wear, such as shirts, pants, and dresses; things worn at certain times
▶ *I will fold these* **clothes** *and put them away. Throw your dirty* **clothes** *into the hamper. Where are my school* **clothes**?

CLOTHING articles worn to cover the body, especially when considered as a whole
▶ *All my winter* **clothing** *is in storage. Trevor got a job in a store that sells men's* **clothing**.

APPAREL articles of clothing
▶ *Women's* **apparel** *is sold on the third floor.*

GARMENT piece of clothing
▶ *All of her outer* **garments** *were soaked by the rain. A hat is a* **garment** *to wear on your head.*

ATTIRE clothes, especially very fine clothes for a particular purpose ▶ *The painting was of a man in the elegant* **attire** *of a sixteenth-century nobleman. We wore formal* **attire** *to the graduation.*

> **tip**
>
> Note that **clothes** is a plural noun and always takes a plural verb: *My* **clothes** *are on fire!* **Clothing** is a collective noun; it may refer to all of the clothes you are wearing, but it always takes a singular verb: *Warm* **clothing** *is necessary in the winter.* **Apparel** and **attire** are also collective nouns that take a singular verb. In this entry, only **garment** can be both singular and plural.

▶ **CLUMSY** adj careless and ungraceful in movement or behavior ▶ *A bear looks* **clumsy** *when it walks. I felt* **clumsy** *after dropping three dishes. Philip's* **clumsy** *apology did not work.*

AWKWARD without grace or skill in movement or behavior ▶ *At first she was an* **awkward** *dancer, but the lessons helped. I feel* **awkward** *when I forget someone's name.*

UNGAINLY not very graceful or delicate in movement or appearance ▶ *He is a tall, lumbering fellow with an* **ungainly** *walk. Her handwriting is large and* **ungainly**.

A hat is a **garment** to wear on your head.

▶ **COLD** adj having a low temperature
▶ *It was a very **cold** day, even for January, and the furnace stayed on all the time.*

COOL a little cold ▶ *The refreshing **cool** breeze felt good after working in the garden on such a hot afternoon.*

CHILLY cold enough to make you shiver
▶ *We wanted to watch the eclipse of the moon, but we all got **chilly** and went inside.*

FROSTY so cold that crystals of ice form on cold surfaces ▶ *We woke on a **frosty** morning to see the sun glistening on the windowpanes.*

ICY extremely and painfully cold *(used especially of wind, storms, and water)*
▶ *An **icy** wind seemed to cut right through our jackets as we walked across the open fields.*

FREEZING extremely cold; cold enough to turn water to ice ▶ *The water in the lake was **freezing** when we went for our early morning swim.*

FRIGID intensely or extremely cold
▶ *My mom says we're in for a **frigid** winter this year.*

▶ **COLOR** n a property of an object that reflects light of a certain wavelength, which we perceive as being red, blue, yellow, or a blend of these ▶ *Each room in the apartment was painted a different **color**.*

tip

There are many words for different colors, shades, and hues. The following are just a few:

RED: pink, scarlet, crimson, maroon, vermilion

ORANGE: tangerine, apricot, peach, coral

YELLOW: lemon, gold, sandy, saffron

GREEN: chartreuse, lime, olive, emerald

BLUE: navy, azure, turquoise

PURPLE: violet, magenta, lilac, mauve, plum

BLACK: ebony, jet, sable

GRAY: lead, slate, smoky, ashen

BROWN: tan, chestnut, beige, fawn, khaki

WHITE: ivory, milky, snowy, chalky, silvery

▶ **COME** vb to move toward something
▶ *Peter could see his sister **coming** up the stairs.*

ARRIVE to get to a destination
▶ *The train **arrived** at the station fifteen minutes late. We should **arrive** before dark.*

REACH to go as far as
▶ *We **reached** home just as it began to rain.*

APPROACH to draw closer to
▶ *A woman in a large hat **approached** me and asked if I was enjoying the park.*

APPEAR to show up
▶ *A pair of chickadees **appears** every day as soon as I put seed in the bird feeder.*

▶ **COMFORTABLE** adj providing or enjoying comfort and relaxation
▶ *This is a **comfortable** chair. I am quite **comfortable** in this room, thank you.*

COZY warm, pleasant, and comfortable
▶ *We entered a **cozy** room with a cheery fire in the fireplace. I felt quite **cozy** lying in bed watching the snow fall.*

SNUG small and comfortable
▶ *The cabin was warm and **snug**.*

▶ **COMMON** adj not special in any way; happening often ▶ *I just use **common** earthworms for bait. Knee injuries are a **common** complaint among football players.*

ORDINARY average, or not distinguished in any way; most often used or usual
▶ *Although it was my birthday, it was just an **ordinary** school day. She quit yelling and returned to her **ordinary** tone of voice.*

TYPICAL having traits or qualities that are normal for a type or class; behaving in the usual way ▶ *My family lives in a **typical** small town. It was **typical** of Toby to forget my birthday.*

FAMILIAR common, well-known, or easily recognized; having intimate knowledge of
▶ *Flights of geese are a **familiar** sight at this time of year. Are you **familiar** with the rules of soccer?*

EVERYDAY happening frequently; all right for most days ▶ *My diary is filled mostly with the boring, **everyday** events of my life. Can I wear my **everyday** clothes to the party?*

WIDESPREAD happening in many places or among many people
▶ *There was **widespread** flooding after the storm. There is **widespread** concern about global warming.*

▶ **COMPARE** vb to judge one thing against another and notice similarities and differences ▶ *They look alike, but if you **compare** these two violins carefully, you will notice that one has a sweeter tone than the other.*

CONTRAST to identify the differences between things ▶ *I want you to **contrast** the attitudes of the two main characters in this story.*

DISTINGUISH to tell the difference between things ▶ *Can you **distinguish** between a frog and a toad? I can't **distinguish** the twins from each other.*

▶ **COMPLAIN** vb to express dissatisfaction, annoyance, or pain ▶ *Don't **complain** about having to do the dishes. Alex has been **complaining** of a toothache for three days.*

PROTEST to express disapproval ▶ *Many people **protested** when the town council voted to shut down the public swimming pool.*

GRIPE to express irritation ▶ *There's no use **griping** about your homework; it just has to be done.*

GRUMBLE to complain by muttering and mumbling ▶ *All the time Jason was trimming the hedge we could hear him **grumbling** to himself about having to work on Saturday.*

WHINE to complain in a high voice ▶ *If you kids don't stop **whining** about the food, you won't get any dessert.*

NAG to complain or find fault constantly ▶ *Okay, if you don't **nag** me every day about cleaning my room, I'll make sure it gets straightened up every Thursday.*

tip

All of these words except **gripe** express a slightly different notion of complaining. **Gripe** is a close synonym of **complain** and is very common in informal speech, but you should avoid using it in your writing.

see **MUMBLE, OBJECT**

▶ **COMPLETE** adj having all the parts that are needed or wanted ▶ *A list of the **complete** works of Johann Sebastian Bach includes more than one thousand items. She is in **complete** control of the situation.*

FULL having everything that is needed or all that can be held, done, or accomplished ▶ *Is this a **full** deck of cards? That box is **full** of junk. The cherry trees are in **full** bloom.*

TOTAL making up the complete amount; absolute or utter ▶ *What is the **total** cost of this car? The party was a **total** surprise to Vanessa.*

There's no use **griping** about your homework; it just has to be done.

WHOLE containing all the parts or elements; complete, with nothing missing ▶ *I ate a **whole** loaf of bread. The **whole** class applauded. I have the **whole** series, all twenty-five books.*

ENTIRE having all the parts, especially in one absolute or unbroken unity ▶ *We will have to replace the **entire** engine. I wasted the **entire** day. I want your **entire** attention.*

▶ **COMPLICATED** adj containing lots of different parts or ideas and thus difficult to use or understand ▶ *The rules for this game are very **complicated**.*

COMPLEX having interconnected or related parts that are hard to separate, understand, or solve ▶ *A molecule of water (H_2O) is fairly simple, but a molecule of caffeine ($C_8H_{10}N_4O_2$) is **complex**. This is a **complex** problem.*

INTRICATE detailed and hard to understand because of its many interwoven or puzzling parts ▶ *Medieval Celtic art is full of extremely **intricate** designs. We got some very **intricate** directions for getting there.*

▶ **CONFUSE** vb to cause someone to misunderstand or not know what to do; to mistake one thing for another ▶ *There were so many signs and lights that I was **confused** about which way to turn. I **confused** Roy with his twin brother.*

PUZZLE to confuse or make unsure; to attempt to solve a problem or puzzle ▶ *I am **puzzled** by her silence; is she ignoring me or doesn't she know I am here? I am **puzzling** over my math.*

BEWILDER to confuse very much, so that it is hard to think clearly ▶ *The instructions to this game completely **bewilder** me.*

CONFOUND to baffle or frustrate; to make someone feel very confused ▶ *We tried to get some advice, but we were **confounded** by regulations and red tape.*

We got some very **intricate** directions for getting there.

n = noun   vb = verb   adj = adjective   adv = adverb   prep = preposition   conj = conjunction

▶ **CONSIDER** vb to think about, in order to understand something ▶ *Ms. Johnson will* **consider** *your request for more time to do your project if you show her that you are working hard on it.*

PONDER to consider carefully; to think deeply about ▶ *For three days Nick* **pondered** *the problem of how to make some money over the summer.*

CONTEMPLATE to focus your attention on something and think about it ▶ *When I* **contemplate** *the beauty of nature, sometimes I want to be a poet and sometimes a biologist.*

REFLECT to think quietly about something that has happened ▶ *As I* **reflect** *upon the past year, I realize I could have worked harder.*

WEIGH to consider carefully in order to reach a balanced understanding ▶ *A jury has to* **weigh** *all the evidence in a case before reaching a verdict.*

see **STUDY**

▶ **CONTAIN** vb to have in it ▶ *My purse* **contains** *three dollars, some change, and a broken pencil. This envelope* **contains** *the name of the winner.*

HOLD to have room for; to be able to contain ▶ *This bottle* **holds** *a gallon, but it contains only about a pint.*

INCLUDE to have as part of a whole ▶ *This list* **includes** *the names and addresses of everyone in the school. His hobbies* **include** *bicycling and playing the cello.*

▶ **CONTINUAL** adj happening again and again; happening without a pause and often without end ▶ *He was kept awake by the* **continual** *noise of trains going by. She lived in* **continual** *fear of getting sick.*

CONTINUOUS uninterrupted in space or time ▶ *A* **continuous** *expanse of wheat stretched as far as the eye could see. Anita could hear a* **continuous** *ringing sound.*

CONSTANT happening all the time or again and again ▶ *I can't concentrate with these* **constant** *interruptions.*

INCESSANT uninterrupted and unending ▶ *Their* **incessant** *chattering gets on my nerves.*

ETERNAL lasting forever; seeming never to stop ▶ *There are many myths of* **eternal** *life. His* **eternal** *complaints can be very annoying.*

PERPETUAL without ending or changing ▶ *These two kittens are in* **perpetual** *motion.*

▶ **CONTINUE** vb to go on; to remain in existence ▶ *We will* **continue** *working until we have finished our report. The rain* **continued** *as we walked home.*

LAST to go on, especially for a particular length of time ▶ *The movie* **lasted** *for two and a half hours. Do you think this storm will* **last** *much longer?*

ENDURE to continue or last for a long time, especially in spite of difficulty, resistance, or opposition ▶ *Our friendship has* **endured** *for many years, even though we live in different parts of the country.*

▶ **CONTRADICT** vb to say the opposite of what has been said; to show or suggest the opposite ▶ *My brother **contradicted** me when I said he was wrong. The results of the two surveys **contradicted** each other.*

DENY to say that something is not true ▶ *Laura **denied** that she had taken the cookies.*

REFUTE to prove that someone or something is wrong ▶ *My records **refuted** the bank's claim that I owed them money.*

▶ **CONTROL** vb to have authority over; to make someone or something do what you want ▶ *Mr. Harris still **controls** the corporation he started 19 years ago. Margo was able to **control** the puppet and make it dance.*

COMMAND to have control over a group of people, especially in the armed forces; to deserve and get ▶ *He **commands** the naval base in Virginia. She is such a firm and fair teacher she **commands** the respect of her students.*

DIRECT to supervise the running or working of something ▶ *Nancy **directs** the fund-raising campaign for the new school.*

MANAGE to be in charge of a store or business ▶ *Terry **manages** a small electrical company.*

see **GOVERN**

▶ **CORRECT** adj free from error or fault; matching a standard or convention ▶ *Make sure you have the **correct** phone number. She always has **correct** behavior.*

ACCURATE free from error, especially because of taking great care ▶ *The policeman spoke to everyone in the building to get an **accurate** description of the intruder. My watch is **accurate** to the nearest second.*

RIGHT matching the facts or the truth; suitable ▶ *Are we traveling in the **right** direction? She is the **right** person for the job of class treasurer.*

PRECISE correct in the smallest details ▶ *Astronomers can calculate the **precise** moment when an eclipse will begin. His homework is very neat and **precise**.*

TRUE agreeing with fact or reality ▶ *Is it **true** that you are going to India next summer? The movie was based on a **true** story.*

EXACT perfectly correct ▶ *The carpenter made **exact** measurements of the space where the bookshelves will go. The cashier gave me the **exact** change.*

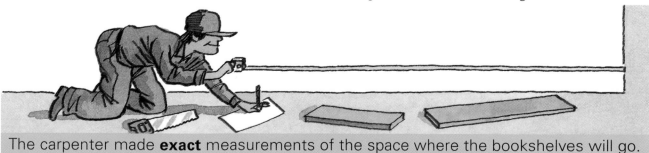

The carpenter made **exact** measurements of the space where the bookshelves will go.

▶ **COUNTRY** n a part of the world with its own borders and government
▶ *Canada, the United States, and Mexico are all **countries** in North America.*
*We are moving to a different **country**.*

NATION a large group of people living in the same region and often sharing the same language, customs, and government
▶ *The whole **nation** was saddened by the death of the ex-president. Leaders from the two **nations** have met to discuss peace.*

STATE a group of people united under one government; any of the political units that make up some countries ▶ *The European **states** have reached an agreement about trade. Alaska became the forty-ninth **state** in the U.S. on January 3, 1959.*

REPUBLIC a country in which the people elect representatives who manage the government ▶ *Many nations first became **republics** in the twentieth century.*

> **tip**
> Some synonyms for **country** identify the type of government that a country has: *The United States is a **democracy**, Norway is a **monarchy**, and Belarus is a **republic**.*

▶ **COURAGE** n the mental or emotional strength that helps you to face danger or difficulty ▶ *It took great **courage** to save those children from the burning building.*

BRAVERY the quality of being brave or unafraid ▶ *Alison was awarded a medal for **bravery** after she rescued a drowning man from the river.*

FORTITUDE the strength of mind to face difficulty, misfortune, or pain with courage ▶ *Cleaning up after the flood took all the **fortitude** and determination Michael could summon in himself.*

NERVE the ability to remain calm in the face of trouble or danger ▶ *It took a lot of **nerve** to climb the face of such a steep cliff.*

GUTS inner strength ▶ *Do you have the **guts** to jump off the high diving board?*

> **tip**
> **Guts** is a common word in informal speech, but it should not be used in your serious writing. Use one of the other, more specific, synonyms instead.

▶ **CRIME** n an act that is against the law; activity that is against the law ▶ *Shoplifting is a **crime** and will be prosecuted. **Crime** is a serious problem in some neighborhoods.*

OFFENSE an act that is against the law, especially an act that is not very serious

▶ *It is an* **offense** *to park here and you will probably get a parking ticket if you do. He was punished after his third* **offense**.

VIOLATION an act of breaking a rule or law ▶ *In basketball, traveling—running with the ball—is a* **violation** *of the rules.*

▶ **CROSS** adj in a bad mood or temper ▶ *My mother got very* **cross** *when she saw the mess we made in the kitchen.*

GROUCHY in a grumbling or complaining mood ▶ *Just because you didn't get to go to the mall doesn't mean you have to be* **grouchy** *for the rest of the day.*

IRRITABLE easily annoyed ▶ *I'm always* **irritable** *when I am sleepy.*

CRANKY easily angered or upset, especially when tired or hungry ▶ *The twins are only four and they get* **cranky** *if they are up after their bedtime.*

FUSSY whining or easily upset ▶ *The baby is* **fussy** *when she is hungry.*

see ANGRY

▶ **CROWD** n a large number of persons gathered together ▶ *There was quite a large* **crowd** *at the concert last night.*

MOB a crowd that is disorganized or hard to control ▶ *An angry* **mob** *gathered outside the factory to protest the layoff of so many workers.*

MULTITUDE a large number of persons or things ▶ *Alice had a* **multitude** *of questions on the first day of school. The senator received letters from a* **multitude** *of people.*

HOST a very large number of persons or things together ▶ *We were attacked by a* **host** *of mosquitoes every evening at dusk.*

THRONG a crowd, especially a moving crowd of people pushing one another ▶ *We almost missed our plane because of the* **throngs** *of holiday travelers jamming the airport.*

HORDE a rough or rude crowd ▶ **Hordes** *of news reporters were pushing and shouting questions at the governor.*

SWARM a large group continuously moving ▶ *A* **swarm** *of tourists rushed off the buses and into the gift shop next to the museum.*

▶ **CRY** vb to show your sorrow, pain, or grief by shedding tears and making sad, involuntary sounds ▶ *Donna began to* **cry** *when she was told that she could not go to the party.*

WEEP to shed tears and cry, often quietly ▶ *Carla began to* **weep** *with joy when her son was rescued. Everyone* **wept** *during the funeral.*

SOB to breathe in short bursts or gasps while you are crying ▶ *The little boy sat on the steps* **sobbing** *because he had lost his new ball.*

WAIL to let out a long cry of sadness or distress ▶ *The baby began to* **wail** *when her mother left the room.*

WHIMPER to make weak, crying noises ▶ *The puppy* **whimpered** *when I stopped petting it.*

WHINE to complain about something with a long, high-pitched sound or voice ▶ *Jerry* **whines** *when he doesn't get his way.*

▶ **CURIOUS** adj eager to learn or to find out
▶ *I am very **curious** about what is in that little box.*

INQUISITIVE always asking questions
▶ *She was **inquisitive** as a child, always wanting to know how things worked.*

PRYING too curious, especially about other people's things or affairs
▶ *Aaron didn't want his brother's **prying** eyes looking through his diary.*

▶ **CUT** vb to slit, pierce, or separate into parts by using a sharp instrument
▶ *Henry liked to **cut** designs out of colored paper. She **cut** her finger on a piece of glass.*

CHOP to cut with a sharp blow
▶ *We can use this hatchet to **chop** off the dead branches. Will you please **chop** the vegetables into small pieces for the stew?*

SLICE to cut a thin piece or wedge
▶ *Can you **slice** the pie into five equal pieces? He **sliced** the end of his finger while he was preparing dinner.*

CARVE to cut wood or stone into a shape; to cut a large portion of meat into pieces suitable for eating
▶ *He **carved** a life-sized statue of a moose out of a tree trunk. Will you **carve** the turkey, please?*

▶ **DAMP** adj a little bit wet, often unpleasantly so ▶ *You should iron this shirt while it is still **damp**. Wipe clean with a **damp** sponge.*

MOIST not completely dry; containing some moisture ▶ *We could feel a **moist** breeze from the ocean. His eyes were **moist** from crying for so long.*

HUMID full of water vapor *(used especially of uncomfortably warm, moist air)* ▶ *It was hard to keep working on such a hot, **humid** afternoon.*

CLAMMY damp, sticky, and cool ▶ *He was so nervous his hands were **clammy** with sweat.*

DANK unpleasantly damp and chilly ▶ *The basement walls were **dank** and spiders lurked in the corners.*

see WET

▶ **DANGER** n a situation in which someone or something may suffer hurt, pain, loss, or damage ▶ *It hasn't rained for two months and there is a great **danger** of forest fires. She was in **danger** when her car skidded on the ice.*

RISK the chance or possibility of being in danger ▶ *The **risk** of injury among football players is fairly high. Doctors are willing to run the **risk** of getting ill in order to help others.*

THREAT a sign of danger or harm; a possible source of danger ▶ *The **threat** of an avalanche was growing as the weather became warmer. The floodwaters are a **threat** to everyone's health.*

PERIL the possibility of being in great danger; something that may cause harm ▶ *The whole neighborhood was in **peril** as the fire spread in our direction.*

HAZARD a possible source of danger or harm ▶ *The fallen trees and power lines were a **hazard** to drivers after the storm. Lung disease is one of the **hazards** of smoking.*

MENACE something that threatens harm or evil ▶ *Some people think that skateboards are a **menace** to pedestrians.*

JEOPARDY great danger· ▶ *Anyone who tries to climb that mountain in winter is placing his or her life in **jeopardy**.*

▶ **DARK** adj partly or completely without light ▶ *The room was getting **dark** so I turned on the lights.*

GLOOMY dark and unpleasant ▶ *Three days of **gloomy** weather was making us all grumpy and irritable.*

MURKY dark or dim because of fog, smoke, or dirt ▶ *Our flashlights could not pierce the **murky** air. We went diving for clams but the water was too **murky** for us to see anything.*

DUSKY a little dark and shadowy ▶ *We love to play games outdoors during the **dusky** autumn evenings.*

see DIM

▶ **DEAD** adj no longer living ▶ *I collected some **dead** wood for our campfire. Shakespeare has been **dead** for more than four hundred years.*

DECEASED having died recently *(used especially in legal situations)* ▶ *Marian inherited a fortune from her **deceased** aunt.*

DEPARTED having died recently *(used especially in religious situations)* ▶ *The soldiers had a ceremony to honor their **departed** friends and comrades.*

LATE having died recently *(used before a name or title that identifies the person)* ▶ *The **late** Bill Monroe was a great musician. I was sorry to hear about the passing of your **late** brother.*

LIFELESS having no life ▶ *The shore was littered with the **lifeless** bodies of seagulls that had been killed by the oil spill.*

EXTINCT having no living descendant ▶ *The passenger pigeon has been **extinct** since the last one died in September 1914.*

▶ **DEADLY** adj capable of killing or likely to kill ▶ *Malaria is a **deadly** disease. These chemicals could cause a **deadly** explosion.*

FATAL causing death; likely to have very bad or harmful results ▶ *There was a **fatal** accident on the highway last night. The tennis champion made one **fatal** mistake and lost the tournament.*

MORTAL causing death; very hostile ▶ *The soldier received a **mortal** wound and died the next day. The two countries have always been **mortal** enemies.*

I collected some **dead** wood for our campfire.

LETHAL causing or capable of causing death ▶ *Lethal poisons should be clearly labeled.*

▶ **DECIDE** vb to make a choice about what to do ▶ *We decided to go to the beach rather than work this afternoon.*

SETTLE to end a dispute or argument; to reach an agreement ▶ *We settled our argument by flipping a coin.*

RESOLVE to deal with a problem or difficulty successfully ▶ *The tensions in the war-torn region were resolved when the leaders agreed to talk seriously together.*

DETERMINE to control or influence directly ▶ *The weather will determine whether or not we can go on a picnic tomorrow.*

RULE to make an official decision or judgment ▶ *The judge ruled that the father should be allowed to see his children.*

CONCLUDE to arrive at a decision or realization based on the facts that you have ▶ *When I saw my book sitting on a shelf in Bill's room, I concluded that he must have taken it.*

see CHOOSE

▶ **DECORATE** vb to make something prettier or more attractive by adding something to it ▶ *We decorated the room with streamers and balloons for the party. The box was decorated with beautiful carvings.*

ADORN to make more beautiful, especially by adding something that is beautiful itself ▶ *Her hair was adorned with flowers. The pharaoh's tomb was adorned with gold and jewels.*

BEAUTIFY to make beautiful or more beautiful ▶ *Maria wanted to beautify her house by planting flowers and shrubs around it.*

TRIM to decorate by adding ornaments or contrasting colors ▶ *We trimmed the tree on Christmas Eve. The room was a pale blue trimmed in white.*

▶ **DEFEAT** vb to win victory over ▶ *My sister's basketball team defeated last year's champions and went on to win the tournament.*

CONQUER to get control of, as if by winning a war; to gain control over by mental or physical force ▶ *The Romans conquered most of Europe. He conquered his fear of heights by climbing a ladder every day for a month.*

BEAT to defeat in a game, contest, or struggle ▶ *My little brother can beat both my dad and me in chess games—at the same time!*

OVERCOME to get the better of after a hard struggle ▶ *Roger was determined to overcome his disability and two years later he won the wheelchair marathon.*

OVERPOWER to get the better of by using greater power or strength ▶ *The mutineers overpowered the captain and took over the ship.*

SUBDUE to bring completely under control or authority ▶ *The police were unable to subdue the protesters by using fire hoses and tear gas.*

▶ **DELAY** vb to put something off until later; to make someone or something late; to be late ▶ *Tamika **delayed** doing her homework until the last minute. The rain **delayed** Joe's arrival. Don't **delay** or we'll miss the bus.*

POSTPONE to put something off until later or another time ▶ *The outdoor concert was **postponed** until next week because of the storm.*

CANCEL to call something off without expecting to do it at a later time ▶ *Juan's party was **canceled** when he came down with chicken pox the day before his birthday.*

▶ **DELICIOUS** adj very pleasing to taste or smell ▶ *This apple pie is **delicious**.*

TASTY having a pleasant taste ▶ *The coffee cake was decorated with **tasty** pieces of fruit.*

APPETIZING looking or smelling good to eat ▶ *The **appetizing** aroma of baking bread filled the house.*

LUSCIOUS very satisfying, and usually very sweet, to the taste or smell ▶ *Catrin made a **luscious** chocolate cake for her mother's birthday.*

SAVORY pleasant to taste, especially because of the seasoning ▶ *The whole family loves my **savory** stew flavored with rosemary and bay leaves.*

▶ **DESCEND** vb 1 to move from a higher position to a lower one ▶ *Scarlet's gown trailed behind her as she **descended** the staircase. Slowly the helicopter **descended** to the ground.*

SINK to descend or drop slowly, especially into water, snow, or mud ▶ *We watched the sun **sink** below the horizon. The ship hit an iceberg and **sank**.*

SWOOP to rush down or pounce upon suddenly ▶ *The hawk **swooped** down on its prey.*

STOOP to bend down to do something; to condescend or degrade yourself ▶ *Don't **stoop** to his level if he starts an argument. I had to **stoop** to get through the low door.*

▶ **DESCEND** vb 2 to get down from ▶ *Kendra **descended** from the ladder to get more paint.*

DISMOUNT to get off (a horse, a bicycle, or a motorcycle) ▶ *I've learned how to deliver my newspapers without **dismounting** from my bike.*

ALIGHT to get down from a height or out of a vehicle with a light step ▶ *The birds **alighted** on the telephone wire. The president **alighted** from the helicopter with a cheery wave to the crowd.*

see **FALL**

I've learned how to deliver my newspapers without **dismounting** from my bike.

▶ **DESTROY** vb to break up or to damage beyond repair ▶ *The building was destroyed by fire.*

WRECK to damage or destroy by force or violence ▶ *Jan wrecked the car when he hit the fence.*

SPOIL to damage seriously ▶ *The whole drawing was spoiled when I spilled some ink on it.*

DEMOLISH to break into pieces; to destroy completely ▶ *The builders demolished the old school building before starting a new one.*

RUIN to damage something so that it is no longer useful ▶ *My homework was ruined when it got rained on.*

► **DIFFERENT** adj not the same
> ► *Jill's opinion is* **different** *from mine. There are many* **different** *species of insect.*

DIVERSE quite different from one another
> ► *Hal has a* **diverse** *set of friends. Joan has many* **diverse** *interests, including soccer, cooking, and ballet.*

DISTINCT clearly different; separate or not the same ► *The original recording is quite* **distinct** *from the cheap copies. German and Dutch are* **distinct** *languages.*

VARIOUS of several kinds; several or many
> ► *This dress comes in* **various** *colors and patterns. Her family has lived in* **various** *parts of the country.*

tip

Different from is used especially when a direct contrast between things is being stressed: *He is* **different from** *the other boys in his class.*

Different than is also often used, especially when it is followed by a clause or modified by an adverb: *This room is* **different than** *it used to be. In some ways, life in Canada is not very* **different than** *life in the U.S.*

Different to is sometimes found in British writing and speech: *Boys today seem* **different to** *what they were when I was young.*

Hal has a **diverse** set of friends.

▶ **DIM** adj somewhat dark; hard to see
▶ *She sat unnoticed in a **dim** corner of the room. I could barely see the **dim** outline of a building in the fog.*

FAINT not very clear, strong, or distinct
▶ *If you look carefully, you can see some **faint** writing in pencil in the margin of the page.*

INDISTINCT not sharply outlined or detailed
▶ *The face in the photo was so **indistinct** we couldn't tell who it was.*

OBSCURE not easy to see because of darkness ▶ *The trunk was hidden in an **obscure** corner of the attic.*

VAGUE not outlined sharply; not clearly defined ▶ *A **vague** image began to appear on the screen. He has only a **vague** memory of what his father looked like.*

see DARK

▶ **DIRTY** adj not clean; covered with or stained with dirt
▶ *The twins got **dirty** playing in the sandbox.*

FILTHY extremely dirty
▶ *I got **filthy** riding my bike through the mud.*

GRIMY covered with dirt that sticks to the surface ▶ *His hands were so dirty, there was a **grimy** film in the sink after he washed them.*

SOILED stained with dirt or some other substance ▶ *Put your **soiled** gym clothes in the laundry. My knees got **soiled** with grass stains.*

DINGY dull and dirty ▶ *He lived in a **dingy** little room with only one tiny window.*

▶ **DISAPPEAR** vb to go out of sight; to go out of existence ▶ *George **disappeared** into the crowd. Typewriters have almost **disappeared** from the modern office.*

VANISH to go out of sight suddenly or mysteriously ▶ *The submarine **vanished** beneath the waves. There was a puff of smoke and the rabbit **vanished** from the magician's hand.*

FADE to lose color or brightness gradually; to become weaker ▶ *The curtains are **fading** because of the sunlight. The lights **faded** as the ship sailed away. The sound **faded** into silence.*

tip

This poem is funny if your listeners know what a limerick is usually like. Start speaking it fairly loudly and get gradually quieter, so that your listeners can barely hear the last two words:

There once was a young man named Wyatt
Whose voice was remarkably quiet.
*One day it completely **faded** away,...*

▶ **DISASTER** n an event that causes great damage, loss, or suffering; something that turns out completely wrong ▶ *The flood was one of the worst **disasters** in the state. The party became a **disaster** when the dog knocked over the table.*

CATASTROPHE an enormous and sudden disaster ▶ *The famine was the worst **catastrophe** the country had ever suffered.*

CALAMITY a disaster with lasting effects ▶ *It was a terrible **calamity** when the fire spread through the center of town.*

MISFORTUNE an unlucky or unfortunate event; bad luck ▶ *The closing of the park is a great **misfortune** for the neighborhood. It was my **misfortune** to miss the plane.*

ACCIDENT an event or circumstance that is unplanned and that often causes loss or injury ▶ *Samantha broke her wrist in a skating **accident**.*

▶ **DISCOVER** vb 1 to find, especially for the first time ▶ *Under the house we **discovered** an old shoe and a belt buckle from the Civil War.*

DETECT to discover or determine the presence or existence of something ▶ *We left the building as soon as we **detected** smoke in the air.*

UNEARTH to dig up from the ground or a hiding place ▶ *We finally **unearthed** Grandfather's will in a box of papers in his desk.*

UNCOVER to reveal; to make known ▶ *The investigation **uncovered** a major fraud.*

▶ **DISCOVER** vb 2 to find out ▶ *We **discovered** that we both have the same birthday. I soon **discovered** that Li was lying.*

REALIZE to become aware ▶ *Will suddenly **realized** that he was lost. John **realized** that he hadn't been working hard enough.*

LEARN to gain information ▶ *I **learned** that Abdul was going away.*

DETERMINE to find out by investigation or reasoning ▶ *The doctors **determined** that the bone was not broken. The jury is trying to **determine** the truth in the case.*

see **FIND, NOTICE**

▶ **DISHONEST** adj not honest; given to lying, cheating, or stealing ▶ *It is **dishonest** to cheat. The people of the town were shocked to learn how **dishonest** their last mayor had been.*

UNTRUTHFUL not true; given to lying ▶ *Brian gave an **untruthful** explanation of what happened. He's been so **untruthful** lately that it's hard to believe anything he says.*

UNTRUSTWORTHY not to be trusted; not dependable ▶ *I won't loan her my tools because she is **untrustworthy** and might lose them.*

DECEITFUL tending to cheat or lie; meant to deceive or mislead ▶ *Ted wrote a **deceitful** letter to his parents, saying his money had been stolen when he had really spent it all on candy.*

CROOKED not straightforward and truthful; cheating or swindling ▶ *The **crooked** used car dealer put the odometer back to 1,000 miles to make me think the car was almost new.*

DEVIOUS dishonest in a cunning and secretive way ▶ *He came up with a **devious** plan to cheat on his taxes.*

▶ **DO** vb to perform or complete an action ▶ *Dad was **doing** the dishes while I **did** my homework.*

ACCOMPLISH to do something successfully ▶ *We **accomplished** all our chores before lunch, so we were able to go swimming all afternoon.*

ACHIEVE to do something successfully, especially after a lot of effort ▶ *The band has finally **achieved** its goal and raised enough money to take a trip to Washington.*

CARRY OUT to put into practice (a plan or idea) ▶ *Once we got the tools and wood, we were able to **carry out** our plan to fence in the backyard.*

see ACT

Once we got the tools and wood, we were able to **carry out** our plan to fence in the backyard.

DOCTOR

▶ **DOCTOR** n someone trained and licensed to treat sick and injured people; *abbreviated as* **Dr.** *when used as a title before a name* ▶ *Fortunately, there was a **doctor** nearby when my father became ill.* **Dr.** *Kenny prescribed an antibiotic for my sore throat.*

PHYSICIAN a doctor of medicine *(as opposed to a* dentist, *a* chiropractor, *or other specialist)* ▶ *As soon as we moved to town we had to find a new family **physician**.*

M.D. a doctor of medicine—from the Latin *medicinae doctor (often used after a doctor's name)* ▶ *The sign on the door read "Sarah Blackwell, **M.D.**"*

G.P. a doctor who does not specialize in one area of medicine — *abbreviated from "general practitioner"* ▶ *Peter decided to be a **G.P.** rather than a surgeon.*

tip

There are many types of **doctors** who specialize in one area: A **pediatrician** takes care of children. A **dentist** takes care of teeth. An **orthodontist** is a dentist who specializes in making teeth straight and making sure they meet correctly. A **surgeon** operates to remove or treat disease inside your body. An **internist** treats diseases without using surgery. A **psychiatrist** treats problems with the mind or emotions. An **obstetrician** takes care of women during pregnancy and childbirth. A **gynecologist** specializes in the treatment of the female reproductive system. An **orthopedist** treats problems with bones, joints, and muscles. A **chiropractor** adjusts the spine and joints. An **acupuncturist** treats pain and disease using special needles inserted into various parts of your body.

Dr. Kenny prescribed an antibiotic for my sore throat.

▶ **DOG** n a domestic mammal with four legs, often kept as a pet or as a work animal, related to wolves, coyotes, and foxes
▶ *Dogs have been domesticated for at least ten thousand years. We treat our dog like a member of the family.*

HOUND any of various kinds of dog that have been bred to hunt by sight or smell
▶ *We could hear the hounds baying in the woods.*

MONGREL an animal, especially a dog, that is a mixture of different breeds
▶ *Our dog is just a mongrel, but we love her.*

MUTT a dog of mixed breed
▶ *Our dog Dylan is just a mutt that we found at the city pound.*

PUPPY a young dog ▶ *It is best to get a puppy when it is about eight weeks old.*

CANINE any of the family of animals that includes dogs, wolves, jackals, foxes, and coyotes ▶ *Canines are carnivorous animals.*

tip

There are more than one hundred different kinds or breeds of **dog**. The following are just a few, identified by type of breed in italics: *Sporting breeds:* **pointer, retriever, setter, spaniel;** *Hounds:* **Afghan hound, basset hound, beagle, bloodhound, dachshund, foxhound, greyhound;** *Working breeds:* **boxer, collie, Doberman pinscher, German shepherd, Great Dane, rottweiler, Samoyed,** schnauzer, sheepdog, Welsh corgi; *Terriers:* **Airedale terrier, border terrier, fox terrier, Irish terrier;** *Toy breeds:* **affenpinscher, Chihuahua, Pekingese, Pomeranian, toy poodle;** *Nonsporting breeds:* **bulldog, chow chow, dalmatian, Lhasa apso, poodle.**

▶ **DOOR** n a barrier that opens and closes the way into or out of a room, building, or cabinet ▶ *Please close the door on your way out.*

DOORWAY an opening for going into or out of a room or building ▶ *We tried for twenty minutes before we were able to move the sofa through the doorway.*

ENTRANCE the way into a place
▶ *The main entrance to the hotel is on 57th Street.*

ENTRY a door, hall, pathway, or driveway that leads into a place ▶ *We stood in the entry to the church to take shelter from the rain.*

EXIT a way out of a place
▶ *As soon as the lights came on, everyone in the theater headed for the nearest exit.*

GATEWAY an opening in a wall or fence with a gate fitted into it ▶ *We drove through the open gateway and up a long drive to the mansion.*

▶ **DOUBT** n a feeling of not being sure
▶ *Fran had many doubts about being able to finish her project on time.*

UNCERTAINTY lack of certainty
▶ *We can't go sailing when there is so much uncertainty about the weather.*

SUSPICION a thought, based more on feeling than on fact, that something is wrong or bad
▶ *George had a slight suspicion that there was a slow leak in his tire.*

SKEPTICISM strong doubt; the tendency to believe that something is untrue until it is proved true ▶ *Her statement was met with skepticism by the whole class.*

DISTRUST a lack of trust or faith ▶ *Her constant lying has filled me with distrust.*

▶ **DOUBT** vb to be uncertain
▶ *I doubt that we will get home before dark.*

QUESTION to express uncertainty or doubt
▶ *I question the truth of that last statement.*

SUSPECT to have doubts about
▶ *The police officer suspected that she was not telling the truth. She said she wants to help, but I suspect her sincerity.*

MISTRUST to be suspicious of; to doubt the truth or correctness of ▶ *I mistrust my own judgment, so I asked for advice from my counselor.*

DISTRUST to have no trust in
▶ *I have distrusted his friendship ever since he accused me of taking his money.*

▶ **DOUBTFUL** adj not at all clear; very much in doubt ▶ *It is doubtful that we will get to the airport in time to catch our plane.*

DUBIOUS feeling some doubt
▶ *Jane is feeling a bit dubious about going to Paris on her own this summer.*

QUESTIONABLE open to question or doubt; suspected of being false, wrong, or immoral
▶ *Tony came in with a questionable excuse this morning. Her lawyer has a very questionable reputation.*

UNCERTAIN unsure; likely to change
▶ *I am uncertain about whether we should go now or wait for Alice. Both the weather and our picnic plans are uncertain.*

▶ **DRY** adj not wet ▶ *Jack came in out of the rain and put on some dry clothes.*

ARID extremely dry because of a lack of rain
▶ *We live on the edge of an arid desert. The arid climate means that farming is not possible in this region.*

PARCHED deprived of moisture; very thirsty
▶ *The parched plants withered and died. I am parched after playing baseball in the hot sun.*

DEHYDRATED with the water or moisture removed; not having enough water in your body ▶ *We took packages of dehydrated foods on our camping trip. Ellie was sick and got dehydrated from not eating or drinking.*

▶ **DULL** adj not exciting, interesting, or lively
▶ *We spent a dull afternoon with nothing to do but listen to the rain on our tent. He gave a really dull talk that lasted an hour.*

UNINTERESTING not holding your interest or attention ▶ *The senator's speech was so uninteresting I fell asleep halfway through it.*

He gave a really **dull** talk that lasted an hour.

BORING causing you to be restless or tired because of being dull or uninteresting ▶ *This is the most **boring** book I have ever tried to read. Oscar is very **boring** at parties; he never wants to do anything fun.*

TEDIOUS very boring and tiring ▶ *A week in bed can get very **tedious**. Working on an assembly line is a **tedious** job.*

MONOTONOUS dull or tedious because it is always the same ▶ *It soon became **monotonous** putting the stamps on six hundred envelopes.*

TIRESOME tiring, boring, and annoying ▶ *Her constant complaining grew increasingly **tiresome** as the week wore on.*

▶ **DUMB** adj not able to speak, either permanently or temporarily ▶ *I was struck **dumb** by his foolishness.*

MUTE not able to speak, especially from birth; choosing not to speak ▶ *He has been **mute** his entire life. I sat still and **mute** as he asked one meaningless question after another.*

SPEECHLESS temporarily unable to speak; no longer able to speak ▶ *He was **speechless** with rage. The illness left him partly paralyzed and totally **speechless**.*

SILENT not making any sound ▶ *The class remained **silent** as she told the exciting story of her adventures.*

tip

For the informal use of **dumb**, meaning "not very smart," see **STUPID**.

▶ **DUTY** n an action a person must do or ought to do ▶ *It is your* **duty** *to clean up the garage every week. The* **duties** *of the secretary include ordering supplies.*

RESPONSIBILITY a task or duty that you are responsible for doing ▶ *It is the president's* **responsibility** *to defend the Constitution. It is my* **responsibility** *to bring food for the picnic.*

OBLIGATION a task or duty that you are required to do ▶ *Everyone has an* **obligation** *to serve on a jury. You have an* **obligation** *to repay the money soon.*

see JOB

It is your **duty** to clean up the garage every week.

▶ **EAGER** adj impatiently interested in beginning something; very interested in doing something ▶ *Todd was **eager** to go camping over the weekend. Rachel is an **eager** softball player.*

ENTHUSIASTIC filled with a strong feeling of excitement or interest ▶ *Petra is an **enthusiastic** student who always finishes her work ahead of time.*

KEEN intensely interested ▶ *She is a **keen** musician and practices for an hour and a half every day.*

AVID extremely eager ▶ *He is an **avid** stamp collector. After being away for a year, Sally was **avid** for news of her friends.*

ANXIOUS eager to the point of worry ▶ *Ben was **anxious** to please his new teachers.*

▶ **EARTH** n the planet we live on; the ground ▶ *Three fifths of the **earth** is covered with water. The **earth** shook as the train rumbled by.*

WORLD the earth; a particular part of the earth; all the people on earth ▶ *We took a trip around the **world**. The Americas are called the New **World**. The whole **world** has heard of Elvis.*

UNIVERSE the earth, the planets, the stars, and all things that exist in space ▶ *Astronomers are trying to determine the size and age of the **universe**.*

COSMOS the universe, especially when considered as an orderly system ▶ *The laws of physics help to explain the structure of the **cosmos**.*

NATURE everything in the world that is not made by people, such as plants, animals, or the weather ▶ *Most branches of science are concerned with the study of **nature**.*

▶ **EASY** adj not difficult; done with ease ▶ *This fifty-piece puzzle is a lot **easier** than the one with a thousand pieces. Andrea thinks it will be **easy** to swim across the lake.*

EFFORTLESS seeming to require no effort or energy ▶ *Mark has been skating all his life and makes it look graceful and **effortless**.*

SIMPLE not hard to do, answer, or solve ▶ *The test was so **simple** that the whole class got a perfect score.*

see OBVIOUS, PLAIN

▶ **EAT** vb to take in food through your mouth; to have a meal ▶ *You have to **eat** right to stay healthy. We will **eat** dinner at six o'clock.*

CONSUME to eat or drink in great amounts ▶ *Risa **consumes** a box of cereal every two days.*

DEVOUR to eat quickly, hungrily, and completely ▶ *After working hard all morning, Janice **devoured** her lunch in six minutes.*

DINE to have a meal, especially dinner, in a formal way ▶ *We **dined** by candlelight at the best restaurant in town.*

FEAST to eat a large, fancy meal, especially on a special occasion ▶ *On Thanksgiving we **feasted** on turkey, sweet potatoes, beans, cranberry sauce, and salad, with pumpkin pie for dessert.*

FEED to give food to; to take in food (in this sense, not usually used of humans) ▶ *Don't forget to **feed** the children. The seagulls were **feeding** on our picnic leftovers.*

GRAZE to eat growing grass or other plants (not usually used of humans) ▶ *The cattle were **grazing** peacefully in the south pasture.*

tip

The words **breakfast** and **lunch**, but not *dinner* or *supper*, can also be used as verbs meaning "to eat breakfast or lunch": *Tom **breakfasted** at nine o'clock. We will **lunch** at the hotel.*

The following example is from Lewis Carroll's description of the mythical snark in "The Hunting of the Snark":

Its habit of getting up late you'll agree
That it carries too far, when I say
*That it frequently **breakfasts** at five-o'clock tea,*
And dines on the following day.

▶ **EDGE** n the line where something begins or ends ▶ *The kitten knocked a book off the **edge** of the table. Michael lives near the **edge** of town. This glass has sharp **edges**.*

RIM the outer edge around something ▶ *A fly walked around the **rim** of the glass. We hiked to the **rim** of the volcano. The hotel was perched on the canyon's **rim**.*

MARGIN the area near or along the edge of something, especially the blank area of a printed page ▶ *I found a mysterious note in the **margin** of my math book. He lived on the **margin** of land between the woods and the sea.*

BRINK the edge of something steep ▶ *We stepped to the **brink** of the cliff and could see the entire valley stretched below us.*

BORDER an outer edge; the dividing line between one country and another
▶ We rowed around the **border** of the lake. Our car was stopped for inspection when we crossed the **border** into Canada.

BOUNDARY a line, fence, or wall that separates one area from another
▶ That row of poplar trees marks the **boundary** between Mr. Thomas's farm and ours.

see **CIRCUMFERENCE**

▶ **EFFECT** n the change that happens because of an act or action ▶ Exercising every day has had a positive **effect** on my health. Simon is suffering from the **effects** of frostbite.

RESULT something that happens because of something else ▶ Sara studied hard and as a **result** she got an A on the test. The scar on Ted's knee is the **result** of a fall off his bike.

OUTCOME what happens at the end of an event or series of events ▶ Have you heard the **outcome** of the elections yet? The end of the war was the direct **outcome** of the peace talks.

CONSEQUENCE the often bad or unfortunate effect of a particular action or series of actions ▶ I failed the test and as a **consequence** I had to stay home. If you break the rules, you have to suffer the **consequences**.

UPSHOT a final and sometimes unexpected effect ▶ They got into an argument over some little thing and the **upshot** of it was that she canceled the wedding altogether.

> **tip**
>
> **Effect** can also be used as a *verb* meaning "to bring about; to cause to happen": *The negotiators were able to **effect** a compromise to settle the strike. Do you think the new rules will **effect** any change in their behavior?* Be careful not to confuse the *verb* **effect** with the *verb* **affect**. See the note at **AFFECT** vb.

▶ **EMBARRASS** vb to make someone feel awkward and uncomfortable
▶ Elisabeth was **embarrassed** by everyone's praise after her violin recital. I didn't mean to **embarrass** you by shouting your name.

SHAME to make someone feel awkward, uncomfortable, or ashamed because of doing something wrong ▶ Ben was **shamed** into cleaning his room when his favorite uncle came to visit.

ABASH to lose your self-confidence suddenly ▶ I was so **abashed** when the president of the United States shook my hand that I couldn't say anything!

DISCONCERT to confuse someone or cause them to lose their confidence or concentration ▶ His constant interruptions during the test were very **disconcerting**.

▶ **EMPTY** adj having nothing or no one inside ▶ *When I opened the box it was* **empty**. *He doesn't like to come home to an* **empty** *house.*

VACANT not occupied by anyone; completely empty ▶ *The hotel had one* **vacant** *room left for us. I got on the bus and sat in the first* **vacant** *seat I came to. My mind is* **vacant**.

HOLLOW having an empty space inside ▶ *A* **hollow** *tree trunk makes an ideal home for many small forest animals.*

UNOCCUPIED not lived in ▶ *That old house has been* **unoccupied** *for twelve years.*

UNINHABITED having no one living there ▶ *We camped for a week on an* **uninhabited** *island.*

▶ **ENEMY** n someone who hates and wants to harm or destroy another; the country or army you are fighting against in a war ▶ *Did your husband have any* **enemies** *who would want to burn down his business? They saw the* **enemy** *coming over the hill.*

OPPONENT someone who is against you in a fight, contest, game, debate, or election ▶ *The two* **opponents** *shook hands before the match began. His* **opponents** *won only eighteen percent of the vote.*

RIVAL someone whom you are competing against ▶ *The softball teams from the two neighboring towns have been fierce* **rivals** *for the past ten years.*

ADVERSARY someone who argues or fights against you ▶ *The United Nations has been trying to negotiate a peace settlement between the two* **adversaries**.

When I opened the box it was **empty**.

ANTAGONIST someone who opposes you or struggles against you for power or control ▶ *The two antagonists scowled at each other after the referee stopped them from fighting.*

▶ **ENERGY** n the strength to do active things without getting tired ▶ *I have lots of energy today, so I think I'll ride my bike in the park.*

VIGOR great physical energy or strength ▶ *Eddie raked the leaves with vigor.*

VITALITY energy and strength ▶ *She is full of vitality and will be a good gymnast.*

LIVELINESS a state of being energetic, alert, and active ▶ *We were amused by the liveliness and playfulness of the puppies.*

see STRENGTH

▶ **ENOUGH** adj as much or as many as needed ▶ *There were enough apples to make a pie. Do you have enough room to be comfortable?*

AMPLE enough or more than enough for what is needed ▶ *Make sure we have an ample supply of candy to give out on Halloween. There was ample food for everyone.*

SUFFICIENT as much as needed for a particular purpose ▶ *We have sufficient food and water to last a week. Do we have a sufficient number of books to go around?*

ADEQUATE enough or good enough ▶ *We have an adequate supply of firewood. Your grades are adequate, but you can do better.*

tip

Note that **enough** cannot be used after *a, an,* or before a singular noun such as *supply, amount, quantity,* or *number,* as the other words in this list can.

▶ **ENSURE** vb to make sure or certain that something happens ▶ *Please ensure that the door is locked when you leave.*

INSURE to pay a company that agrees to pay you in the event of sickness, fire, accident, or other loss ▶ *We insured the boat against fire and theft.*

ASSURE to make certain of something; to promise something, or to say something positively ▶ *I assured myself that the doors were locked. I can assure you that we will be there on time.*

SECURE to guarantee; to make something safe, especially by closing it tightly ▶ *We will buy the house if we can secure a loan from the bank. Will you secure the latch on the gate, please?*

▶ **ENTER** vb to go in or come in
▶ *I took off my hat as soon as I **entered** the building.*

PENETRATE to go inside or through something ▶ *When I stepped on the nail it hurt me but didn't **penetrate** the skin. The tanks **penetrated** the enemy's defenses.*

ENROLL to put your name on a list in order to become a member ▶ *As soon as we moved to town my parents **enrolled** me in the school. I **enrolled** in a swimming class to learn lifesaving.*

see COME, GO

▶ **ENTERTAIN** vb to provide something interesting or enjoyable to do; to be enjoyable and interesting to ▶ *Jonah **entertains** his friends with magic tricks. This book has **entertained** readers for many years.*

AMUSE to make someone laugh or smile; to keep someone happy and not bored ▶ *I was **amused** by Mark's Halloween costume—a windshield wiper! Penny likes to draw cartoons to **amuse** her little sister.*

DIVERT to distract attention from whatever troubles them, especially with something pleasurable ▶ *In order to stop thinking about her toothache, Miranda **diverted** herself by playing the guitar.*

CHEER to make someone glad or happy who had been sad or unhappy; to become happier (usually used with **up**) ▶ *When I was sick, Randall tried to **cheer** me up by telling me funny stories. I **cheered** up after you found the watch I had lost. I was **cheered** by the good news.*

▶ **ENTHUSIASM** n excitement or interest
▶ *The candidate's speech filled his supporters with **enthusiasm**. We began our project with great **enthusiasm**.*

PASSION strong enthusiasm or love
▶ *He has a **passion** for football.*

ZEAL strong enthusiasm and eagerness
▶ *Mrs. Evans performs her volunteer work with great **zeal**.*

FERVOR intense feeling
▶ *Margaret spoke with **fervor** about gaining equality for women. The singing aroused a strong religious **fervor** in his breast.*

ZEST enthusiasm and liveliness
▶ *Rebecca is always cheerful and has a great **zest** for life.*

▶ **ENVY** vb to wish that you could have something that another person has or do something that he or she has done
▶ *I **envy** John because he is going to South America this summer. Don **envies** Phil's ability to sing.*

Don **envies** Phil's ability to sing.

COVET to want very much something that belongs to someone else
▶ *I really **covet** Doug's new bicycle.*

RESENT to feel anger or annoyance at
▶ *I **resent** that you always interfere in my private affairs. Molly **resented** George's promotion, because she has worked here much longer than he has.*

see WANT

▶ **ERASE** vb to rub out with an eraser; to get rid of completely ▶ ***Erase** the extra pencil marks on your drawing. I tried to **erase** that thought from my mind.*

OBLITERATE to destroy something completely ▶ *In AD 79, a volcano **obliterated** the city of Pompeii, Italy. The spilled ink has **obliterated** all of the writing on this page.*

DELETE to remove something from a piece of writing or computer text
▶ ***Delete** the last two sentences. I think you should **delete** any reference to his personal life.*

▶ **ESCAPE** vb to break free from a place where you have been kept against your will; to avoid ▶ *Two convicts have **escaped** from prison. We managed to **escape** the rush-hour traffic.*

FLEE to run away from harm or danger ▶ *Thousands of refugees were **fleeing** from the approaching army.*

ELUDE to escape or get away from ▶ *I **eluded** my friends during our game of tag.*

see AVOID

▶ **EVENT** n something that happens, especially something interesting or important ▶ *Every Tuesday we study current **events** in social studies. Playing in the White House concert was the biggest **event** of her life.*

INCIDENT an event connected with other more important ones ▶ *Getting stuck in the mud was just one **incident** in a week of adventures.*

OCCURRENCE something that takes place or happens ▶ *That is the third **occurrence** of theft this week.*

ADVENTURE an exciting or dangerous experience ▶ *Our hike across the mountain became quite an **adventure** when we got lost!*

I **eluded** my friends during our game of tag.

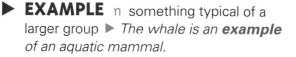

▶ **EXAMPLE** n something typical of a larger group ▶ *The whale is an **example** of an aquatic mammal.*

INSTANCE a person, act, or thing named in order to prove or support a general point ▶ *Nancy gave me several **instances** of when I had interrupted her.*

CASE an example that demonstrates existence of something ▶ *This is a **case** of deliberate disobedience! I thought she was my cousin, but it was a **case** of mistaken identity.*

SAMPLE a small amount of something that shows what the whole of it is like ▶ *The nurse took a blood **sample** to test for disease. The sales representative showed her **samples** to the manager of the store.*

MODEL a thing or person that is a good example ▶ *Ted is a **model** of good behavior.*

▶ **EXCLUDE** vb to block or prohibit the entrance of; to leave out ▶ *They were **excluded** from membership in the club. This list **excludes** prices.*

ELIMINATE to leave out or get rid of; to remove from a competition by a defeat ▶ *Let's try to **eliminate** pollution from the river. Our team was **eliminated** from the tournament in the semifinals.*

SUSPEND to stop something for a short time; to punish someone by stopping them from taking part in an activity for a while ▶ *The construction was **suspended** while archaeologists examined the discovery. Bill was **suspended** from the team for a week.*

EXPEL to send or force something out ▶ *You **expel** air from your lungs when you exhale. His behavior was so bad he was **expelled** from school.*

▶ **EXPENSIVE** adj having a high price, especially one that is greater than the thing is worth or more than you can afford to pay ▶ *Richard bought an **expensive** new CD player. She spent all her savings on an **expensive** vacation.*

COSTLY costing a lot of money, especially because of its richness or actual value ▶ *The crown is covered with **costly** gems. Harvey made a **costly** mistake when he left his camera in the taxi.*

VALUABLE worth a lot of money, or very important in another way ▶ *Myra's stamp collection is probably very **valuable**. We got some **valuable** information from our travel agent.*

INVALUABLE extremely valuable or useful ▶ *This letter signed by Thomas Jefferson is **invaluable**. Roger has been an **invaluable** employee for twenty years.*

DEAR highly valued or much loved; very expensive or more expensive than usual ▶ *She has been a **dear** friend for most of my life. Meat and sugar were very **dear** during the war.*

▶ **EXPLAIN** vb to make something plain or easier to understand; to give the reason or cause for something ▶ *The lifeguard* **explained** *the rules before we jumped in the pool. Can you* **explain** *why the seasons change?*

CLARIFY to make something clear or easier to understand ▶ *After Mr. Duffy handed out the assignment we asked him to* **clarify** *what he meant by "metaphor."*

INTERPRET to give the meaning of something in language that can be understood; to give your own understanding of something ▶ *Can you* **interpret** *this poem so that it makes sense to me? I* **interpret** *his smile to indicate he likes you.*

JUSTIFY to explain or show why something is right, fair, or reasonable ▶ *How can you* **justify** *spending so much money on clothes?*

DEMONSTRATE to show other people how to do something or use something ▶ *After she explained how to use the new computers, she* **demonstrated** *how to do it.*

FAIR adj reasonable and honest
▶ *I think it was a **fair** decision to have everyone share the cost. A referee has to be **fair** to both teams.*

JUST in accordance with the law or with moral principles; being morally upright or good ▶ *A **just** society will not tolerate prejudice. He is a **just** man and will treat everyone fairly.*

IMPARTIAL not favoring one person or one point of view over another ▶ *The case was tried by an **impartial** jury. I don't care who wins the game; I'm just an **impartial** observer.*

EQUAL the same for each member of a group ▶ *Everyone will have an **equal** opportunity to play during the game.*

UNBIASED without bias or prejudice ▶ *My **unbiased** opinion is that you are both wrong!*

see **RIGHT**

The case was tried by an **impartial** jury.

► **FAITHFUL** adj constant in affection or allegiance to someone or something ► *Janice has been a **faithful** friend my whole life. My dog is a **faithful** companion.*

LOYAL faithful and constant, especially in allegiance to a leader, a country, an institution, or to a principle ► *When the revolution began, some colonists remained **loyal** to the king. She has been a **loyal** supporter of the team for years.*

TRUE strongly and steadily faithful or loyal ► *He will be **true** to his word no matter what happens. A **true** friend would help her through her troubles.*

DEVOTED very loving, faithful, or loyal ► *Mark is a **devoted** father who spends a lot of time with his children.*

STEADFAST firm and steady; not changing ► *I couldn't have done this without the **steadfast** support of my friends. She stared at him with a **steadfast** gaze.*

► **FAKE** adj not real or genuine ► *Her earrings are made of **fake** diamonds. He got caught trying to buy cigarettes with a **fake** ID card.*

FALSE not genuine; meant to deceive ► *I lost a tooth in the accident and now I have a **false** tooth. He was using a **false** name.*

ARTIFICIAL not occurring naturally; not natural or made from natural materials ► *These are **artificial** flowers, made of silk. **Artificial** coloring is added to some foods to make them look better.*

IMITATION made to look like something else that is genuine or of a higher quality ► *The car seats are **imitation** leather.*

COUNTERFEIT made to look like something else in order to deceive people ► *She was caught with a suitcase full of **counterfeit** money.*

► **FALL** vb to move downward quickly because of the force of gravity ► *Sandra **fell** off her bike. We picked up all the apples that had **fallen** from the tree during the storm.*

DROP to fall suddenly; to let something fall ► *The acrobat **dropped** to the floor. The dog **dropped** the ball at my feet.*

COLLAPSE to fall down suddenly from weakness or illness ► *The building*

I lost a tooth in the accident and now I have a **false** tooth.

collapsed *after the earthquake.
The dancer* **collapsed** *during his
performance.*

PLUNGE to move swiftly downward or
forward ▶ *Phyllis* **plunged** *into the water.
The temperature* **plunged** *after sunset.*

TOPPLE to fall over, usually from a height;
to make something fall ▶ *The radio tower*
toppled *in the hurricane. Rebel troops*
toppled *the government without a fight.*

TUMBLE to fall suddenly and helplessly
▶ *The children* **tumbled** *down the hill,
laughing all the way. The kitten* **tumbled**
off the chair and ran away.

see DESCEND

▶ **FAMILY** n a group of people
related to one another, especially parents
or guardians and their children
▶ *My wife's* **family** *came to this country
from Wales when she was a girl.*

RELATIVE a member of your family
▶ *Four of our* **relatives** *came to visit
us for the weekend.*

RELATION a member of your family;
relative ▶ *I want to invite all my friends
and* **relations** *to the party.*

▶ **FAMOUS** adj known to many people
▶ *Neil Armstrong is a* **famous** *astronaut.
The rock group became* **famous** *and went
on a tour of the country.*

NOTED famous for accomplishments
▶ *Toni Morrison is a* **noted** *American
novelist. Professor Wilson is a* **noted**
authority on ants.

PROMINENT widely known for high
position, reputation, or accomplishments
▶ *She belongs to one of the most*
prominent *families in the state.
George's father is a* **prominent** *lawyer.*

EMINENT well-known and respected;
standing out above others ▶ *Marie Curie
was an* **eminent** *scientist known especially
for her discovery of radium.*

NOTORIOUS famous for undesirable reasons
▶ *Al Capone was a* **notorious** *gangster in
the 1930s. The movie became* **notorious**
for its violence.

▶ **FAR** adj not near ▶ *Kim was waving from
the* **far** *side of the river. He has traveled to
the* **far** *regions of the earth.*

DISTANT not close in space or time; not
closely related ▶ *We could hear the* **distant**
*thunder growing louder. Archaeologists study
the* **distant** *past. Myra is a* **distant** *cousin.*

REMOTE far away or isolated
▶ *My sister and I grew up in a* **remote**
village in the mountains.

tip

Far is often used as an adverb
meaning "to or for a great
distance": *Don't swim* **far** *from
the shore. How* **far** *have you
traveled today?*

Use **distant** when you want to include
an actual measure of how far away
something is: *Their farm is about eight
miles* **distant** *from the nearest store.*

▶ **FAST** adj moving or able to move with great speed ▶ *Alice is a **fast** runner. She also likes to drive **fast** cars.*

RAPID fast-moving; not taking much time; repeating often in a short time ▶ *The boat was swept away in the **rapid** current. He made a **rapid** recovery. You have a **rapid** heartbeat after exercising.*

QUICK not taking much time ▶ *Ben made a **quick** trip to the store.*

SPEEDY very fast; fast and efficient ▶ *I hope their delivery service is **speedy**, because I hate cold pizza!*

SWIFT moving quickly and smoothly or easily ▶ *In one **swift** motion he caught the glass before it hit the floor. It will take a **swift** runner to win this race.*

tip

Fast can also be used as an adverb: *I ran as **fast** as I could.* All of the other words in this list can be made into adverbs by adding **-ly**. **Speedy** also adds an **i** to make it easier to pronounce: **speedily**.

▶ **FAULT** n a defect or lack of strength, especially in character or personality ▶ *Jake's biggest **fault** is that he lies.*

FAILING a minor fault ▶ *One of Tim's **failings** is that he is always late.*

WEAKNESS a minor fault that results from a lack of self-control; a special desire for something ▶ *Her greatest **weakness** is that she can never say no to her friends. Dennis has a **weakness** for chocolate.*

VICE immoral or harmful behavior ▶ *The mayor's office turned out to be full of **vice** and corruption at the highest level.*

▶ **FEAR** n the unpleasant feeling you have when you are in danger or when you expect something bad to happen ▶ *I was filled with **fear** as the sled rushed down the hill. The deer stood in our headlights, motionless with **fear**.*

ALARM a sudden fear that something bad will happen ▶ *There was a loud crash of thunder and I woke up in **alarm**. Don't worry, there's no cause for **alarm**.*

FRIGHT fear caused by sudden danger ▶ *You gave me quite a **fright** when you jumped out from behind the door. Her face was pale with **fright**.*

DREAD a strong feeling of fear and helplessness about something in the future ▶ *The whole city was filled with **dread** as the enemy troops drew closer. Andrei is in constant **dread** of being attacked by dogs.*

TERROR an intense feeling of great fear ▶ *We were all filled with **terror** as the fire spread and smoke filled the room.*

PANIC a sudden intense fear that results in confused attempts to flee ▶ *In spite of widespread **panic**, all the passengers were rescued before the ship sank.*

There was a loud crash of thunder and I woke up in **alarm**.

HORROR a feeling of great fear or disgust caused by something terrible, grotesque, or ugly ▶ *We watched in **horror** as the flash flood swept away entire houses.*

▶ **FEMININE** adj having or being a quality thought to be typical of women ▶ *Her handwriting is very **feminine**.*

FEMALE of or relating to women or girls or to the sex that gives birth to young animals or lays eggs ▶ ***Female** athletes are now getting more respect than they used to. Many **female** birds have dull coloring for camouflage.*

LADYLIKE having the manners or behavior expected of a lady; like a lady ▶ *Use your fork, Angela; it is not **ladylike** to eat with your fingers!*

WOMANLY having the qualities expected of a woman, especially such desirable traits as maturity or strength of character ▶ *The main character in the novel is a strong, **womanly** figure who struggles hard to keep her family together.*

see MASCULINE

▶ **FEW** adj some but not many
▶ *We can't spend much for lunch because I have only a **few** dollars with me. This is one of the **few** books I really like.*

SEVERAL more than two, but not many
▶ ***Several** days passed before Tim returned. I would like **several** stamps. The storm knocked down **several** trees in the park.*

COUPLE two; very few, though perhaps more than two ▶ *I will be home in a **couple** more days.*

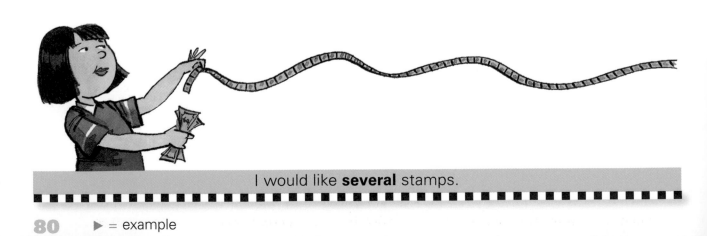

tip

Note that **few** and **couple** are used with *a*, but **several** is not.

Especially in writing, **couple** is more often used as a noun followed by *of*: *I will be home in a **couple of** weeks. I saw a **couple of** robins on the grass today.*

Similarly, **few** and **several** can also be used as nouns followed by *of*: *I would like a **few of** these roses, please. She gave me **several of** my favorite kinds of candy.*

▶ **FIGHT** vb to try to hurt someone by hitting, kicking, or using weapons; to try to defeat someone or something
▶ *If you **fight** with my brother you will have to **fight** me, too! I've been **fighting** a cold for three days now.*

BATTLE to fight with many people on each side, especially to fight in a war; to fight hard against something for a long time
▶ *The two armies are **battling** over control of the government. Phyllis has been **battling** cancer for two years.*

STRUGGLE to fight violently or with great effort ▶ *Bull elephant seals must **struggle** constantly with younger males to keep control of the herd.*

COMBAT to fight against someone or something, especially in a war
▶ *The rebels have been **combating** government forces in the hills. Penicillin is used to **combat** infection.*

CLASH to fight with sudden force or argue vehemently ▶ *The armies **clashed** in one last attempt to gain ground from each other.*

CONFLICT to disagree; to be in opposition
▶ *Todd's ideas always **conflict** with mine.*

see **ARGUE, ATTACK**

I would like **several** stamps.

All of these words can also be used as nouns: *Moira got into a **fight** with her sister. The **battle** lasted for two days. After a long **struggle** we finally won. He was lucky that he never had to go into actual **combat**. They are both stubborn, and a **clash** of wills was inevitable. The **conflict** was resolved after many weeks of negotiation.*

▶ **FIND** vb to get something by chance or by searching for it ▶ *I **found** a dollar on my way home from school. Ellie finally **found** her shoe under the bed.*

LOCATE to find out where something is ▶ *Can you **locate** Utah on the map? I wanted to call home, but I couldn't **locate** a phone booth.*

COME ACROSS to find or meet by chance ▶ *I **came across** these old photographs while I was cleaning the closet. He **came across** an old friend at the post office.*

SPOT to see or notice ▶ *Just when he was about to give up the search, he **spotted** the kitten up in a tree. She couldn't **spot** her mother in the crowd.*

see **DISCOVER**

▶ **FINISH** vb to come to the end of something you were doing ▶ *Estelle **finished** the book in three days. Can you help me with my homework when you **finish** the dishes?*

COMPLETE to bring to an end; to make whole or perfect ▶ *I will have time to relax after I **complete** my history project.*

END to come or bring to a stop ▶ *We had to leave before the concert **ended**. I wish you would **end** this constant fighting and arguing.*

CONCLUDE to finish in a particular way ▶ *The debate **concluded** with a unanimous vote in favor of building a new science lab.*

TERMINATE to bring to an end in time or space ▶ *José's job as a lifeguard **terminates** on the last day of August.*

WIND UP to bring to a conclusion ▶ *We decided to **wind up** the school year with a class picnic and pool party.*

see **STOP**

▶ **FIRM** adj not moving, bending, or giving way easily under pressure ▶ *I like to sleep on a **firm** mattress. The house is built on a **firm** foundation.*

HARD not easily dented, pierced, or cut ▶ *Coconuts have a **hard** shell.*

SOLID firm enough to keep its own shape; not liquid or gas ▶ *They had to dig the tunnel through **solid** rock. This orange juice is frozen **solid**!*

STIFF difficult to bend or stretch ▶ *These new shoes are still too **stiff** to be comfortable.*

STEADY not shaky or wobbly ▶ *Make sure the ladder is **steady** before you climb up.*

see **TOUGH**

▶ **FIT** adj adapted or qualified for some use, purpose, or situation; acceptable from a particular point of view ▶ *The boat is now **fit** for sailing. Is this salad **fit** to eat? I don't think he is **fit** to be a father.*

SUITABLE right for a particular purpose ▶ *Bring some clothes **suitable** for rainy weather.*

PROPER right for a given purpose or occasion ▶ *The restaurant requires **proper** attire; no bathing suits are allowed.*

APPROPRIATE especially well suited or fit for some purpose, use, or situation ▶ *Are you sure these books are **appropriate** for very young children? You should have the **appropriate** gear for rock climbing.*

▶ **FIX** vb to restore to proper condition ▶ *I'll be down as soon as I **fix** my hair. Do you know how to **fix** a flat tire?*

REPAIR to make work again; to put back together something that is broken ▶ *Steve said he could **repair** our lawn mower. It took me all afternoon to **repair** the broken window.*

MEND to fix or repair something torn, broken in pieces, or worn threadbare ▶ *I think we can **mend** that cup handle with a little glue. I learned how to **mend** my own socks.*

PATCH to put a small piece of material on a hole, rip, or worn place in order to mend it ▶ *Martha **patched** the holes in my favorite blue jeans.*

▶ **FLOWER** n the colored part of a plant that produces seeds or fruit; a plant that has flowers ▶ *Can you name the parts of a **flower**? We gave my mother a bouquet of **flowers** on her birthday.*

BLOSSOM a flower on a fruit tree or other plant ▶ *The apple **blossoms** make the orchard a beautiful white. Those peony **blossoms** are huge!*

BLOOM a flower on a plant; the state of having blossoms ▶ *What a lovely rose **bloom**. The lilacs are in **bloom** this week.*

BUD a small shoot on a plant that grows into a leaf or flower ▶ *As the **buds** get larger and turn from red to green, I know that it will soon be spring. I gave her a single rose**bud**.*

I gave her a single rose**bud**.

▶ = example

tip

There are many garden plants grown especially for their flowers. Some of the most widely known are **daisy, violet, African violet, tulip, daffodil, crocus, hyacinth, iris, zinnia, lily, petunia, rose, sunflower, snapdragon, magnolia, marigold, carnation, geranium, phlox, poinsettia, chrysanthemum, orchid, pansy,** and **gladiolus**.

▶ **FLY** vb to travel through the air ▶ *Last night I dreamed I could **fly** like a bird. We **flew** to Nebraska on our vacation.*

SOAR to fly very high in the air ▶ *I like to watch the larks **soaring** in the evening sky. We could see the trail left by a jet **soaring** across the sky.*

GLIDE to descend gradually through the air without using much engine power; to move smoothly and easily ▶ *The plane **glided** toward the landing strip. The skaters **glided** across the ice.*

FLOAT to move slowly through the air; to rest on water ▶ *We watched several hot-air balloons **float** over the hills. The gulls **floated** on the gentle waves.*

▶ **FOG** n thick water vapor or clouds near the surface of the earth ▶ *We decided not to drive home until the **fog** lifted.*

MIST a cloud of tiny water droplets in the air ▶ *A light **mist** floated over the lake at dawn.*

SMOG a mixture of fog and smoke that hangs in the air over cities and industrial areas ▶ *The **smog** over Los Angeles can be quite thick.*

HAZE smoke, dust, or moisture in the air that prevents you from seeing very far ▶ *We could barely see the mountains through the **haze**.*

We decided not to drive home until the **fog** lifted.

▶ **FOLLOW** vb 1 to come after or take place after in time or in order ▶ *February* **follows** *January. W* **follows** *V in the alphabet. The reception will* **follow** *the wedding.*

SUCCEED to follow after another in order, especially to take over from someone in an important position ▶ *Kim* **succeeded** *her mother as president of the company.*

ENSUE to follow immediately; to take place as a result ▶ *The play was very thought-provoking and a lively discussion* **ensued** *on our way home.*

▶ **FOLLOW** vb 2 to go behind ▶ *The students* **followed** *the teacher into the classroom. We have been* **following** *that truck for twenty minutes.*

PURSUE to follow someone in order to catch him or her ▶ *The policeman* **pursued** *the thieves on foot across the vacant lot.*

CHASE to run after someone in order to catch him or her or to make him or her go away ▶ *We* **chased** *Philip for three blocks before we caught up with him. We* **chased** *the dog off the soccer field.*

TRAIL to follow the scent or tracks of an animal or person; to follow slowly behind others ▶ *The hound kept its nose to the ground as it* **trailed** *the raccoon. Pedro was* **trailing** *a long way behind.*

TRACK to follow the tracks or marks left by a person or animal ▶ *The hunters* **tracked** *the herd of bison across the plains.*

▶ **FOOLISH** adj not showing good sense; not wise ▶ *It was rather* **foolish** *of me to leave my suitcase on the bus. I felt* **foolish** *when I couldn't answer any of her questions.*

RIDICULOUS extremely foolish ▶ *It was* **ridiculous** *to think that she wouldn't recognize me—I'd only been gone a month. That is a* **ridiculous** *hat!*

SILLY lacking good sense or judgment; laughable ▶ *I would have gotten an A on my math test if I hadn't made some* **silly** *mistakes.*

ABSURD making no sense at all ▶ *It is* **absurd** *to try to climb this mountain wearing sandals.*

see **FUNNY, STUPID**

▶ **FORBID** vb to order someone not to do something ▶ *I* **forbid** *you to climb those trees.*

BAN to officially forbid someone from doing something or something from happening; to exclude ▶ *The government has* **banned** *any further travel to the war zone. I don't believe books should be* **banned** *from libraries.*

PROHIBIT to officially forbid or prevent something ▶ *Smoking is* **prohibited** *in public buildings.*

▶ **FORCE** vb to cause by using strength or power ▶ *Dad* **forced** *me to eat the rest of my dinner. Slaves were often* **forced** *to work long days in the hot sun without a rest. She* **forced** *the window open.*

REQUIRE to have to do ▶ *You are* **required** *to take a driving test before you can get a driver's license.*

COMPEL to cause by using great force or pressure ▶ *Stanley felt* **compelled** *to get a second job to pay for his new car. I can't* **compel** *you to give the money back, but you should.*

COERCE to force someone against his or her will, often by using threats ▶ *We had to shout and stamp our feet to* **coerce** *the horse into the truck.*

MAKE to cause or force ▶ *Pepper* **makes** *me sneeze. Mommy,* **make** *her give me my hat back!*

▶ **FOREIGN** adj to do with or coming from another country ▶ *James collects* **foreign** *stamps. Have you ever been to a* **foreign** *country? Can you speak a* **foreign** *language?*

ALIEN different and strange ▶ *Jenna found her new school very* **alien**. *Penguins cannot live in this warm,* **alien** *environment.*

IMPORTED brought into a country from elsewhere ▶ *This guitar is made from* **imported** *Brazilian rosewood.*

EXOTIC from a faraway country; strange and exciting ▶ *The music of India sounds very* **exotic** *to most Americans. She was wearing an* **exotic** *perfume.*

▶ **FOREIGNER** n a native or citizen of a country other than the one he or she is in ▶ *Many* **foreigners** *visit this country every year. It is hard being a* **foreigner** *and not knowing the language.*

ALIEN a person who lives in one country and is a citizen of another country ▶ *All* **aliens** *in this country are supposed to register with the immigration bureau.*

IMMIGRANT a person who has come from another country to stay permanently ▶ *Alexa's grandmother was a Russian* **immigrant**.

OUTSIDER someone who is not a member of a particular group ▶ *For a while Jamie felt like an* **outsider** *at his new school, but then he made some good friends.*

▶ **FORGET** vb not to remember; to lose a thought or idea from your mind ▶ *I forgot to clean up my room yesterday, so I'll do it now. I used to know your phone number, but I forgot it.*

NEGLECT to fail to take care of; to fail to do, especially from carelessness ▶ *Barbara has been neglecting her pet guinea pig lately. Phil neglected to turn off the iron.*

OMIT to leave out; to fail to do something ▶ *You may omit chapter 6 in your reading homework. I omitted telling you that your mother called.*

OVERLOOK to fail to notice; to choose to ignore ▶ *Daisy overlooked the extra costs. I overlooked Dylan's rude remarks.*

▶ **FORGIVE** vb to stop being angry with; to decide not to punish ▶ *I will forgive you for breaking the window if you will help me repair it.*

EXCUSE to overlook or forgive a fault that is not very important; to forgive for a small fault or mistake ▶ *Excuse the interruption, but dinner is ready now. Please excuse me for stepping on your toe.*

PARDON to release from punishment; to forgive a small fault or discourtesy ▶ *The thief was pardoned for his crime and let out of prison. Pardon me, sir; is this seat taken?*

ABSOLVE to remove blame or guilt from ▶ *A careful investigation absolved everyone at the party of any blame for the damage.*

ACQUIT to clear of a charge or accusation; to find not guilty ▶ *The jury acquitted*

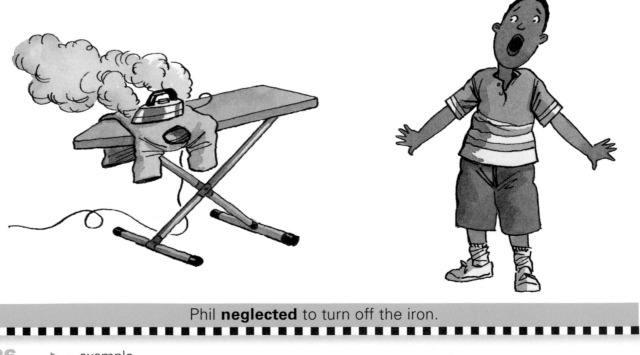

Phil **neglected** to turn off the iron.

Mr. Gonzalez when they learned that he was not even in the country when the crime took place.

▶ **FORM** vb to make up or create
▶ *These three lines* **form** *a triangle. First,* **form** *the clay into a ball. She* **formed** *her own advertising company.*

SHAPE to give a particular form, shape, or outline to ▶ *These events will* **shape** *the course of our lives for years to come.*

MOLD to give form or shape to, often by pouring or pressing material into a container ▶ *These figures were* **molded** *out of bronze. A good teacher helps to* **mold** *the minds of her students.*

FASHION to create, make, or construct ▶ *She* **fashions** *jewelry out of antique coins. We* **fashioned** *a makeshift shelter out of pine boughs.*

see **BUILD, INVENT, MAKE**

▶ **FREE** vb to set loose from something that limits or confines ▶ *The captives were* **freed** *from prison after the war. We were trying to* **free** *the squirrel from the trap it was caught in.*

RELEASE to set loose from confinement or obligation ▶ *The whole school was* **released** *early because a storm was coming. She* **released** *me from my promise to go.*

LIBERATE to give liberty to; to set free ▶ *We would like to* **liberate** *people from the struggles of poverty. Electricity will* **liberate** *oxygen and hydrogen from water.*

EMANCIPATE to free a person or group from slavery or the control of others ▶ *In 1863, Abraham Lincoln signed a proclamation* **emancipating** *the slaves.*

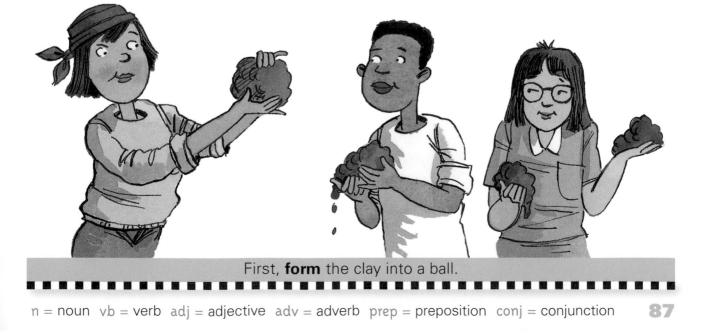

First, **form** the clay into a ball.

▶ **FREEDOM** n the state of being free from the control of others ▶ *The **freedom** of the press is an important right in a democracy. After its wing had healed, we gave the bird its **freedom**.*

LIBERTY freedom or release from slavery, imprisonment, or the control of others ▶ *You are now at **liberty** to come and go as you please. The colonists decided to fight for their **liberty**.*

INDEPENDENCE freedom from the influence or control of others ▶ *His job at the bakery gave Tom greater **independence** from his family.*

▶ **FRIEND** n someone you know and like; someone who is not your enemy ▶ *All his **friends** came to the party.*

GIRLFRIEND the girl or woman in a romantic relationship; a female friend of a girl or woman ▶ *Tom and his **girlfriend** went to the dance together. Alicia is inside playing with her **girlfriend**.*

BOYFRIEND the boy or man in a romantic relationship ▶ *Natalie has been going out with her **boyfriend** for a year.*

COMPANION a person who spends a lot of time with you ▶ *Allen has been my constant **companion** for six years.*

ASSOCIATE someone you work with or see often ▶ *Her **associates** included the mayor and everyone on the committee.*

ALLY a country or person who agrees to help and support another ▶ *Canada and Mexico are close **allies** of the United States.*

▶ **FRIENDLY** adj having feelings of goodwill and kindness toward others; kind and helpful ▶ *Janice is a **friendly** neighbor who looks after our pets when we are away. Her offer to take me fishing was a **friendly** gesture.*

KIND gentle, helpful, and sympathetic ▶ *The nurses at the hospital were very **kind** to me when I had my tonsils out.*

SOCIABLE liking to be in the company of others ▶ *His younger brother is very **sociable** and has lots of friends.*

CORDIAL friendly in a polite way ▶ *We had a very **cordial** conversation with the mayor.*

NEIGHBORLY friendly to the people who live near you ▶ *The people on this block are all very **neighborly**, and came to meet us the day we moved here.*

see **NICE**

▶ **FROG** n a small green or brown amphibian with webbed feet and long back legs for jumping and swimming ▶ ***Frogs** live in or near water.*

TOAD an amphibian that looks like a frog but has a rougher, drier skin and lives mostly on land ▶ ***Toads** lay their eggs in water. We found a **toad** under one of the plants in our flower garden.*

BULLFROG a large frog that makes a deep croaking sound ▶ *All evening we could hear the **bullfrogs** along the shore of the lake.*

SPRING PEEPER a small brown tree frog in eastern North America that makes a shrill peeping sound, especially in the spring

▶ *When you hear the **spring peepers** you will know that spring has really arrived.*

TADPOLE a young frog or toad in the larva stage that lives in water, breathes with gills, and has a tail for swimming but no legs ▶ *We could see dozens of **tadpoles** swimming in the shallow water.*

▶ **FULL** adj containing as much or as many as possible or usual ▶ *I drank a **full** glass of milk. Amy's room is **full** of books. My schedule is too **full** for me to go skiing this weekend.*

PACKED as full as possible ▶ *The orchestra played to a **packed** house. The theater was **packed** with people—not a seat was empty.*

LOADED containing very much or very many; completely full ▶ *Fresh oranges are **loaded** with vitamin C. It took three of us to pull the **loaded** wagon up the hill.*

FILLED containing the full amount ▶ *The lifeboats were already **filled** to capacity.*

CROWDED containing very many people or animals ▶ *The street was **crowded** with sightseers trying to get into the museum.*

STUFFED uncomfortably full ▶ *No more to eat, please—I feel **stuffed**.*

▶ **FUNCTION** n a purpose, role, or job ▶ *The **function** of the heart is to pump blood around the body. The treasurer's **function** is to keep track of our funds.*

OFFICE an important and usually powerful position ▶ *She is running for the **office** of governor.*

see DUTY, JOB

She is running for the **office** of governor.

▶ **FUNNY** adj causing laughter or smiles
▶ *That movie was so **funny** I couldn't stop laughing. My dad likes to tell jokes that aren't really very **funny**.*

AMUSING funny in a quiet, pleasant, or playful way ▶ *Isabella told us an **amusing** story about how her dog was chased by the squirrels in her yard.*

HUMOROUS causing laughter or smiles in a pleasant or friendly way ▶ *James Thurber wrote **humorous** stories about life in his family.*

WITTY funny or amusing in a clever way
▶ *Oscar is always making **witty** remarks about people.*

HILARIOUS very funny and causing much laughter or merriment
▶ *She is a **hilarious** comedian; she kept us all in stitches for an hour.*

COMICAL causing amusement or laughter, especially because of something unexpected or startling ▶ *Charlie is always making **comical** faces when the teacher isn't looking.*

RIDICULOUS funny or silly, especially in a way that can be made fun of
▶ *Michael wore a **ridiculous** costume actually made out of fruit!*

see FOOLISH

Michael wore a **ridiculous** costume actually made out of fruit!

g

▶ **GAME** n an activity with rules that can be played by one or more people ▶ *Let's play a **game** of Capture the Flag. My little sister beat me at chess three **games** in a row.*

SPORT a game involving physical activity ▶ *Soccer is the only **sport** Marilyn likes to play. I don't like to watch **sports** on TV—I'd rather play myself.*

PASTIME a hobby, a sports activity, or an entertainment that passes the time in an enjoyable way ▶ *His favorite **pastimes** are basketball, computer games, and playing the cello.*

COMPETITION the act or process of competing in a game, a sport, or business ▶ *The strong **competition** between the two schools makes this football game more exciting than usual.*

CONTEST a struggle for victory; a competition in which each person performs without direct contact with others ▶ *The game ended in a fierce **contest** for the winning point. Angelo won the statewide essay writing **contest**.*

RECREATION the enjoyment of something after working; the games, sports, or hobbies that people enjoy in their spare time ▶ *I like to swim and to read for **recreation**. My mother's favorite **recreation** is waterskiing.*

▶ **GATHER** vb to get or bring together in one place or group; to come together in a group ▶ *We **gathered** blackberries from bushes beside the road. A large crowd **gathered** outside the courthouse.*

COLLECT to gather something, especially as a hobby ▶ *Sean has been **collecting** stamps for more than 10 years.*

ASSEMBLE to gather in one place; to put all the parts of something together ▶ *The whole school **assembled** in the cafeteria. Follow the instructions to **assemble** this model.*

ACCUMULATE to collect things or to pile up, especially over a period of time ▶ *We have been **accumulating** cans and bottles for recycling. A layer of dust has been **accumulating** in the cabin all winter.*

see SAVE

▶ **GENTLE** adj kind and sensitive; not harsh, rough, stern, loud, or violent ▶ *My dog looks scary, but he is very **gentle**. She uses a very **gentle** soap to wash the baby. I heard a **gentle** knock on the door.*

MILD gentle and not aggressive; not extreme or severe ▶ *Clark is a **mild**-mannered newspaper reporter. The weather has been unusually **mild** this fall.*

SOFT pleasantly quiet and gentle; moving without much force ▶ *There was **soft** music playing in the elevator. A **soft** breeze blew across the bay.*

TENDER gentle and loving ▶ *She gave the baby a **tender** kiss.*

▶ **GET** vb to have newly in your possession ▶ *I have to **get** a new box of pencils. I **got** a letter from my cousin today.*

RECEIVE to have given or sent to you ▶ *I **received** a message from my brother saying that I should go straight home after school.*

OBTAIN to get, especially by searching, working, or asking ▶ *Hector **obtained** the information he needed from the encyclopedia.*

ACQUIRE to get gradually or after working continuously for a long time ▶ *John **acquired** his ability to speak Japanese by living in Japan for eight months.*

GAIN to get after great effort; to get more of ▶ *She **gained** the governor's office after a long campaign. I **gained** five pounds last month.*

WIN to achieve by work, effort, or good luck ▶ *Julius **won** his brother's respect. Miriam **won** a bicycle in the raffle.*

see **CATCH, SEIZE**

▶ **GIFT** n something that is given without cost ▶ *Marsha received birthday **gifts** from all her friends. She gave the statue to the museum as a **gift**.*

PRESENT a gift offered to show good will ▶ *He gave his teacher a **present** of flowers. We give **presents** to each other at Christmas and Hanukkah to show our love.*

DONATION a gift of money or goods, especially to an organization or to help someone ▶ *We are collecting **donations** of food and clothing to help the flood victims.*

GRANT a sum of money given by the government or another organization for a special purpose ▶ *Medical research at the university is supported by **grants**. I was awarded a **grant** to study in South America.*

▶ **GIVE** vb to hand or deliver; to pay ▶ *Bryan **gave** Tom a pair of skates. I will **give** you a dollar if you can fix this for me.*

PRESENT to give in a formal way, especially as a gift or prize ▶ *I would like to **present** you with this medal for bravery.*

DONATE to give as a gift
▶ *We donated our piano to the school. The company donated a portion of its profits to charity.*

GRANT to give or to allow, especially in answer to a request ▶ *We were granted permission to leave. His boss granted him two weeks off when his daughter was born.*

BESTOW to award ▶ *The judges bestowed the blue ribbon on the winner of the contest.*

▶ **GLASS** n a transparent material made from melted sand; a container for drinking, made from glass or plastic ▶ *Glass is used in windows, bottles, and lenses. Would you like a glass of water?*

CUP a small container for holding liquids, often with a handle ▶ *I poured myself another cup of hot chocolate.*

MUG a large, heavy cup with a handle ▶ *We each had a mug of hot cider when we came inside.*

TUMBLER a tall drinking glass with straight sides ▶ *Fran drinks at least one tumbler of milk at each meal.*

▶ **GO** vb to be in motion toward or away from ▶ *After school I will go straight home. We watched the boats going up and down the river.*

PROGRESS to move forward; to improve ▶ *The parade progressed slowly down the block. How are you progressing on your essay?*

PROCEED to go forward; to continue ▶ *When the plane lands, proceed directly to the baggage claim section. You may now proceed with your work.*

see **LEAVE, MOVE, TRAVEL**

I poured myself another **cup** of hot chocolate.

▸ **GOOD** adj a term of approval suggesting that something is of high quality, useful, well-behaved, clever, kind, or otherwise favorable ▸ *You did a **good** job cleaning the garage. This pencil is **good** for drawing. Cynthia is a **good** girl. I feel **good** today.*

FINE very good; better than average; in good health ▸ *Kim is doing a **fine** job on her English essay. The weather is **fine** for hiking. I was sick, but I feel **fine** today.*

EXCELLENT much better than average ▸ *George has been getting **excellent** grades all year. This cathedral is an **excellent** example of medieval architecture.*

OUTSTANDING extremely good ▸ *Alexa gave an **outstanding** performance as the wicked queen in the play.*

ADMIRABLE deserving admiration or praise ▸ *I think it is **admirable** of her to volunteer to visit with elderly patients at the nursing home after school.*

RESPECTABLE reasonably good ▸ *In spite of being sick for two weeks, Brian got a **respectable** grade in science.*

SPLENDID exceptionally good ▸ *I have a **splendid** idea—let's all go swimming!*

see **FAIR, GREAT, NICE**

▸ **GOVERN** vb to be in charge, usually of a country or an organization ▸ *In a democracy the people themselves decide who will **govern** them.*

RULE to have power and authority, usually over a country ▸ *The tyrant **ruled** the country with an iron hand.*

REIGN to rule as a monarch ▸ *Queen Victoria **reigned** over England for 64 years.*

see **CONTROL**

▸ **GRAND** adj large and impressive; very worthy or dignified ▸ *A **grand** staircase leads up from the entranceway.*

MAGNIFICENT very impressive or beautiful ▸ *The museum has a **magnificent** collection of Roman sculptures. The play was a **magnificent** success.*

The weather is **fine** for hiking.

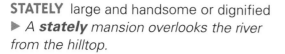
STATELY large and handsome or dignified ▶ *A stately mansion overlooks the river from the hilltop.*

MAJESTIC having great dignity; having great power and impressive beauty ▶ *The castle towers rise with majestic beauty reflected in the water below. The majestic waves crashed over the rocks.*

SPLENDID very beautiful and brilliant or gorgeous ▶ *The ceiling of the chapel is covered with splendid paintings.*

▶ **GRATEFUL** adj feeling gratitude, especially in return for favors received from someone else ▶ *The librarian was very grateful for the help we gave her putting books back on the shelves.*

THANKFUL feeling or expressing thanks or gratitude, especially for your good fortune ▶ *Helena was thankful for dry clothing after the flood. We are truly thankful that no one was hurt during the storm.*

PLEASED feeling pleasure or happiness about something that has happened ▶ *Mark was feeling very pleased with himself for getting straight A's. I am pleased to see that you are feeling better.*

APPRECIATIVE feeling appreciation or grateful recognition ▶ *Mr. Thomas was very appreciative of our help and gave us each a dollar for shoveling the snow off his steps and sidewalk.*

INDEBTED owing a debt of gratitude, especially for a favor ▶ *I am indebted to my teachers for giving me a good education.*

OBLIGED feeling that you ought to repay a kindness or debt ▶ *I am much obliged to you for driving me to the airport. I felt obliged to pay for the lamp that I broke.*

▶ **GREAT** adj very big, large, or important; *as a general term of approval—very good* ▶ *There is a great oak tree in our yard. Jefferson was a great man. We had a great time at your party. It's a great day for gardening.*

WONDERFUL causing awe or wonder; *as a term of approval it is stronger than great—excellent or unusually good* ▶ *The porpoise is a wonderful and amazing creature. In my opinion, she would be a wonderful governor.*

TERRIFIC very great or extreme; *as a term of approval it is stronger than wonderful—very good or excellent* ▶ *Rod set off at a terrific speed. It was a terrific idea to buy this canoe!*

SUPERB extremely great, grand, or good ▶ *That was a superb meal, perfectly cooked and beautifully presented. She is a superb actress and can play many different parts.*

REMARKABLE extraordinary and worth noticing or remarking on ▶ *The computer chip is a remarkable invention.*

see GOOD, GRAND, NICE

▶ **GREEDY** adj wanting or taking all that you can get; desiring more than you need ▶ *I realize now that I was being* **greedy** *when I took more ice cream than I could eat.*

SELFISH concerned too much with yourself; not willing to share ▶ *I don't want to go on vacation with Mark, because of his* **selfish** *behavior. She was too* **selfish** *to let me borrow her skates.*

POSSESSIVE wanting to keep something to yourself without sharing it ▶ *Cara is very* **possessive** *of her toys.*

COVETOUS wanting something very much that belongs to someone else ▶ *Tom admitted that he is* **covetous** *of my new watch.*

ACQUISITIVE eager to acquire things, especially wealth ▶ *Ross has an* **acquisitive** *nature and already owns several companies.*

AVARICIOUS greedy for money and stingy ▶ *He was an* **avaricious** *man who never did anything to help the poor.*

see **JEALOUS**

▶ **GROUP** n a number of things that go together or are similar in some way ▶ *She joined a small* **group** *of people waiting for the bus. Hawaii is made up of a* **group** *of islands in the Pacific.*

BUNCH a cluster of things growing together; a group of similar things; a group of people ▶ *We bought* **bunches** *of grapes and bananas. He kept a* **bunch** *of keys on his belt. She's the best singer in the* **bunch**.

GANG a group of people with similar interests or goals, usually with a leader; an organized group of criminals or youths ▶ *He was the foreman of a* **gang** *of migrant workers. Henry refused to join any of the* **gangs** *in his neighborhood.*

PACK a group of animals that hunt together; a group of people with similar interests; a group of things packaged together ▶ *We saw a* **pack** *of wolves. A* **pack** *of kids came running down the street. Jodie gave me a* **pack** *of cards. He told a* **pack** *of lies.*

SET a collection of things that make a whole ▶ *I just bought a hand-carved chess* **set**. *Alice got a* **set** *of tools for her birthday. We have a* **set** *of encyclopedias at home.*

CLASS the people or things that can be grouped together because they are similar; a group of people being taught together ▶ *There are several* **classes** *of cars, including luxury cars, sports cars, and economy cars. My Spanish* **class** *has 18 students in it.*

BAND a group of people who do something together; a group of musicians who play together ▶ *A* **band** *of robbers was caught by the police. Gracie sings and plays piano in a jazz* **band**.

see **BAND, TROOP**

▶ **GROW** vb to get larger in size, length, or amount ▶ *Martha has* **grown** *three inches this year. You will* **grow** *smarter if you study every day.*

DEVELOP to grow gradually and naturally; to build up, make larger, or make stronger ▶ *She is* **developing** *into quite a good violinist. We need to* **develop** *a plan of action. He is* **developing** *his muscles.*

Gracie sings and plays piano in a jazz **band**.

EXPAND to spread out, stretch, or make larger in size ▸ *She wants to* **expand** *her horizons by traveling around Asia.*

INCREASE to grow or become greater in size or number; to make larger in size or number ▸ *The amount of snowfall has* **increased** *this year to eighty inches. We should* **increase** *the number of members in the band.*

MATURE to reach full growth; to become adult ▸ *Edmund is* **maturing** *very rapidly.*

▶ **GUESS** vb to give an answer that may be right but that you cannot be sure of; to think something, without being certain ▸ *I can only* **guess** *that he is about fourteen years old. I* **guess** *I can do it.*

SUPPOSE to assume that something is true or possible; to guess ▸ *Let's* **suppose** *that people were able to fly like birds. I* **suppose** *she's right.*

PRESUME to take something for granted or to assume; to dare ▸ *You are*

Dr. Livingstone, I **presume***. Do you* **presume** *to suggest that I am too old to get a job?*

IMAGINE to picture in your mind; to guess or suppose ▸ *I can't* **imagine** *what it would be like to be able to fly! I* **imagine** *Andrea has left already.*

BELIEVE to feel sure that something is true ▸ *Twana* **believed** *her cousin's story.*

ESTIMATE to make a rough guess; to form an opinion ▸ *Jodie* **estimated** *that they would arrive by ten o'clock. Leon* **estimated** *that his little brother would be able to stay awake.*

SPECULATE to wonder or guess about something without knowing all the facts ▸ *I've been* **speculating** *about your ability to sail a boat by yourself.*

THINK to have as a thought; to imagine ▸ *I* **think** *she's a great teacher. I* **thought** *I heard someone knocking at the door, but it was only the wind.*

▶ **HABIT** n something that you do regularly, often without thinking about it ▶ *I'm trying to break myself of the* **habit** *of biting my nails.*

CUSTOM a tradition in a culture or society; something that you do regularly ▶ *In this country it is the* **custom** *to say "You're welcome" if someone says "Thank you" to you.*

PRACTICE a repeated or customary action; an action that is repeated regularly, especially to improve a skill ▶ *How old is the* **practice** *of sending birthday cards? Catrin has violin* **practice** *after school.*

ROUTINE a regular way or pattern of doing things ▶ *Taking out the garbage is part of my daily* **routine**.

▶ **HAPPEN** vb to take place or come to pass ▶ *A lot has* **happened** *since you left. What will* **happen** *if you are late to school?*

OCCUR to take place or come into existence ▶ *The accident* **occurred** *on the corner of Main Street and Park Street. A tornado will* **occur** *only under certain weather conditions.*

TRANSPIRE to become known; to happen or occur ▶ *It soon* **transpired** *that the money had been stolen. Nothing of significance* **transpired** *at the conference.*

▶ **HAPPY** adj pleased and contented ▶ *The children were very* **happy** *to learn that their mother was coming home from the hospital.*

GLAD having a feeling of pleasure or joy ▶ *It makes me* **glad** *to see the family all together again.*

The accident **occurred** on the corner of Main Street and Park Street.

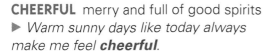
CHEERFUL merry and full of good spirits ▶ *Warm sunny days like today always make me feel **cheerful**.*

JOYFUL full of great joy or happiness because of something that has happened ▶ *Everyone was feeling **joyful** on the last day of school.*

JOYOUS full of joy or happiness by nature ▶ *We want to wish you a **joyous** holiday season.*

tip

Both **happy** and **glad** are often used in statements simply to be polite: *I am **happy** to see that you could come today. She was **glad** to hear that you are going to California.*

▶ **HARD** adj taking or requiring great physical or mental effort; not easy ▶ *It was **hard** work washing all those windows. We had a really **hard** test in math class today.*

DIFFICULT taking or requiring skill, cleverness, or courage to do or understand ▶ *It was **difficult** for Rachel to decide whether to go with her friends or stay with her sister. This book is **difficult** to read.*

TOUGH very hard or difficult ▶ *Marcy had to make some **tough** decisions about which of her friends she could rely on.*

DEMANDING requiring a lot of time, attention, or effort ▶ *Cecilia's job was very **demanding** and she often had to work on weekends.*

STRENUOUS requiring great physical energy or effort ▶ *We were all breathing hard after a half hour of **strenuous** exercise.*

It was **hard** work washing all those windows.

▶ **HATE** vb to feel very strong or intense dislike toward someone or something ▶ *She eventually came to **hate** the coal mines where her father and brothers had worked for their entire lives.*

DETEST to have an intense, often violent, feeling of not liking someone or something ▶ *I **detest** the way Angela is always saying mean things about her friends behind their backs.*

ABHOR to have a strong feeling of disgust for someone or something ▶ *Michelle **abhors** violence of any kind.*

DESPISE to look down on as not good or worthy ▶ *I **despise** anyone who picks on little children.*

LOATHE to have a strong feeling of disgust or intolerance for ▶ *I **loathe** traveling long distances by bus.*

DISLIKE to have a feeling of displeasure about ▶ *I don't **dislike** him because of his looks, but because of the way he treats people.*

> **tip**
>
> **Dislike** is the least intense of these words, although **hate** is often used where a weaker word such as **dislike** would express the true feeling better. If you are looking for a more precise word than **hate** to express a very strong or intense feeling, you should consider one of the other words in this list rather than use **hate** so much that it loses its force.

▶ **HEAL** vb to make well or healthy again; to get better ▶ *This ointment will help to **heal** the burns on your arm. Your broken leg will **heal** if you keep it in a cast for six weeks.*

CURE to bring back to good health; to get rid of a disease or illness ▶ *The doctor worked hard to **cure** her patients during the flu epidemic. She prescribed some pills to **cure** Ian's fever.*

REMEDY to use a specific medicine or treatment to cure, relieve, or correct an illness or injury ▶ *We should be able to **remedy** the problem with a careful program of exercise and physical therapy.*

> **tip**
>
> **Heal** usually refers to the making better of or getting better from a sore, wound, or injury. **Cure** usually refers to getting rid of a disease or illness.

▶ **HEAVY** adj 1 weighing a lot; weighing more than usual for one of its kind ▶ *These boxes are too **heavy** for one person to carry. He is a **heavy** man with large muscles. She carried a **heavy** load.*

CUMBERSOME heavy or bulky and difficult to move around ▶ *The couch is too **cumbersome** to move upstairs.*

HEFTY quite heavy; large and strong ▶ *This is a **hefty** dictionary. He is **hefty** enough to be a football player.*

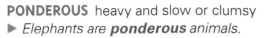

PONDEROUS heavy and slow or clumsy ▶ *Elephants are **ponderous** animals.*

MASSIVE large and solid, and thus often heavy as well ▶ *We sat around a **massive** oak table that could seat 20 people.*

▶ **HEAVY** adj 2 serious or profound; serious and sad or depressing ▶ *They were having a **heavy** conversation about the future. Boy, that was a **heavy** movie!*

WEIGHTY of great importance or seriousness ▶ *She likes to talk about death, the meaning of life, and other **weighty** topics.*

PONDEROUS hard to understand, and dull ▶ *The politician gave a **ponderous** speech that lasted an hour.*

▶ **HEIGHT** n a measurement of how high something is ▶ *The **height** of the Sears Tower in Chicago is 1,454 feet. I looked down from a **height** of 40 feet.*

ALTITUDE the height of something above the ground ▶ *The plane is flying at an **altitude** of 34,000 feet.*

ELEVATION height above sea level; a high place or a hill ▶ *Pike's Peak rises to an **elevation** of 14,110 feet. From this **elevation** we can see across the city to the harbor.*

STATURE the height of a person or animal ▶ *Ben is very short in **stature** but he can run faster than anyone else in the school.*

▶ **HELP** vb to make things easier or better for someone ▶ *Can I **help** you with your homework? Will you **help** me carry these books upstairs?*

ASSIST to give help as an assistant ▶ *On weekends my father lets me **assist** him in repairing the boat.*

AID to give help or relief ▶ *We sent several truckloads of food and supplies to **aid** the victims of the flood.*

SUPPORT to help and encourage ▶ *We **supported** him in his efforts to clean up the park.*

▶ **HIDE** vb to keep secret or put in a secret place; to go where you cannot be seen ▶ *Ray **hid** the package under his bed. She tried to **hide** her disappointment. Francine was **hiding** behind a tree in the backyard.*

CONCEAL to hide purposefully in order to keep secret or unseen ▶ *Jeremy tried to **conceal** the stray dog from his mother, but she heard it whimpering in his room.*

DISGUISE to make look or sound different from usual, so as not to be recognized ▶ *The criminal escaped from the police by **disguising** himself as a woman.*

COVER UP to keep from being known ▶ *The official tried to **cover up** the fact that he had accepted a bribe.*

CAMOUFLAGE to disguise by blending in with the surroundings ▶ *The stripes on a zebra actually help to **camouflage** it from lions and other predators.*

How **high** is that bird flying?

▶ **HIGH** adj a great distance from the ground or from ground level; measuring from top to bottom ▶ *How **high** is that bird flying? I have never seen such a **high** mountain. The dresser is forty-two inches **high**.*

TALL not short or low; higher than usual; having a certain height ▶ *The city is full of **tall** buildings. Margaret is five feet two inches **tall**.*

LOFTY very tall and imposing ▶ *Several **lofty** skyscrapers dominated the skyline.*

TOWERING very high or tall ▶ *There are several **towering** players over seven feet tall on the team.*

▶ **HIRE** vb 1 to agree to pay (someone) for services or work ▶ *I think we had better **hire** a plumber to fix this broken pipe. The factory is **hiring** one hundred new workers this week.*

ENGAGE to arrange and pay for the services of ▶ *The company had to **engage** a lawyer just to handle the many complaints they were getting.*

EMPLOY to provide work and pay for ▶ *The company already **employs** a thousand people. Soon we will have to **employ** a gardener to take care of all these plants.*

tip

Hire and the more formal term **engage** both refer to the taking on of new workers. **Employ** often refers to a business's relationship with the people who already work there, though it can also be used to refer to the taking on of new workers.

I **rented** a tuxedo to wear to the wedding.

▶ **HIRE** vb 2 to pay money for the use of
▶ We **hired** a car during our vacation
in Scotland.

RENT to pay for or get paid for the temporary
right to use ▶ Every summer we **rent** a
cottage by a lake for a week. I **rented** a
tuxedo to wear to the wedding. We **rent**
our apartment.

CHARTER to hire for private use
▶ The school **chartered** a bus for the
annual trip to the museum.

LEASE to agree by a written contract to
give or get the use of property for a certain
period of time ▶ We **leased** the apartment
to a family from Brazil. My father decided to
lease a new car rather than buy one.

▶ **HIT** vb to give a blow with the hand, a
weapon, or other object; to knock or bump
into ▶ As soon as I stepped into my
brother's room, he **hit** me with a pillow.
The stone **hit** the window with a crash.

STRIKE to hit or try to hit
▶ We started a fire by **striking** some
flint with a piece of steel.

PUNCH to hit with your fist
▶ He **punched** me in the stomach
and knocked the breath out of me.

POUND to keep hitting noisily and with force
▶ The rain **pounded** on the roof. I woke up
because someone was **pounding**
on the door.

SLAP to hit with the palm of your hand
▶ When I **slapped** him on the back he
dropped his ice-cream cone.

BATTER to hit over and over
▶ The island was **battered** by three
hurricanes in a single month.

see KNOCK

▶ **HOLE** n an empty place or a gap in a surface ▶ *We planted the tree in a* **hole** *three feet deep. There is a* **hole** *in my sock.*

HOLLOW a shallow hole or depression ▶ *The squirrels built a nest in the* **hollow** *of that tree. We picnicked in a quiet* **hollow** *in the woods.*

CAVITY a hole or empty space in something solid; an empty or hollow space in your body ▶ *The stream has carved out a* **cavity** *under the rocks. He has a* **cavity** *in his tooth. Your sinuses are* **cavities** *in your skull.*

PIT a hole in the ground; a small hollow or depression ▶ *We dug a* **pit** *to bury our garbage in. The hail made* **pits** *all over our car.*

▶ **HOLY** adj to do with or belonging to God or a higher being; held in great reverence ▶ *The temple is on one of the* **holiest** *sites in Hindu tradition. The five books of Moses are* **holy** *to both Jews and Christians.*

SACRED thought of as holy; used for religious purposes; very important and deserving great respect ▶ *The Ganges is a* **sacred** *river in India. Handel composed much* **sacred** *music. I consider this to be a* **sacred** *promise.*

DIVINE to do with or from God or a god ▶ *People no longer believe in the* **divine** *right of kings. He attends* **divine** *worship early every morning.*

HALLOWED revered because of tradition or past events ▶ *The battlefield at Gettysburg is* **hallowed** *ground.*

▶ **HOMONYM** n one of two or more words that have the same pronunciation and often the same spelling, but different meanings ▶ *Bass ("a low voice") and base ("the bottom of something") are* **homonyms***, as are fret ("to worry") and fret ("a ridge on a guitar neck").*

HOMOGRAPH one of two or more words that have the same spelling but different meanings and possibly different pronunciations ▶ *The nouns bass ("fish") and bass ("a low singing voice") are* **homographs***, as are wind ("a current of air") and wind ("to coil").*

HOMOPHONE one of two or more words that have the same pronunciation but different spellings and different meanings ▶ *To, too, and two are* **homophones***.*

Homonyms: *a* **lock** *of hair —* *a* **lock** *on a door;* **broke** *(past tense of break) —* **broke** *("out of money");* **so** *tired —* **sew** *a dress; a* **few** *things —* **phew***, what a smell!*

Homographs: *the* **bow** *of a ship —* *to* **bow** *from the waist — to tie a* **bow***;* **finish** *("to end") —* **finish** *("to paint");* **fast** *("rapid") —* **fast** *("to not eat").*

Homophones: **site** — **sight** — **cite***;* **weigh** — **way***;* **cell** — **sell***;* **have** — **halve***;* **key** — **quay***.*

Note that **homonyms** can be either **homographs** or **homophones**, but **homographs** and **homophones** are different from each other.

▶ **HOPE** vb to wish for, especially for something that you believe will happen or can be done ▶ *I hope they get here before noon. Angela hopes to go to college to study biology.*

EXPECT to wait for someone or something to arrive; to think that something ought to happen ▶ *We're expecting guests for dinner. Aunt Jane expects you to behave perfectly.*

ANTICIPATE to prepare for and look forward to ▶ *We have been anticipating her visit for months. They expect a large crowd at the concert but they don't anticipate trouble.*

▶ **HORSE** n a large, strong animal that has hooves and that people ride or use to pull such things as wagons, coaches, carriages, and plows ▶ *Europeans were the first to bring horses to North America in 1519.*

PONY a breed of horse that is small when fully grown; any horse, especially a small one ▶ *Sarah actually got a pony for her birthday!*

FOAL a young horse, donkey, or zebra ▶ *The mare and her foal grazed peacefully in the pasture.*

COLT a young horse, donkey, or zebra, especially a male ▶ *I love to watch the colts running in the paddock.*

FILLY a young female horse, especially one under five years old ▶ *The two fillies raced around the track at great speed.*

STALLION a mature male horse ▶ *The prince rode a great stallion at the head of his troops.*

MARE a mature female horse ▶ *Our mare will have her foal in a few weeks.*

Sarah actually got a **pony** for her birthday!

▸ **HOT** adj having a high temperature
▸ *This soup is too* **hot** *to eat. Today is the* **hottest** *day of the year. It must be* **hotter** *than ninety-five degrees.*

SWELTERING uncomfortably hot *(used of the weather or its effects)*
▸ *I've got to get out of this* **sweltering** *heat. We were* **sweltering** *as we cut down the brush beside the road.*

SULTRY uncomfortably hot and moist *(used of the weather)* ▸ *The afternoon was so* **sultry** *I just sat in the shade all afternoon and read a book.*

TORRID very hot and dry *(used of the weather or of hot, dry areas)* ▸ *Some plants have adapted to life in* **torrid** *desert regions by storing moisture in their roots.*

WARM a bit hot ▸ *This sweater keeps me nice and* **warm***. I prefer the* **warm** *weather of spring and early summer.*

LUKEWARM slightly warm *(used of liquids)*
▸ *I sat and read in the bath until it was only* **lukewarm***. We gave the shivering cat a saucer of* **lukewarm** *milk.*

TEPID slightly warm; not warm enough *(used of liquids)* ▸ *I hate drinking* **tepid** *tea.*

▸ **HOUSE** n a building where people live; the people who live in a house
▸ *My parents bought a new* **house***. The smoke alarm woke up the whole* **house***.*

HOME the place where you live or belong
▸ *I am going* **home** *right after my violin lesson. My sister's* **home** *is in Nebraska.*

APARTMENT a set of rooms to live in, usually a unit of a larger building
▸ *We live in an* **apartment** *on West 10th Street.*

DWELLING the place where someone lives, such as a house or an apartment
▸ *What kind of a* **dwelling** *do you live in?*

I've got to get out of this **sweltering** heat.

RESIDENCE the place where somebody lives, especially a house ▶ *Joan grew up in a large residence on Water Street.*

CABIN a small, simple house, usually of one story and often built of wood ▶ *We rented a cabin by a lake for our vacation.*

SHACK a small, roughly built house ▶ *They grew up in a little shack in the mountains.*

HUT a small, primitive house ▶ *The village consisted of a circle of huts built of grass, sticks, and mud.*

▶ **HUMAN BEING** n a member of the species of animal *(Homo sapiens)* that includes all people ▶ *Yuri Gagarin was the first human being to travel into space.*

HUMAN a human being ▶ *Malaria is transmitted to humans by a certain kind of mosquito.*

PERSON a single human being ▶ *She is a very kind person.*

INDIVIDUAL a single person, especially in contrast with others ▶ *Helen is a remarkable individual; she can play the violin quite well, she is an excellent teacher, and she has written six books!*

tip

Person is the word most commonly used when you don't need to refer to the species of animal that we belong to.

see HUMANITY, MAN, WOMAN

▶ **HUMANITY** n the human race; all human beings ▶ *The doctors were honored for their services to humanity.*

HUMANKIND the human race; all human beings ▶ *She has a vast knowledge and understanding of humankind.*

MANKIND the human race; all human beings ▶ *The story of mankind is a history of our struggle against the elements and against each other.*

MAN *(when used without the or a)* the human race; all human beings ▶ *The evolution of man is a fascinating subject.*

tip

These four words all mean the same thing, but many people now object to the word **mankind** and to this sense of **man** because the word **man** is more frequently used to mean "an adult male person." Because this more common use refers to males and not to females, many people feel that the sense of **man** and **mankind** as used above also tends to exclude women. Thus, it may be more thoughtful to use **humanity**, **humankind**, the phrase **the human race**, or the plural **human beings** when you want to refer to the race in general.

see HUMAN BEING, MAN, WOMAN

Even though he had won a great prize, he was **humble** and gave credit to the many people who had helped him.

▶ **HUMBLE** adj not proud; aware of your own faults or shortcomings
▶ *Even though he had won a great prize, he was **humble** and gave credit to the many people who had helped him.*

MEEK quiet, humble, and obedient, sometimes too much so
▶ *He was a **meek** little man who never spoke up to give his opinion.*

MODEST not boastful about your abilities, possessions, or achievements
▶ *She was a world-famous violinist but she was very **modest** about her accomplishments.*

▶ **HUNT** vb to look carefully for something; to chase and kill wild animals for food or sport ▶ *Lisa **hunted** for her watch. Most nations have agreed to stop **hunting** whales.*

SEARCH to explore or examine very carefully in order to find something
▶ *The police were **searching** the woods for clues.*

SEEK to look for or try to discover; to try; to ask for or request ▶ *He was only **seeking** some peace and quiet. Diane is **seeking** to win the election. I will need to **seek** the help of an expert.*

INVESTIGATE to find out as much as possible about something
▶ *Researchers are **investigating** the possible causes of the disease. The police are **investigating** a burglary.*

SCOUR to examine an area thoroughly to find something ▶ *We **scoured** the neighborhood looking for our dog. Paulo **scoured** his room for the lost book.*

▶ **HURRY** vb to do things quickly
▶ *You will have to **hurry** if you want to finish cutting the grass before dark.*

RUSH to go somewhere very quickly; to do something very quickly
▶ *We were late, so we had to **rush** to get to the post office before it closed. He **rushed** through his homework in half an hour.*

HASTEN to move quickly
▶ *If we **hasten** to town we will be able to see the parade.*

HUSTLE to push someone roughly in order to make him or her move; to do something rapidly and energetically
▶ *The guard **hustled** the prisoners out of the room. Andy **hustled** to finish the job by noon.*

► **IDEA** n a plan, image, belief, or opinion ▶ *It was a good **idea** to finish our homework before we went to the party.*

THOUGHT an idea that comes into your mind as the result of thinking or reasoning ▶ *When Josh finished the book, he wrote down his **thoughts** on the story.*

CONCEPT a general or typical idea of something, without details ▶ *With just a few strokes of her pencil she is able to express the **concept** of a bird in flight.*

IMPRESSION a general or superficial idea that comes into your mind because of something that you learn, see, or hear ▶ *I get the **impression** that you didn't have a good time yesterday. The football player gives the **impression** of great strength.*

NOTION an idea that is vague or quickly formed without careful thinking ▶ *What gave you the **notion** that you could borrow my skis without asking?*

see **THEORY**

► **IMITATE** vb to act the same as; to use as a model ▶ *Julio always **imitates** his big brother because he looks up to him. Can you **imitate** this style of drawing?*

COPY to make something look or sound like the original; to do the same as someone else ▶ *I **copied** the carving the best I could in pencil.*

MIMIC to imitate someone else's actions or speech, especially to make fun of them ▶ *It got annoying when Sally started **mimicking** everything I said.*

MOCK to make fun of someone in an unpleasant way, often by imitating ▶ *She got in trouble for **mocking** the teacher behind his back.*

Can you **imitate** this style of drawing?

▶ **IMPORTANT** adj having great value, worth, or impact ▶ *It is **important** to study the causes of diseases. I have an **important** meeting with my boss to discuss getting a raise.*

SIGNIFICANT especially meaningful or excellent ▶ *It was a **significant** moment in her life when she was chosen to be an astronaut. Matisse was a **significant** modern artist.*

PRINCIPAL most important or main ▶ *Peggy was given the role of one of the **principal** characters in the play.*

CHIEF of greatest importance or significance ▶ *A teacher's **chief** objective is to educate students.*

MAJOR great in importance, quantity, or seriousness ▶ *Robert Frost is one of the **major** poets of the twentieth century. She was sick for a month with a **major** illness.*

MAIN most important ▶ *My **main** reason for doing this is to make you happy.*

see NECESSARY

▶ **INFORMATION** n things that you learn from reading, studying, or talking with others ▶ *Can you find me some **information** about the birds that live in this part of the country?*

FACT a piece of information that is true ▶ *Is it a **fact** that Julio was elected class president? Evolution is a **fact** that is best explained by Charles Darwin's theory of natural selection.*

KNOWLEDGE the things that you know ▶ *The quiz tested our **knowledge** of geography.*

NEWS fresh or recent information or facts ▶ *The **news** about the space shuttle was very exciting. Tell me all the **news** about your trip!*

DATA information or facts, used as a basis for study, discussion, or calculation ▶ *Researchers collected and analyzed all the **data** they could find in order to try to understand the effects of the disease.*

EVIDENCE information and facts that help prove something or lead you to believe something is true ▶ *All the **evidence** suggests that he is the person who stole our money.*

tip

Even though **data** comes from the plural of the Latin word *datum*, it is not always used in plural constructions in English. In general speech and writing it is a collective abstract noun used with a singular verb: *All of our **data** is stored on computer disks.* It is also often used, especially by some scientists and editors, with plural verbs and pronouns: *These **data** are the most interesting collected so far.*

▶ **INSIDE** adj on the surface, side, or part away from the outside; private or secret ▶ *I put my wallet in my **inside** coat pocket. Wait till I tell you the **inside** story of what really happened!*

INTERIOR in the middle of, rather than on the outside or edge; away from the coast or border ▶ *His office was an **interior** room with no windows. Settlers of the **interior** regions of the country depended on river travel.*

INTERNAL happening or existing inside something ▶ *We are studying the **internal** organs of the body.*

INNER inside or near the center; private ▶ *The **inner** part of the earth's core is extremely hot. No one can know your **inner** thoughts.*

INDOOR used, done, or built inside ▶ *There is a new **indoor** swimming pool at the school.*

> **tip**
>
> **Inside** and **interior** are often used as nouns: *The **inside** of the house is as beautiful as the outside. We grew up in the **interior** of the country, but every summer we would travel to the ocean for a week's vacation.*
>
> **Inside** may also be used as a preposition (*I put your things **inside** the suitcase*) or an adverb (*Greg went **inside** when it started raining*).

▶ **INTEND** vb to have in mind to do ▶ *I **intended** to visit you yesterday, but I was sick.*

MEAN to have in your mind as a purpose ▶ *I didn't **mean** to step on your toe.*

PROPOSE to say what you have in mind to do ▶ *Dolores **proposed** that we all go skating. I **propose** to tell her exactly what I think.*

PLAN to have in mind as a purpose or project ▶ *We are **planning** to clean the garage on Saturday.*

▶ **INTEREST** n a feeling of wanting to know more about something ▶ *She has had an **interest** in horses ever since she read The Black Stallion. Your pictures of Peru have aroused my **interest**.*

CURIOSITY a strong desire to know more about something or about things in general, often leading to inquiry ▶ *Just out of **curiosity**, who won the game? The young child was full of **curiosity** and kept asking me questions.*

CONCERN a strong personal interest ▶ *The need for repairs to the school is of **concern** to us all.*

► **INTERESTING** adj attracting and holding your attention and interest ► *She has led a very **interesting** life. It would be **interesting** to know what you think.*

FASCINATING extremely interesting or attractive ► *I think botany is a **fascinating** subject. She is so **fascinating** I can't stop thinking about her.*

EXCITING producing a strong interest and excitement ► *We watched an **exciting** film about the first trip to the moon. Nothing very **exciting** happened at school today.*

INTRIGUING arousing a strong interest and curiosity ► *The discovery of a meteorite from Mars with fossils in it raises some **intriguing** questions about the origins of life.*

ENGROSSING taking up all your attention ► *This job is so **engrossing** I didn't hear you come in.*

ABSORBING taking up all your attention and drawing you in ► *I found the book so **absorbing** that I felt as if I were there, and I completely lost track of time.*

I think botany is a **fascinating** subject.

▶ **INVENT** vb to think up something new
▶ *Wilbur and Orville Wright **invented** the first successful airplane.*

DEVISE to invent or create by thinking
▶ *Henry Ford **devised** a method of mass production for automobiles. We **devised** a clever plan for getting the piano upstairs.*

DESIGN to draw something that could be built or made ▶ *The architect **designed** a new house.*

see **BUILD, DISCOVER, FORM, MAKE**

▶ **IRONY** n a way of speaking or writing that means the opposite of what the words say
▶ *"What a beautiful day!" said David with **irony**, as the blizzard raged around us.*

SATIRE a type of clever, mocking humor that points out the faults in certain people or ideas ▶ *Many of Mark Twain's writings are full of **satire** and make us realize how foolish people can be.*

PARODY an imitation of a serious piece of writing, film, or music that makes fun of the original work ▶ *Most of the poems in* Alice's Adventures in Wonderland *are **parodies** of popular nineteenth-century poems for children.*

"What a beautiful day!" said David with **irony**, as the blizzard raged around us.

JAIL n a building where persons accused of crimes are confined ▶ *The two men were sent to jail for stealing credit cards.*

PRISON a building where criminals convicted of major crimes are confined ▶ *The members of the gang that robbed the bank were sent to prison for 15 years.*

PENITENTIARY a prison run by a state or federal government ▶ *He served 10 years in the state penitentiary for kidnapping.*

BRIG a place on a ship where prisoners are confined ▶ *The captain had the mutineers put in the brig until the ship reached port.*

JEALOUS adj feeling angry or annoyed because someone has something you want or likes someone other than you ▶ *Lena was jealous of Ethan because he got a new pair of skates. It makes me jealous when my sister gets too much attention.*

ENVIOUS wishing that you could have something that someone else has ▶ *I have always been envious of his money and good looks.*

RESENTFUL feeling hurt or angry about something that has been done or said to you ▶ *I am resentful of your constant interference in my private affairs.*

see **GREEDY**

JOB n something you have to do, especially regularly or for pay ▶ *It's my job to feed the guinea pig every morning. Chaim got a job delivering newspapers.*

TASK a small job that you have been given to do ▶ *Ms. Reyes gave us the task of decorating the classroom for the party.*

CHORE a small job that you must do regularly ▶ *I have to do three chores before school—make my bed, pick up my room, and take out the garbage.*

ERRAND a trip to do a small job, often for someone else ▶ *We can go swimming as soon as I get back from running errands for my mother.*

WORK a regular job, often for pay ▶ *My mother got work as a nurse at the hospital.*

see **FUNCTION, DUTY, WORK**

▶ **JOIN** vb to put together or bring together; to come together ▶ *Let's all join hands and sing the camp song. The sides of a picture frame should join at a right angle.*

CONNECT to join two things; to join or become joined to or with another
▶ *If we connect these hoses, they will reach the pool. The big end of this one connects to the small end of that one.*

ATTACH to join by tying, sticking, screwing, clipping, or in some other way
▶ *The basketball hoop is attached to the wall above the garage door with three long bolts.*

LINK to join in a series like a chain
▶ *The protestors linked elbows as they marched down the street. Each of these computers is linked to the printer.*

FASTEN to join one thing firmly to another
▶ *Fasten these posters to the bulletin board with thumbtacks.*

UNITE to join to make one
▶ *All of these puzzle pieces can be united into a single picture.*

COUPLE to join two related things
▶ *Railroad cars are coupled with a special device.*

see MIX

▶ **JOKE** n a trick or a short story with a funny ending meant to make people laugh
▶ *Tom loves to play jokes on his friends on April Fools' Day. Maria has a new joke to tell almost every day.*

JEST a remark that is not spoken seriously
▶ *I didn't mean to insult you; it was only a jest when I said you were funny-looking.*

GAG a joke or trick, especially one that is prepared in advance of a performance
▶ *The old movie is full of sight gags such as people falling and getting pies in their faces.*

WISECRACK a remark that is meant to be funny, especially in a mocking or satirical way
▶ *I am really getting annoyed about your constant wisecracks.*

PRANK a mischievous trick
▶ *We are all getting tired of Philip's pranks.*

PRACTICAL JOKE a trick played on someone that is meant to embarrass or surprise them
▶ *Bryn played a practical joke on me and I got squirted when I turned on the faucet.*

> **JUDGE** n someone who is appointed to decide a question, especially one who decides how a guilty person should be punished; someone who determines the winner or winners in a contest or competition
> ▶ The **judge** sentenced the criminal to a year in prison. You be the **judge** of which is the best pie. The **judges** awarded the gymnast the highest possible score for her performance.

REFEREE someone who supervises a sports match or a game and makes sure that the players obey the rules
▶ The **referee** ejected two of the players from the game because they were fighting.

UMPIRE a person appointed to rule on plays in baseball and some other sports
▶ The **umpire** signaled that the runner was safe on second base.

OFFICIAL someone who holds a high position in an organization; someone who enforces the rules in sports and games
▶ Robin has worked as a government **official** for 10 years. The **official** called a penalty on one of our players.

The **referee** ejected two of the players from the game because they were fighting.

▶ **JUMP** vb to move off the ground by bending and suddenly straightening the legs ▶ *How high can you jump? The puddle is too big to jump across.*

SPRING to move suddenly upward, forward, or backward ▶ *When the phone rang, I sprang out of my chair. As soon as she turns on the light, everyone spring up and yell, "Surprise!"*

LEAP to jump, especially high or far ▶ *The horse leaped over the fence and ran away.*

VAULT to jump high, especially over a barrier using your hands for help ▶ *She vaulted over the wall and landed in a flower bed.*

HOP to jump with one foot and land on the same foot; to make a small jump ▶ *I hurt my ankle and had to hop all the way home. We hopped over the little stream and continued our walk.*

She **vaulted** over the wall and landed in a flower bed.

n = noun   vb = verb   adj = adjective   adv = adverb   prep = preposition   conj = conjunction   **117**

k

KINDNESS n the state or quality of being gentle, helpful, and sympathetic toward others ▶ Marie's **kindness** and generosity have made her beloved by all of us.

MERCY greater kindness than is expected or even fair, especially in punishing wrongdoers ▶ The principal showed **mercy** by not punishing us as long as we cleaned up the mess we made.

CHARITY a kind understanding of others; money or other help that is given to people in need ▶ The president showed great **charity** by welcoming thousands of refugees into the country. We gladly accepted her **charity**.

see PITY

KING n a man from a royal family who is the ruler of a country ▶ The **kings** of France and England were at war for many years.

QUEEN a woman from a royal family who is the ruler of a country; the wife of a king ▶ Elizabeth II became the **queen** of England in 1952.

MONARCH a ruler, such as a king or queen, who often inherits his or her position ▶ Many countries are ruled by **monarchs**.

SOVEREIGN someone who has the highest authority, especially as the ruler of a country ▶ He was a powerful **sovereign** who extended his rule over the surrounding territories and islands.

EMPEROR the male ruler of an empire ▶ Augustus Caesar was the first Roman **emperor**.

EMPRESS the female ruler of an empire; the wife of an emperor ▶ Catherine the Great was **empress** of Russia.

KNOCK vb to hit or bump; to make a noise by hitting something ▶ I **knocked** a vase off the table. She **knocked** on the door.

BANG to hit hard against ▶ The musician **banged** the cymbals together. I **banged** my knee on the corner of the bed.

TAP to hit gently or lightly ▶ I **tapped** gently on the window to get her attention. The doctor **tapped** my knee with a little mallet.

RAP to hit sharply and quickly ▶ Bettina **rapped** on the door several times with her umbrella.

THUMP to hit heavily; to beat heavily and rapidly ▶ His boots **thumped** to the floor as he pulled them off. I could feel my heart **thumping** after the race.

see HIT

▶ **KNOT** n a fastening made by looping and twisting one or more pieces of string, rope, or thread ▶ *It is handy to know several different kinds of knots if you go camping.*

TANGLE string, rope, thread, or hair twisted together in a confused mass ▶ *I spent all morning trying to get a big tangle out of my fishing line.*

SNARL a knotted or tangled mass, especially in thread or hair ▶ *Amy doesn't like having to brush the snarls out of her hair every morning, so she got her hair cut short.*

tip

There are many types of **knots**. Some of the most common are **square knot, granny knot, overhand knot, slipknot, bow,** and **figure-eight knot.**

▶ **KNOW** vb to be familiar with a person, place, or piece of information ▶ *He knows the names of everyone in the school. Do you know how to play chess?*

UNDERSTAND to know what something means or how something works ▶ *I don't understand your question. She understands automobile engines better than anyone else in the family.*

REALIZE to be aware that something is true ▶ *Do you realize how happy your letter makes me?*

RECOGNIZE to see someone and know who the person is; to understand and accept a situation as true or right ▶ *Margaret recognized Camilla. They recognize their duty to vote in the election.*

I

▶ **LAST** adj coming at the end of a series; most recent ▶ *I was sorry when I reached the **last** page of the book. Has it been six months since your **last** visit to the dentist?*

LATEST most recent
▶ *Have you read her **latest** book?*

FINAL occurring at the end of a series and not to be followed by another
▶ *We watched the eclipse up to its **final** moments. I said, "No," and that's **final**!*

ULTIMATE last in a series
▶ *We visited Paris and Rome, but our **ultimate** destination was Athens.*

CONCLUDING coming at the end; final
▶ *This is the **concluding** book in the series.*

CLOSING coming at the end (of a speech or piece of writing)
▶ *His **closing** remarks took 10 minutes! That is a very funny **closing** paragraph.*

▶ **LAUGH** vb to make sounds with the voice that express joy, amusement, or scorn
▶ *The show was so funny I **laughed** for an hour. Why do you **laugh** when somebody tickles you?*

GIGGLE to laugh in a quiet and silly or nervous way ▶ *We all began **giggling** when the teacher's tie got caught in his desk drawer.*

I said, "No," and that's **final**!

CHUCKLE to laugh quietly in a low tone
▶ *I chuckled quietly as I read the comics to myself.*

SNICKER to laugh in a sly way
▶ *My new boots were so large, I just knew that everyone was snickering behind my back.*

ROAR to laugh loudly
▶ *The crowd roared when the clowns kept tripping over each other's shoes.*

GUFFAW to laugh very loudly
▶ *Our enjoyment of the movie was spoiled by a man behind us who guffawed at every little joke.*

tip

All of these words can also be used as nouns: *I like the sound of my brother's **laugh**. Her **giggle** gave away the secret of her hiding place. She gave a **snicker** as I turned away. His loud **guffaw** could be heard a block away. The audience gave a **roar** every time I got hit by a pie.*

My new boots were so large, I just knew that everyone was **snickering** behind my back.

n = noun   vb = verb   adj = adjective   adv = adverb   prep = preposition   conj = conjunction   **121**

▶ **LEAD** vb 1 to show the way by going before or with; to mark the way ▶ *You can **lead** a horse to water, but you can't make him drink. You **lead** the way and I will follow. This road **leads** to town.*

GUIDE to point out the way ▶ *The settlers hired a scout to **guide** them through the mountains.*

DIRECT to turn or point someone toward a place or a goal ▶ *Can you **direct** me to the post office? Her shout **directed** my attention to the speeding car.*

CONDUCT to show the way to by going with ▶ *The bride's brother **conducted** us to our seats at the wedding.*

STEER to control the movement of ▶ *You **steer** the sled after I push to get us started.*

TAKE to lead or accompany ▶ *I **took** my dog for a walk. Let's **take** Mom out to dinner.*

▶ **LEAD** vb 2 to be the head or leader of; to be in charge of ▶ *The conductor **leads** an orchestra as it plays.*

DIRECT to be in charge of; to control ▶ *She **directs** one of the largest companies in the state.*

MANAGE to have charge of; to run the business of ▶ *Mom **manages** a restaurant.*

SUPERVISE to watch over and control the work of ▶ *The manager **supervises** two hundred workers on each shift.*

▶ **LEAVE** vb to go away ▶ *We had to **leave** before the party was over.*

DEPART to go away; to turn aside from ▶ *Our plane **departs** at 2:35. On the last day of school we **departed** from our usual schedule.*

EXIT to go out ▶ *Please **exit** through the doors at the front of the theater.*

WITHDRAW to move back; to remove yourself ▶ *The teams **withdrew** from the field at halftime. She wanted to **withdraw** from school, but I changed her mind.*

DESERT to leave without permission; to leave, forsake, or abandon ▶ *The soldier was punished for **deserting** his post. She would never **desert** a friend in need.*

ABANDON to leave behind because you have to; to leave behind even though you shouldn't ▶ *We **abandoned** our broken-down car and walked the last mile. She **abandoned** her friends when the work got hard.*

see **GO**

▶ **LEGAL** adj allowed by law; to do with the law ▶ *It is not **legal** to drive without a valid license. We found my grandfather's **legal** papers in his desk.*

LAWFUL permitted, established, or recognized by law ▶ *This lease is not a **lawful** agreement unless it is signed by both the landlord and the tenant.*

LEGITIMATE in accordance with the law or with sound reasoning ▶ *All the **legitimate***

*heirs to the estate have been named in her will. You have a **legitimate** complaint.*

see **VALID**

▶ **LEGENDARY** adj perhaps based on fact, but not entirely true; famous and often the subject of exaggerated stories ▶ *She wrote a book about the **legendary** exploits of Daniel Boone. Babe Ruth has become a **legendary** figure in baseball.*

MYTHICAL based on myth; imaginary ▶ *Achilles is a **mythical** hero of ancient Greece. The movie is about a **mythical** island where dinosaurs survive.*

FICTITIOUS made up or imaginary; not true ▶ *All of the characters in my story are **fictitious**. Her excuse turned out to be entirely **fictitious**.*

▶ **LENGTHEN** vb to make longer; to become longer ▶ *Will you please **lengthen** the hem of my green dress? The days **lengthen** as summer gets nearer.*

STRETCH to pull to full length or size ▶ *We **stretched** a ribbon across the road at the finish line.*

EXTEND to reach over a certain distance; to make longer in time ▶ *The ladder **extends** to the third floor. We **extended** our vacation an extra week.*

PROLONG to make something last longer ▶ *My grandmother **prolonged** her visit a few more days.*

▶ **LET** vb not to forbid or prevent; to give permission to; to cause to happen ▶ ***Let** me go! My mother **lets** me stay up late on weekends. A small crack in the glass **let** all the water leak out of the fishbowl.*

ALLOW to give permission to; to tolerate ▶ *You will be **allowed** to use your books during the test, but you don't have to.*

PERMIT to give permission or consent to, usually willingly ▶ *This card **permits** me to take books out of the library.*

AUTHORIZE to give official permission for something ▶ *This document **authorizes** you to take money out of my bank account.*

▶ **LEVEL** adj having no part higher than another and parallel to the horizon; at the same height ▶ *A pool table should be absolutely **level**. She is getting so tall that her head is **level** with my shoulder.*

FLAT having a surface that is level and without many low or high spots ▶ *The **flat** and featureless prairie stretched out for miles in every direction.*

SMOOTH not rough or bumpy ▶ *Use fine sandpaper to make the edges as **smooth** as possible. This is a very **smooth** stretch of road.*

EVEN level and smooth; staying about the same ▶ *After climbing hills all day, it was a relief to walk on **even** ground. Run the race at an **even** speed; don't start off too fast.*

▶ **LIE** n a statement that is intended to be untrue or to deceive ▶ *It was a **lie** when you said that you were home last night; I saw you at the movies.*

FALSEHOOD an untrue statement; absence of accuracy or truth ▶ *You will make things worse by adding a **falsehood** to your story. We now see the **falsehood** in believing the earth is flat.*

FIB a small, trivial, or forgivable lie ▶ *He told a little **fib** rather than hurt his sister's feelings.*

▶ **LIFT** vb to bring to a higher position ▶ *Please **lift** the chair so that I can straighten the rug. These boxes are too heavy to **lift**.*

RAISE to move to a higher position; to increase in size, amount, strength, or in some other way ▶ ***Raise** your hand if you know the answer. Let's **raise** the price on our lemonade. Don't **raise** your voice at me!*

ELEVATE to lift up; to place in a higher position ▶ *The nurse **elevated** the patient's feet with a pillow. After a week of rain, some sunshine should **elevate** our spirits.*

HOIST to lift or pull up, especially by using a rope, cable, crane, or other lifting device

He told a little **fib** rather than hurt his sister's feelings.

▶ *A giant crane* **hoisted** *the steel beams to the top of the new building. When the wind picked up, the crew* **hoisted** *the sails.*

BOOST to push up from below
▶ *George* **boosted** *me up so I could see over the fence.*

▶ **LIKE** vb to be pleased with; to be attracted to; to take pleasure in
▶ *Miranda* **likes** *baseball more than she thought she would. Do you* **like** *my brother? I* **like** *to do my homework early.*

ENJOY to get pleasure from; to experience with joy ▶ *Stephanie* **enjoys** *taking walks with Bill. Laura* **enjoyed** *the movie until it got too scary.*

FOND, BE FOND OF to have a liking for
▶ *José is* **fond** *of animals, but he likes cats best of all.*

CARE FOR to have a liking for; to love
▶ *I don't really* **care for** *bean salad. Philippe* **cared for** *his aunt very deeply.*

see LOVE

▶ **LIST** n a series of items, names, or numbers, often written in a particular order ▶ *Tom made a* **list** *of everything he needed at the store. Is your name on the passenger* **list**?

CATALOG a book or pamphlet that lists items sold by a company or describes art in an exhibition; a list of all the books in a library ▶ *The seed* **catalogs** *begin to arrive in January. Many libraries now have an online* **catalog**.

PROGRAM a booklet that gives you information about a concert or theater performance ▶ *The* **program** *gives the names of the musicians and the pieces they will play.*

SCHEDULE a printed list or timetable
▶ *Do you have a* **schedule** *of events for the month of April? Get a bus* **schedule** *so we can figure out when to leave.*

ROSTER a list, especially of names
▶ *The teacher took attendance using the class* **roster**.

José is **fond** of animals, but he likes cats best of all.

n = noun   vb = verb   adj = adjective   adv = adverb   prep = preposition   conj = conjunction   **125**

▶ **LIVE** vb to have as your home
▶ *Marcie lives in the city.*
We lived on a boat for three weeks.

RESIDE to live in or have a home in
▶ *Senator Morris resides in Washington most of the year.*

DWELL to live or reside, especially for a long time ▶ *She dwelled way back in the mountains for so long that she forgot how noisy the city could be.*

STAY to live or reside for a fairly short time ▶ *We stayed at a fancy hotel for the weekend. My grandmother stays in Florida during the winter.*

▶ **LIVELY** adj full of life and energy; moving quickly ▶ *We had a lively discussion about how we should spend the money. Shana's party was lively and exciting.*

ACTIVE always moving and doing things
▶ *Glyn kept active all summer by playing baseball, soccer, and basketball, and going swimming.*

ENERGETIC full of energy
▶ *My great-grandfather was so energetic that he played golf every day until he was ninety-two!*

VIGOROUS using lots of energy or strength
▶ *We were all tired after a vigorous game of hockey. I need more vigorous exercise. Gordon gave a vigorous pull on the rope.*

▶ **LONELY** adj unhappy about being alone
▶ *He began to feel lonely after being sick in bed for three days and not having any visitors.*

LONESOME lonely, especially for a certain person or place ▶ *Her first day at camp she felt lonesome for her mother.*

HOMESICK missing home and family
▶ *He felt homesick the first night he was away, but he felt better when he got a letter from his parents.*

see **ALONE**

▶ **LONG** adj more than the average length, distance, or time; from one end to the other; taking a lot of time ▶ *We took a long walk. The path was about a mile long. Is the movie very long?*

LENGTHY very long; longer than necessary
▶ *He gave a lengthy explanation of his plan.*

TALL higher than usual; not short or low; having a certain height ▶ *Megan is a tall girl for her age. That is a very tall building. Danny is over six feet tall.*

▶ **LOOK** vb to direct your eyes in order to see
▶ *Look at the flowers I planted under the window. You will find the answers to the puzzle if you look on page 12.*

SEE to view with your eyes
▶ *Can you see any whales in the distance?*

WATCH to keep your eyes on
▶ *We watched the movie for two hours. You have to watch the ball if you expect to hit it.*

GAZE to keep your eyes on something for a long time, especially in admiration, surprise, or deep thought ▶ *Alice gazed at the painting for an hour. Hugh was bored and just sat gazing out the window.*

STARE to look at without moving your eyes, especially when surprised, frightened, or in deep thought ▶ I *stared* at the paper for 15 minutes before I began to write. Phil got nervous when he noticed the teacher *staring* at him.

GLANCE to look at something quickly or briefly ▶ Antonio *glanced* at his watch every few minutes. I *glanced* out the window and saw a Baltimore oriole sitting in the tree.

▶ **LOSE** vb 1 to be unable to find; to be deprived of; to not have control of
▶ I think I *lost* the dollar I had in my pocket. Many people *lost* their homes in the hurricane. Jack *lost* his temper.

MISPLACE to put something down and then forget where it is ▶ I *misplaced* my glasses and now I can't find them because I can't see!

▶ **LOSE** vb 2 to fail to win; to be defeated
▶ We *lost* the championship game by a single point. You *lost* because you weren't concentrating on the game.

FORFEIT to lose or have taken away because of some fault or as a penalty
▶ We *forfeited* the game because not enough team members showed up to play. Because of your poor behavior, you will have to *forfeit* your trip to the beach.

▶ **LOUD** adj making a great deal of sound
▶ Does the radio have to be on so *loud*? Arthur has a very *loud* voice for such a small boy.

NOISY full of noise; making a lot of noise
▶ The party was so *noisy* that it was hard to hear what anyone was saying. Every morning a flock of *noisy* crows wakes me up.

DEAFENING extremely loud
▶ The plane took off with a *deafening* roar. We were startled by a *deafening* clap of thunder.

Does the radio have to be on so **loud**?

▶ **LOVE** n a strong liking for
▶ *He was helped through his troubles
by his parents' **love** and support.
Sandy's **love** of baseball lasted all her life.*

AFFECTION a tender or fond liking
▶ *Samuel and his sister shared a warm
affection for each other. Miranda had a
deep **affection** for her violin teacher.*

DEVOTION a strong feeling of attachment
or loyalty ▶ *James felt a deep **devotion**
to his family.*

PASSION a strong feeling of love
▶ *They promised to love each other with an
undying **passion**. Her **passion** for helping
people led her to become a doctor.*

FONDNESS a liking; a tender love or
affection ▶ *I have a particular **fondness**
for raspberries and cream. Mary's **fondness**
for her niece is obvious.*

▶ **LOVE** vb to have a deep feeling of
love or affection for; to like very much
▶ *I **love** my sister and I don't want her
to leave. Anne is a good student who
loves sports and music.*

ADORE to love or honor very much; to like
very much ▶ *Ellen and Peter **adore** each
other and are getting married next month.
Oh, I just **adore** the way those shoes look
on you!*

ADMIRE to have respect and affection for
▶ *I **admire** the dedication of the teachers in
this school.*

WORSHIP to love and honor God or a god;
to love intensely; to idolize ▶ *The Romans
worshiped many gods. Juan is so much
in love with Rosa, he **worships** the ground
she walks on.*

see **LIKE**

Ellen and Peter **adore** each other and are getting married next month.

▶ **MAKE** vb to produce or bring into being
▶ *We helped Dad **make** dinner. We **made** a snowman in the front yard.*

CREATE to produce, especially by using your imaginative skill ▶ *Pablo Picasso **created** a true work of art from old bicycle parts.*

MANUFACTURE to make from raw materials, either by hand or by machine
▶ *Toni works for a company that **manufactures** vending machines.*

PRODUCE to make, grow, or manufacture; to bring into view ▶ *Her new firm **produces** clothing. Our farm **produces** grain for cattle feed. He **produced** a letter from his pocket.*

see BUILD, FORM, INVENT

▶ **MAN** n an adult male person
▶ *Who is that **man** in the gray coat? He is a successful **man**.*

GENTLEMAN a polite term for **man**; a man with good manners ▶ *Good evening, ladies and **gentlemen**. Alexander is quite a **gentleman**; he is always polite and gracious.*

BOY a male child or young man
▶ *There are 11 **boys** in my class.*

GUY a man or boy; sometimes used in the plural for people of either sex
▶ *Some **guy** on the street handed me this piece of paper. All you **guys** are going to be late if you don't hurry.*

FELLOW a man or boy
▶ *Do you know that **fellow** sitting by the window?*

HUSBAND a married man, especially when referred to in relation to his wife
▶ *Her **husband** is a famous writer.*

MALE a person or animal of the sex that fathers young, but does not give birth
▶ *Adult **males** usually have lower voices than females. While the female penguin goes to eat, the **male** protects their egg.*

tip

Guy and **fellow** are both very common words in speech but they are too informal to use in your serious writing. Choose whichever of the other synonyms is close to the specific idea you have in mind.

see HUMAN BEING, HUMANITY, WOMAN

▶ **MANY** adj consisting of or amounting to a large number ▶ *Brenda has **many** friends. They have lived here for **many** years.*

NUMEROUS consisting of very many things or persons ▶ *The librarian has had **numerous** requests for books about Mars.*

VARIOUS an indefinite number of ▶ *We visited **various** museums on our trip to New York.*

COUNTLESS so many that you can't count them ▶ *We had **countless** arguments.*

▶ **MASCULINE** adj having or being a quality thought to be typical of men ▶ *He has a very **masculine** physique.*

MALE of or relating to men or boys or to the sex that fathers young ▶ ***Male** ostriches take care of the young fledglings.*

MANLY having the qualities expected of a man, especially such desirable traits as maturity and strength of character ▶ *Simon tried to be **manly** and not show his disappointment.*

see **FEMININE**

▶ **MAYBE** adv it might or could be that ▶ ***Maybe** I will see you next week. **Maybe** Janice is the one who left you that message.*

PERHAPS it might or could happen or be that; it might or could be ▶ ***Perhaps** she is late because she forgot to set her alarm clock. This is **perhaps** the best job you have ever done.*

POSSIBLY it is possible but uncertain that ▶ *He said that **possibly** he could be there by Tuesday.*

CONCEIVABLY it is possible to imagine that ▶ *Quite **conceivably**, that was the worst movie ever made!*

tip

All of these words express uncertainty about something. **Maybe** and **perhaps** are very close synonyms, and usually it makes no difference which one you use. **Possibly** stresses the uncertainty even more, and **conceivably** suggests the difficulty of even imagining something.

▶ **MEAL** n food that is served and eaten, usually at a particular time of day; the act or time of eating ▶ *That was a really good **meal**. Ralph is always on time for **meals**.*

FEAST a large, fancy meal, particularly on a special occasion ▶ *We had a regular **feast** for the whole family on Thanksgiving.*

BANQUET a formal meal for a large number of people, usually on a special occasion ▶ *There was a huge **banquet** to honor my grandparents on their fiftieth wedding anniversary.*

SNACK a small, light meal ▶ *José likes to have a **snack** when he gets home.*

Various meals served throughout the day are **breakfast** (the first meal of the day), **brunch** (a meal in the late morning that combines breakfast and lunch), **lunch** (the meal that you eat in the middle of the day), **dinner** (the main meal of the day, whether eaten in the middle of the day or in the evening), **tea** (a light afternoon meal, often served with tea to drink), and **supper** (an evening meal).

▶ **MEAN** adj selfish, bad-tempered, or disagreeable, especially in a petty way ▶ *Beverly is sometimes* **mean** *to her younger cousins.*

CRUEL not caring about the suffering of others ▶ *Thea believes that it's* **cruel** *to keep animals in cages.*

VICIOUS fierce and dangerous ▶ *Their dog is so* **vicious** *they have to keep it chained up all the time.*

MALICIOUS having or done from a deep desire or intent to hurt someone ▶ *She is* **malicious** *to her little brother. They were deliberately spreading* **malicious** *gossip about our new neighbors.*

▶ **MELODY** n a pleasant and rhythmic series of musical notes ▶ *Alissa played a little* **melody** *on the piano.*

TUNE a series of musical notes arranged in a pattern; a simple melody that is easy to remember ▶ *I can hum the* **tune** *to the song but I can't remember the words.*

SONG a piece of music with words for singing; the musical sounds of animals such as birds, whales, and insects ▶ *There are two* **songs** *that we sing during the first act of the play. We woke to the* **song** *of a cardinal in the tree outside our window.*

JINGLE a simple, often repetitious melody, song, or poem ▶ *I hate it when I get some silly advertising* **jingle** *stuck in my head.*

THEME a short melody that is repeated in a piece of music ▶ *Many people recognize the opening* **theme** *of Beethoven's Fifth Symphony, even if they've never heard the whole piece.*

Thea believes that it's **cruel** to keep animals in cages.

n = noun vb = verb adj = adjective adv = adverb prep = preposition conj = conjunction **131**

▶ **MELT** vb to change from a solid to a liquid because of heat
▶ *The ice on the lake **melted** during the warm spell we had last week.*

DISSOLVE to seem to disappear when mixed with a liquid ▶ *You can **dissolve** more sugar in warm water than you can in cold water.*

THAW to melt; to become unfrozen
▶ *I took the meat out of the freezer so that it would **thaw** in time for me to cook dinner.*

▶ **METEOR** n a piece of rock from space that enters the earth's atmosphere at high speed and burns as it falls to the earth
▶ *During the **meteor** shower in August we saw 15 **meteors** in less than an hour.*

METEORITE a remaining part of a meteor that hit the earth before it burned up
▶ *Scientists are studying a small **meteorite** that they believe came originally from Mars.*

SHOOTING STAR a burning meteor that appears as a streak of light in the sky
▶ *Kate saw a **shooting star** as she sat in the dark looking at the sky.*

COMET a body of icy rock that travels around the sun in a long path and often has a visible tail of light as it nears the sun
▶ *Two bright **comets** have appeared recently: Hyakutake in 1996 and Hale-Bopp in 1997.*

ASTEROID a very small planet that travels around the sun, especially between the orbits of Mars and Jupiter
▶ *There are thousands of **asteroids** ranging in diameter from less than a mile to almost five hundred miles.*

▶ **MIDDLE** n the point halfway between two other points ▶ *You walk here from your house and I'll walk in your direction and we'll*

I took the meat out of the freezer so that it would **thaw** in time for me to cook dinner.

meet in the **middle**. I eat lunch in the **middle** of the day.

CENTER the point inside a circle or sphere that is the same distance from every part of the edge ▶ *A line from the* **center** *to the edge of a circle is called the radius. We met at a restaurant near the city* **center***.*

CORE the part near the center; the most important part ▶ *Don't eat the* **core** *of the apple. The* **core** *of my argument is the idea that you should always tell the truth.*

HEART the central, main, or most important part ▶ *The library, the museum, and the symphony hall are at the* **heart** *of the culture of a city.*

HUB a focus of activity or interest ▶ *Chicago is an important* **hub** *of transportation for the whole country.*

NUCLEUS a part around which the other parts are grouped; a focus of growth or activity ▶ *Our genes are contained in the* **nucleus** *of each cell. Her collection of eighteenth-century books formed the* **nucleus** *of her library.*

▶ **MIND** n the part of you that thinks, feels, understands, reasons, and remembers ▶ *Larissa needed to clear her* **mind** *so that she could figure out what to do next.*

BRAIN the organ inside your head that controls your body and allows you to think and to have feelings ▶ *The human* **brain** *is able to do many things at the same time.*

INTELLECT the power of the mind to think, understand, and learn ▶ *Albert Einstein was a physicist who was known for his* **intellect***.*

see SOUL

▶ **MINISTER** n a person who is authorized to lead religious ceremonies in a church, especially a Protestant church ▶ *Her father was a Presbyterian* **minister***.*

PRIEST in certain Christian denominations and other religions, a person who can lead religious services and other rites ▶ *Michael decided to study to become a Roman Catholic* **priest***. The Episcopal Church now has many women* **priests***.*

PASTOR a minister or priest in charge of a church or parish ▶ *She took a position as* **pastor** *of a church several miles from here.*

RABBI a Jewish religious leader and teacher ▶ *The* **rabbi** *leads services at the synagogue on Saturdays.*

CLERGY people trained and authorized to conduct religious services ▶ *The mayor invited* **clergy** *of all faiths to discuss how to help the poor in the city.*

▶ **MISTAKE** n a misunderstanding of the meaning; a wrong action or statement, usually from carelessness or ignorance ▶ *I went to the wrong room by* **mistake***. I made a* **mistake** *on one of my math problems.*

ERROR a wrong belief; something done incorrectly ▶ *It is an* **error** *to think that he was just being friendly. I made an* **error** *in subtraction.*

SLIP a slight mistake in speaking or writing ▶ *It was just a* **slip** *of the tongue when I said "Rob" instead of "Tom."*

OVERSIGHT an unintentional omission or a careless mistake ▶ *It was an* **oversight** *not to have sent you an invitation.*

▶ **MIX** vb to bring different things together
▶ *Mix all the ingredients together in a bowl.*
*She never **mixes** business with pleasure.*

COMBINE to unite, join, or mix
▶ *Combine the flour, sugar, and baking*
powder before adding the milk and eggs.

BLEND to bring together or mix different
things so that the things cannot be identified
▶ *I made the orange color by **blending***
*red and yellow. This book **blends** fact*
and fiction.

MERGE to blend gradually
▶ *Native American and Spanish cultures*
***merged** over the centuries to create the*
Mexico of today.

MINGLE to bring together or mix different
things, keeping the things identifiable
▶ *The school year ended with **mingled***
feelings of sadness and joy.

STIR to mix a substance by moving a
spoon or stick around and around in it
▶ *Stir the oatmeal constantly until it*
begins to thicken.

WHIP to beat or stir rapidly, allowing
air to create a frothy mixture
▶ *Whip the whites of four eggs until*
they are stiff.

see JOIN

▶ **MODERN** adj to do with the present
or the recent past; new in style
▶ *Modern medicine saves many lives*
that would have been lost not long ago.
*Do you like **modern** art?*

CONTEMPORARY in the style of the present
time ▶ *Their whole house is filled with*
***contemporary** furniture—and some of it*
is very comfortable!

CURRENT happening now
▶ *I have to do a report on some*
***current** events in today's paper.*

UP-TO-DATE containing the most
recent information; in the latest style
▶ *Is this encyclopedia **up-to-date**?*
She is always dressed in the most
***up-to-date** fashions.*

see NEW

▶ **MONEY** n the coins and bills that people
use to buy things ▶ *I'm getting hungry—do*
*you have any **money**? How much **money***
did that book cost?

CASH money in the form of coins and bills
▶ *My father never likes to carry **cash**; he*
always pays by check or credit card.

Do you like **modern** art?

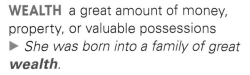
WEALTH a great amount of money, property, or valuable possessions ▶ *She was born into a family of great* **wealth**.

CURRENCY the form of money used in a country ▶ *Each country has its own* **currency**.

PROPERTY wealth measured in land, buildings, and other things that you own ▶ *He lives quite comfortably as a man* of **property**.

▶ **MORAL** adj relating to or able to distinguish between right and wrong in conduct ▶ *Rebecca is a* **moral** *person who insists on treating people fairly and honestly.*

VIRTUOUS having or exhibiting a morally excellent character or nature ▶ *Tom lived a* **virtuous** *life without ever hurting anyone intentionally.*

RIGHTEOUS morally right and justifiable ▶ *Chris responded to that injustice with* **righteous** *indignation.*

ETHICAL in agreement with standards of behavior, especially those of a particular profession ▶ *It is not* **ethical** *for a doctor to discuss a patient's illness with other people.*

▶ **MOVE** vb to change place or position ▶ *Traffic was* **moving** *slowly because of the icy roads. Would you* **move** *your books so I can sit down, please?*

TRANSFER to move from one person or place to another ▶ *I* **transferred** *the ball to my left hand.*

SHIFT to change the place, direction, or position of ▶ *She* **shifted** *her weight to her other foot. I used to respect the mayor, but my opinion of her has* **shifted**.

REMOVE to take off or away ▶ *Please* **remove** *your shoes before you enter the room. They* **removed** *the boxes from the garage.*

see GO, LEAVE, TRAVEL

Tom lived a **virtuous** life without ever hurting anyone intentionally.

▶ **MUMBLE** vb to speak quietly and unclearly, with the mouth nearly closed
▶ *He **mumbled** something about being late and rushed out of the room.*

MURMUR to talk very quietly; to make a quiet, low, continuous sound
▶ *I could hear people **murmuring** in the next room, but I couldn't tell what they were saying. The wind **murmured** in the trees.*

MUTTER to speak or complain quietly and unclearly ▶ *Philip **muttered** something under his breath. She went out **muttering** about how unfair her parents are.*

WHISPER to talk very quietly without using the vocal cords ▶ *I **whispered** a question to the girl in the next row. We had to **whisper** so we wouldn't wake the baby.*

see COMPLAIN, TALK

▶ **MYTH** n a story that expresses a people's beliefs, tells about gods or goddesses, or tries to explain something in nature
▶ *Most religions have a creation **myth** that explains how the world began.*

LEGEND a story handed down from earlier times that may have some basis in historical fact ▶ *The **legends** of King Arthur tell us more about how to behave toward others than they tell us about that early British leader.*

FABLE a story that teaches a lesson and often has animal characters that act like people ▶ *Many **fables** from Africa tell about a clever rabbit who is always trying to outsmart the other animals.*

EPIC a long poem, story, or film that tells the deeds of legendary or historical figures ▶ *The two great Greek **epics** are The Iliad and The Odyssey. Melville's **epic**, Moby Dick, is the tale of a hunt for a white whale.*

see STORY

▶ **NAKED** adj completely or partially without clothing or protection; without anything added ▶ *I was dripping wet and* **naked** *when the phone rang downstairs. I want you to tell me the* **naked** *truth.*

NUDE completely without clothing ▶ *The ancient Greeks produced many wonderful sculptures of* **nude** *figures.*

BARE without the usual clothing or covering ▶ *Don't go out in the rain with a* **bare** *head; wear a hat. All the leaves have fallen and the trees are* **bare**.

BALD without any natural covering, especially of hair on the head ▶ *My father is almost completely* **bald**.

> **tip**
>
> Some people consider **nude** to be a more polite word to use than **naked** when referring to an unclothed human body. **Nude** is also the term regularly used in reference to works of art showing unclothed figures.

▶ **NEAT** adj clean and in good order ▶ *I try to keep my room* **neat**, *but I'm not very successful at it!*

TIDY neat in appearance or habits ▶ *My sister, on the other hand, is very* **tidy**, *and her room always looks clean.*

TRIM neat and in good condition ▶ *Like a picture from a book, the street was lined with trees and a row of* **trim** *little houses.*

ORDERLY neat, with everything in its proper place or time ▶ *Patricia has to keep her desk very* **orderly** *because she is always working on three or four projects at a time.*

▶ **NECESSARY** adj required or needed ▶ *A well-balanced diet is* **necessary** *for good health. Do you have all the* **necessary** *ingredients for a cake?*

ESSENTIAL vital and important ▶ *It is* **essential** *that you read the instructions before you begin.*

INDISPENSABLE absolutely necessary or so important it cannot be done without ▶ *A set of fine tools is* **indispensable** *to a mechanic. There are some excellent players on this team but no one is* **indispensable**!

see IMPORTANT

▶ **NEED** vb to want urgently;
(as an auxiliary verb) to be obliged; must
▶ *The refugees* **need** *food and shelter.*
You **need** *not pay me until the job is done.*
I **need** *to practice for the concert tomorrow.*

REQUIRE to demand as necessary or
to have a great need for ▶ *My hamster*
requires *fresh food and water every day.*

LACK to be without something that you
need ▶ *The flood victims* **lack** *food*
and medicine.

see **WANT**

▶ **NERVOUS** adj easily upset or tense;
fearful or timid ▶ *Thunderstorms make me*
nervous. *I am* **nervous** *about my doctor's*
appointment.

RESTLESS unable to keep still or to
concentrate on anything ▶ *I got very*
restless *waiting for the plane to arrive.*

FIDGETY unable to keep still because
you are bored, nervous, or uneasy
▶ *Barney was very* **fidgety** *before the test.*

EDGY nervous and anxious
▶ *We were all feeling a bit* **edgy**
when the game went into overtime.

UPTIGHT tense, nervous, or uneasy
▶ *Doreen was very* **uptight** *after the*
accident.

▶ **NEW** adj just made or begun; seen,
known, or thought of for the first time
▶ *Eduardo got a* **new** *job. The astronomer*
discovered a **new** *planet. I just thought of a*
new *idea.*

FRESH produced, obtained, or arrived just
now or a short time ago; not yet affected by
time or use ▶ *We need a* **fresh** *approach to*
this problem. I bought a dozen **fresh** *eggs.*

ORIGINAL the first of its kind
▶ *Her* **original** *idea was to build a tree*
house. Jaime came up with an **original**
design for a birthday card.

RECENT happening, made, or done a short
time ago ▶ *The city is still recovering from*
the **recent** *snowstorm.*

I am **nervous** about my doctor's appointment.

I bought a dozen **fresh** eggs.

NOVEL new and unusual or strange
▶ Mark had a **novel** idea for his class report—he wrote it as a play and had us all act it out.

BRAND-NEW very new and unused
▶ I'm breaking in a **brand-new** pair of shoes.

see MODERN

▶ **NICE** adj pleasing or comforting, usually in a mild or general way
▶ What a **nice** day. He is a **nice** boy. That's a **nice** haircut. You did a **nice** job cutting the lawn. I had a **nice** nap.

PLEASANT enjoyable or giving pleasure; likable ▶ We spent a **pleasant** afternoon in the park. She has a very **pleasant** personality.

AGREEABLE pleasing, likable, or enjoyable
▶ Ken is an **agreeable** person. This is an **agreeable** day for sitting in the shade and relaxing.

GOOD-NATURED generally friendly and kind
▶ Rebecca is **good-natured** and always has a cheerful smile for everyone.

DELIGHTFUL very pleasing or charming; giving delight ▶ We spent a **delightful** weekend camping by a beautiful lake. Colin has a **delightful** sense of humor.

FANTASTIC extremely nice or good
▶ Between going to the game and the beach, I had a **fantastic** day.

tip

Nice is a very general word to describe someone you like or something that makes you feel good, but it is not very specific. Be careful not to overuse it. Often a stronger or more specific word is better.

see FRIENDLY, GOOD, GREAT

n = noun   vb = verb   adj = adjective   adv = adverb   prep = preposition   conj = conjunction   **139**

▶ **NOISE** n a sound, especially when it is loud, unmusical, or unpleasant ▶ *There is so much **noise** in here I can't hear what you are saying. Suddenly, they heard rustling **noises** in the hedge.*

DIN a great deal of noise that is hard to endure ▶ *The constant **din** of the traffic made it impossible for me to sleep.*

UPROAR shouting, noise, and confusion ▶ *When the game ended in a tie, the crowd was in an **uproar**.*

CLAMOR a loud, excited shouting and noise, especially of complaint or demand ▶ *The **clamor** of the crowd grew louder when they announced that the concert would be delayed another hour.*

RACKET a loud, clattering combination of noises ▶ *The construction workers are making quite a **racket** with their machinery running and radio blaring.*

HUBBUB the confused sound of many mingled voices ▶ *The **hubbub** in the theater died down when the lights went out and the curtain went up.*

▶ **NORMAL** adj not different from what is usual or expected ▶ *The **normal** time for my recorder lesson is 4:30, but this week it is at 4:00.*

TYPICAL having traits or qualities that are normal for a type or class; conforming to a type or class ▶ *My family lives in a **typical** small town.*

AVERAGE about midway in value, rate, or size ▶ *What is the **average** price of a pair of shoes? John is of **average** height and has black hair.*

see USUAL, COMMON

▶ **NOTICE** vb to see or to become aware of ▶ *Oh, hello! I didn't **notice** you sitting there when I came in. Did you **notice** the smell of fish in the kitchen?*

OBSERVE to watch carefully; to notice by looking or watching ▶ *The police have been **observing** the house for a week. I **observed** a chipmunk dashing into a hole in the tree trunk.*

NOTE to notice and pay attention to ▶ *Please **note** the price increase.*

PERCEIVE to become aware of through one of the senses, especially through sight or hearing ▶ *I **perceived** a change in her voice.*

see DISCOVER, LOOK

▶ **NUMBER** n 1 a word or symbol used for counting and for doing arithmetic ▶ *We learned the **numbers** from 1 to 20 in Spanish class today. Subtract the **number** 2,185 from the total.*

NUMERAL a written symbol that represents a number, such as 8 or VIII ▶ *Did you write the letter b or the **numeral** 6? What is the Roman **numeral** for 42?*

FIGURE a written number; an amount given in numbers ▶ *The final answer should be a number in six **figures**. Ted gave me the final **figures** for the book sale.*

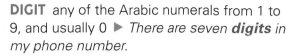
DIGIT any of the Arabic numerals from 1 to 9, and usually 0 ▶ *There are seven **digits** in my phone number.*

▶ **NUMBER** n 2 a usually large group or collection of things or people
▶ *A **number** of fans crowded around the band members when they arrived. Can you guess the **number** of beans in the jar?*

AMOUNT the total number of something
▶ *We got an unusually large **amount** of snow last winter.*

QUANTITY an indefinite number of something; a large number or amount
▶ *The package contains a small **quantity** of jelly beans. Restaurants buy food in **quantity**.*

tip

Number in sense 2 is usually used to refer to nouns that can be made plural: *Shelley made a **number** of mistakes on the test. What is the **number** of students in your class?*

Amount is usually used with nouns that cannot be made plural: *We got a small **amount** of sunshine yesterday. Put just a tiny **amount** of water on the microscope slide.*

We got an unusually large **amount** of snow last winter.

n = noun   vb = verb   adj = adjective   adv = adverb   prep = preposition   conj = conjunction   **141**

O

▶ **OBEY** vb to do what someone tells you to do; to carry out or follow (as laws, rules, or instructions)
▶ Karen always **obeys** her mother.
Drivers should always **obey** the speed limit.

MIND to pay obedient attention to
▶ **Mind** your mother while I'm gone.
I wish he would **mind** his manners.

COMPLY to act in agreement with rules or requests ▶ We **complied** with Mother's request to stay inside while it was raining.

HEED to pay close attention to
▶ I will **heed** your good advice.

BEHAVE to act properly
▶ I wish you would **behave** yourself!

▶ **OBJECT** vb to dislike or disagree with
▶ I **object** to that last statement you made.
Steve always **objects** when we want to go swimming.

PROTEST to object to strongly and publicly
▶ The students **protested** against the school's new dress code.

DISAPPROVE to make an unfavorable judgment on or state an unfavorable opinion of ▶ Do you think your mother will **disapprove** of our plans to go camping?

DISAGREE to have different opinions from
▶ I **disagree** with everything you have said for the last 10 minutes!

see **ARGUE, COMPLAIN**

Steve always **objects** when we want to go swimming.

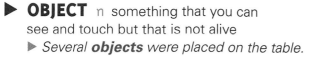

OBJECT n something that you can see and touch but that is not alive
▶ Several **objects** were placed on the table.

THING an event, act, idea, or object
▶ A funny **thing** happened today. She can't think of a **thing** to do. What is that **thing** in your hand?

ARTICLE an object that is a member of a group or class ▶ I got several **articles** of clothing for my birthday.

ITEM one of a number of objects
▶ Here is a list of **items** you will need to bring to camp.

OBVIOUS adj very easy to see or understand ▶ His frown was an **obvious** sign that he was unhappy.

EVIDENT easy to see or recognize
▶ It is **evident** from her success that she knows how to handle money wisely. Her happiness was **evident** from the way she talked.

APPARENT easy to know or understand
▶ It soon became **apparent** that Tim is a much better tennis player than I am.

CLEAR easy to understand; easy to see through; easy to hear
▶ These instructions are **clear** and easy to follow. The window is made of **clear** glass. She spoke in a **clear** voice.

PLAIN easy to see or hear
▶ The book was sitting on the table in **plain** sight.

see EASY, PLAIN

OCEAN n the entire body of salt water that covers about 70 percent of the earth's surface; one of the four main parts of this body
▶ The four **oceans** are the Atlantic, the Pacific, the Indian, and the Arctic. We went to the **ocean** for our vacation.

SEA a large body of salt water that is partly or wholly surrounded by land; the ocean
▶ The Caribbean **Sea** is part of the Atlantic Ocean. The ship ran into a storm at **sea**.

DEEP the ocean, especially below the surface ▶ Divers and scientists are discovering unknown forms of life that live in the **deep**.

OFFER vb to ask someone if he or she would like something; to say you are willing to do something; to suggest
▶ Can I **offer** you some cake? I **offered** to wash the dishes. Zoë **offered** a couple of interesting ideas.

PRESENT to give a gift or prize to in a formal way; to introduce ▶ I would like to **present** you with this medal. Alison **presented** her plan at the committee meeting.

TENDER to offer for acceptance
▶ If you don't like my work, I will gladly **tender** my resignation.

► **OFTEN** adv many times
  ► *We **often** go for walks in the woods. Have you been to the city very **often**?*

FREQUENTLY at frequent or brief intervals
► *My older brother comes to see me quite **frequently**.*

REGULARLY at regular or periodic intervals
► *She goes to the dentist **regularly**.*

REPEATEDLY over and over again
► *I have asked you **repeatedly** not to put your feet on the sofa.*

► **OLD** adj having existed for a long time
  ► *Sarah likes to collect **old** bottles. At the party, my **old** friends got to meet my new friends.*

ELDERLY rather old; older than middle-aged
► *Shana and her friends liked to visit with the **elderly** residents of their building on Sunday afternoons.*

AGED grown very old and usually weak or feeble ► *Fran helped an **aged** man up the stairs.*

ANCIENT very old; dating from long ago
► *My uncle has an **ancient** parrot that must be twenty-five years old. We get our understanding of democracy from the **ancient** Greeks.*

OLD-FASHIONED of a style used in earlier times; out-of-date ► *Marianne loves to wear an **old-fashioned** three-cornered hat. My dad has some very **old-fashioned** ideas about dating.*

ANTIQUE very old and usually of a style used in earlier times
► *Mary wore the **antique** necklace she got from her great-grandmother. A parade of **antique** cars went down the street.*

► **ONCE** adv on one occasion; at an unspecified time in the past
  ► *I met my great-grandfather **once** before he died. This part of the continent was **once** covered by a broad, shallow sea.*

PREVIOUSLY earlier than or before another event ► *Martin had been to the museum **previously**, so he took his friends straight to his favorite exhibit.*

FORMERLY at an earlier time
► *She was **formerly** known as an Olympic athlete, but now she is recognized as a writer as well.*

► **ONLY** adv as a single instance or fact; not more than ► *Dan has lost **only** one race. There were **only** three people in the store.*

JUST exactly or precisely; by a very small amount or margin ► *We had to do the assignment **just** as we were told. We made it to the train **just** on time.*

BARELY no more than ► *They had **barely** enough food to last the weekend.*

HARDLY only just *(used to stress the smallness of an amount or time)*

▶ We had **hardly** closed the door behind us when the storm began. He sneaked all the way downstairs with **hardly** a sound.

MERELY only or simply; and nothing else
▶ Don't blame me; I'm **merely** the messenger.

tip

Only is also used as an adjective meaning "with nothing or no one else": Maria was the **only** person who brought a raincoat.

▶ **OPEN** adj not shut, closed, or sealed
▶ There is an **open** container of milk in the refrigerator. I always leave a window **open** when I sleep.

AJAR slightly or partly open
▶ Amy left the door **ajar** so that she could hear the children in the next room.

UNCOVERED with no cover; with the cover removed ▶ You should always cook spaghetti in an **uncovered** pot.

UNFASTENED not tied, attached, or closed firmly ▶ The dog ran away when its leash came **unfastened**.

UNLOCKED not locked
▶ The thieves found their way into the house through an **unlocked** basement door.

He sneaked all the way downstairs with **hardly** a sound.

▶ **OPPOSITE** adj located or facing directly across; facing or moving the other way; completely different
▶ *The boys sat on **opposite** sides of the room. We ran in **opposite** directions. My brother came to the **opposite** conclusion.*

OPPOSING facing against each other
▶ *A peace treaty ending the civil war was signed by leaders of the **opposing** armies.*

CONTRADICTORY not consistent *(used especially of statements or ideas that cannot both be true)* ▶ *The two witnesses had **contradictory** versions of how the accident happened.*

CONTRARY completely different in nature, direction, or order ▶ *John and Denise have **contrary** views on politics; he is liberal while she is conservative.*

CONFLICTING in conflict with each other
▶ *Phil and I have **conflicting** opinions about how to train the puppy.*

▶ **ORDER** vb to tell someone that he or she has to do something
▶ *Ken's mother **ordered** him to clean his room. My brother **ordered** me to get out of his room.*

COMMAND to order, especially with authority ▶ *The colonel **commanded** the soldiers to search the town.*

DIRECT to supervise people or give them directions ▶ *Jennifer **directed** her classmates in the school play.*

INSTRUCT to teach; to give instructions or orders to ▶ *She **instructed** the class in the basics of algebra. I will **instruct** you on how to behave.*

▶ **OUTSIDE** adj on the surface, side, or part away from the inside
▶ *He trimmed the **outside** edges of the painting with a sharp knife.*

We ran in **opposite** directions.

EXTERIOR on the side or part, especially of a building, away from the inside
▶ The **exterior** walls of the house were heavily insulated.

EXTERNAL happening or existing outside; for use on the outside, especially of the body
▶ Some animals have an **external** skeleton. This medicine is for **external** use only—do not put it in your mouth or swallow it.

OUTER outside or away from the center
▶ The **outer** planets of the solar system are extremely cold.

OUTDOOR used, done, or built outside
▶ I like to swim in the **outdoor** pool at the park. Golf is an **outdoor** sport.

▶ **OWN** vb to have or keep by natural or legal right ▶ Barbara **owns** more than two hundred books. We **own** a dog and two horses. Do they **own** this house?

POSSESS to own or have possession of; to have a characteristic, quality, or power
▶ Her family has **possessed** great wealth for several generations. The state **possesses** the right to punish criminals.

HOLD to have possession or ownership of; to have in your mind as a judgment or belief
▶ Art **holds** the deed to his grandfather's farm. She **holds** very strong opinions.

tip

Outside and exterior are often used as nouns: The **outside** of the box was painted red. The **exterior** of the building was covered with ivy.

Outside may also be used as a preposition (I left my muddy boots **outside** the door) or as an adverb (Vicky went **outside** when it started to snow).

p

PAIN n a feeling that hurts, either physically or emotionally ▶ *I can still feel the pain where I hit my knee on a rock. The pain of losing every game made Philip cry.*

ACHE a dull, steady pain ▶ *I got an ache in my neck from painting the ceiling.*

PANG a sudden sharp or stabbing pain that doesn't last long ▶ *Jean felt a pang in her side when the falling branch knocked her down. After he stole the money, Jason felt the pangs of guilt.*

SORENESS a steady pain, especially from an injury or sore ▶ *The soreness in your arm will probably last a few days after the bandage is taken off.*

TWINGE a quick, sharp minor pain ▶ *My father says he feels twinges in his big toe before it rains.*

STITCH a sharp pain, usually in the side or back ▶ *You can get a stitch in your side if you run fast for a long time.*

SPASM a violent, often painful, jerk of a muscle ▶ *After running three miles, I felt spasms in my leg muscles.*

CRAMP a sudden pain caused by a very tense muscle ▶ *As I was climbing the steep, rocky mountainside I got a cramp in my leg.*

PAMPER vb to take very good care of, with kindness, food, comfort, or anything special ▶ *Grandparents love to pamper their grandchildren.*

SPOIL to pamper too much or too often ▶ *She has been so spoiled by her parents that she gets angry if anyone tells her she can't do what she wants.*

INDULGE to give in to a desire or craving; to let someone have his or her own way ▶ *Dennis rarely indulges his love of chocolate. I will indulge you this once and let you stay up as long as you want.*

HUMOR to keep a person happy by agreeing with him or her or doing what he or she wants ▶ *Let's humor him just so that he stops complaining all the time.*

BABY to pamper someone too much, as if the person were younger than he or she really is ▶ *Ron was an only child and his parents babied him for many years.*

PART n something that makes up less than the whole of a thing ▶ *I finished part of my homework this morning. When we put the clock back together, there were three parts left over!*

PIECE something separated or broken from a whole thing ▶ *Would you like a piece of this pie? My new puzzle has over five hundred pieces. The plate fell and shattered into pieces.*

SECTION a distinct part ▶ *Could I have the comic section of the newspaper, please? The test is in two sections: math and language arts.*

When we put the clock back together, there were three **parts** left over!

PORTION the part that a person has or gets ▶ *Alison's* **portion** *of the inheritance was her grandmother's diamond necklace.*

SEGMENT one of the parts that something is easily divided into ▶ *Chris gave me two* **segments** *of his tangerine.*

FRAGMENT a small part or piece broken off ▶ *The archaeologists were excited to find two* **fragments** *of an ancient stone calendar.*

FRACTION a very small part or amount of something ▶ *I bought this ring for just a* **fraction** *of the usual price.*

SHARE the part that belongs to a single person ▶ *Everyone who helps with the work will get an equal* **share** *of the profits.*

▶ **PARTY** n a group of people who come together to enjoy themselves; the entertainment that these people share

▶ *Will you come to my birthday* **party**? *Let's have a* **party** *after school gets out in June.*

CELEBRATION a ceremony, a party, or an enjoyable activity that marks a happy occasion ▶ *The city has a fireworks display at the Fourth of July* **celebration**. *We'll have a big* **celebration** *when Alice gets home.*

FESTIVITY joyfulness and gaiety; *(in plural)* the things done at a party or celebration ▶ *Our entire holiday was filled with excitement and* **festivity**. *Annie helped plan the* **festivities** *for the party.*

GATHERING an informally organized party or social event ▶ *After the wedding there was a small* **gathering** *of friends and relatives at our house.*

RECEPTION a formal event or party, especially to welcome the guests ▶ *My sister and I were invited to a* **reception** *for new students at the school.*

This picture is a **perfect** likeness of her brother.

▶ **PERFECT** adj without any defect or mistake; completely correct
▶ *This picture is a **perfect** likeness of her brother. I got a **perfect** score on my test.*

IDEAL exactly as you would wish; of the perfect kind ▶ *With this light, steady breeze, today will be **ideal** for sailing.*

FLAWLESS not having any flaw or error
▶ *Catrin gave a **flawless** performance at her violin recital.*

FAULTLESS without any fault
▶ *Now that I have studied carpentry, I can appreciate the **faultless** workmanship of these antique chairs.*

IMPECCABLE without error, fault, or weakness ▶ *Keesha speaks such **impeccable** Spanish you would think she was born in Spain.*

▶ **PERIOD** n a length of time ▶ *Rocky left the room for a short **period**. She was out of the country for a **period** of nine years.*

AGE a period of time in history, especially one marked by some identifying characteristic ▶ *The **age** of the dinosaurs came to an end about 65 million years ago.*

ERA a period of time in history, especially one marked by significant change or development ▶ *The invention of the automobile began a new **era** in the history of transportation. We live in an **era** of great discoveries.*

EON a very long or indefinitely long period of time ▶ *Geologists define an **eon** as one billion years. I haven't seen you for **eons**!*

▶ **PERSONALITY** n all of the qualities or traits that make one person different from another; a famous person ▶ *Sally has a very outgoing **personality**. Peter collects autographs from show business **personalities**.*

CHARACTER all of the qualities or traits that make you the kind of person you are, especially your mental and ethical traits
▶ *Success did not change Risa's basic **character**. Years of volunteer work among the poor helped to create his strong and understanding **character**.*

DISPOSITION a person's general attitude and general mood ▶ *Rebecca has a very cheerful* **disposition***.*

TEMPERAMENT the way you usually think, act, or respond to other people or to situations ▶ *Laura has a very calm* **temperament** *and did not get upset when the storm delayed her flight home.*

TEMPER a person's usual state of mind; a tendency to get angry ▶ *A person with an even* **temper** *rarely gets angry. He has quite a* **temper***.*

▶ **PERSUADE** vb to lead to do or believe something by giving good reasons ▶ *Margaret finally* **persuaded** *everybody to stay until it stopped snowing.*

CONVINCE to overcome doubt by arguing or giving good reasons ▶ *Jessica tried to* **convince** *me that she knew the way home, but I knew that we were hopelessly lost.*

INFLUENCE to have an effect on ▶ *My parents' constant encouragement* **influenced** *me to try out for the baseball team.*

see URGE

▶ **PET** vb to stroke or pat an animal in a gentle, loving way ▶ *I always* **pet** *the dog when he obeys my command.*

CARESS to touch or stroke gently ▶ *The mother* **caressed** *her child's hand as he sobbed.*

CUDDLE to hold closely and lovingly in your arms ▶ *He always* **cuddles** *his teddy bear as he falls asleep at night.*

FONDLE to handle or stroke lovingly or tenderly ▶ *Mary* **fondled** *her infant daughter as she slept on her lap. Greg* **fondled** *the carvings with great care.*

▶ **PITY** n a feeling of sorrow for the suffering of another ▶ *I felt* **pity** *for the homeless on such a cold night.*

SYMPATHY an understanding of and sharing in another's feelings ▶ *I can always turn to my best friend, Rachel, for* **sympathy***.*

COMPASSION a feeling of pity for and a desire to help someone who is suffering ▶ *He felt such* **compassion** *for the victims of the flood that he sent several truckloads of food and clothing to help them out.*

see KINDNESS

▶ **PLACE** n a particular region, area, or space; a city, town, building, room, or other geographical area ▶ *A good* **place** *to hang this picture would be right over my desk. We needed a map to help us get to the right* **place***.*

LOCATION the position or place where something is or will be ▶ *We found a good* **location** *for our lemonade stand, with lots of people walking by.*

LOCALE the place or region where something happens, as in a story ▶ *Mark Twain used the Mississippi River as the* **locale** *for his book,* The Adventures of Tom Sawyer.

SITE the land where something is built or takes place ▶ *The town grew up on the* **site** *of an ancient castle. We pitched our tent on a hilltop* **site** *overlooking the lake.*

► **PLAIN** adj not decorated; easy to understand ► *The present was wrapped in **plain** blue paper. The law was written in **plain** English.*

SIMPLE not having many parts or elements ► *The box was decorated with a **simple** design on the lid. Just answer with a **simple** yes or no!*

UNCOMPLICATED not complicated ► *She wanted to live an **uncomplicated** life in a cabin in the woods.*

see OBVIOUS

► **PLAN** n an idea about how you intend to do something; a drawing that shows how the parts of something are arranged ► *The family sat down together to share their vacation **plans**. Lori showed us the **plans** for her new kitchen.*

DESIGN the shape or style; a drawing showing the main elements of a plan ► *The floor **design** had diamonds and squares. The architect sketched the **design** of the new building.*

PROJECT a plan or a proposal for a plan; an assignment to be done over a period of time by a person or group of people

► *The senate approved the highway **project**. We are starting a **project** in our social science class on protecting the environment.*

PLOT a secret plan, usually to do something wrong or illegal ► *The police foiled a **plot** to kidnap the millionaire's son.*

SCHEME a plan, especially for doing something secret or dishonest ► *The twins tried to drum up a **scheme** for making money without having to work.*

► **PLEASE** vb to be agreeable to; to give pleasure to ► *Do you think the picture I painted will **please** my uncle if I give it to him?*

SATISFY to fulfill the wishes or desires of; to fulfill the needs of ► *It seems that no matter how much work I do, my teacher is never **satisfied**. Alice ate just enough cake to **satisfy** her hunger.*

DELIGHT to give great joy or pleasure to ► *The twins were **delighted** to learn that they were going to the beach tomorrow.*

GRATIFY to give pleasure or satisfaction to; to give in to or indulge ► *I am **gratified** that my lost wallet was returned. Grandmother loves to **gratify** my every wish.*

The architect sketched the **design** of the new building.

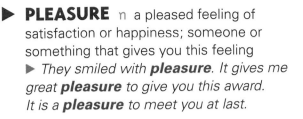

▶ **PLEASURE** n a pleased feeling of satisfaction or happiness; someone or something that gives you this feeling ▶ *They smiled with* **pleasure***. It gives me great* **pleasure** *to give you this award. It is a* **pleasure** *to meet you at last.*

JOY a feeling of great happiness; someone or something that brings great happiness ▶ *Andrea was filled with* **joy** *when she won the race. The walk through the woods was a great* **joy***.*

FUN a good time; something that provides pleasure ▶ *I had* **fun** *with you this afternoon. It is a lot of* **fun** *to play baseball.*

ENJOYMENT the pleasure experienced when enjoying something ▶ *I get a lot of* **enjoyment** *from cooking. The morning was filled with* **enjoyment** *as we laughed and played together.*

DELIGHT a great deal of pleasure, expressed with enthusiasm; someone or something that provides great pleasure ▶ *I could see the* **delight** *on the child's face as she rode the pony. Bryn's recorder playing is a* **delight** *to hear.*

ECSTASY a state of extreme pleasure or happiness ▶ *He was in* **ecstasy** *when he heard that he had been chosen for the all-star team.*

He was in **ecstasy** when he heard that he had been chosen for the all-star team.

▶ **POLITE** adj having good manners; being well-behaved and considerate of others ▶ *Be **polite** to our guests when they arrive, and offer them something to eat.*

COURTEOUS polite and respectful toward others ▶ *On a bus or subway, it is **courteous** to give up your seat to an older person.*

WELL-MANNERED acting properly and with good manners ▶ *All the students were very **well-mannered** during the field trip.*

CIVIL as polite as necessary, but no more ▶ *The salesperson was **civil** to us, but he didn't try very hard to help us.*

GRACIOUS having and showing kindness and courtesy ▶ *It was very **gracious** of you to invite us here for the week.*

see **FRIENDLY, THOUGHTFUL**

▶ **POOR** adj having little money and few possessions ▶ *My father was a **poor** farmer who struggled to make a living every year.*

NEEDY very poor; not having enough to live on ▶ *We gave food and clothing to the **needy** families whose homes were lost in the hurricane.*

PENNILESS extremely poor; without any money at all ▶ *After gambling away his entire savings, Arnie was left homeless and **penniless**.*

DESTITUTE living in poverty; without the necessities of life ▶ *The war has left thousands of families **destitute**.*

BROKE having little or no money ▶ *I've been **broke** ever since I had to pay for repairs to my car.*

▶ **POSSIBLE** adj able to exist, happen, or be done ▶ *It is **possible**, but not likely, that he will arrive early. Satellites make it **possible** to send news around the world in seconds.*

PRACTICAL useful and sensible; showing good judgment ▶ *We developed a very **practical** plan for making money this summer. A **practical** person would never try to do this huge job alone.*

PROBABLE likely to occur or be; reasonably to be expected, though not certain ▶ *Thunderstorms are **probable** this evening. I think Jenna is the **probable** winner of the election.*

FEASIBLE able and likely to be done successfully; believable ▶ *Heavier-than-air flight did not seem **feasible** in the last century. Shana's excuse was not very **feasible**.*

▶ **PREDICT** vb to say what you think will happen, based on what you know now ▶ *She **predicted** the team would lose this game because their best player was injured.*

FORECAST to say what you think will happen, especially to the weather, after studying the available data ▶ *The radio announcer **forecasts** rain for tomorrow evening. Economists **forecast** a drop in oil prices next year.*

FORETELL to know or say what you think will happen ▶ *There was no way to **foretell** that we would both get sick.*

PROPHESY to say what you think will happen, based on mystical knowledge or divine inspiration

▶ *Some people **prophesied** that the world was going to end in the year 1000.*

▶ **PREJUDICE** n a preconceived opinion based on race, religion, or other characteristics ▶ *Racial **prejudice** has been the cause of great suffering for many centuries.*

INTOLERANCE a lack of willingness to respect or accept the customs, beliefs, or opinions of others ▶ *The mutual **intolerance** of the two groups toward each other has made it impossible for them to end the fighting.*

BIGOTRY an intense and often open dislike or hatred of a group, based on prejudice and intolerance ▶ *One of the goals of the struggle for civil rights has been to eliminate **bigotry** and hatred.*

BIAS a mental leaning, either for or against something, that may influence our judgment ▶ *She has a strong **bias** in favor of classical music. A member of a jury should not have any **bias** relating to the case being tried.*

PARTIALITY a mental leaning in favor of something ▶ *She has a **partiality** for the novels of Charles Dickens. I will admit that I have a **partiality** for chocolate cake.*

▶ **PRETTY** adj pleasing to look at or listen to ▶ *The village surrounds a **pretty** little harbor, with sailboats bobbing at anchor. Andrea has a **pretty** smile.*

BEAUTIFUL giving great pleasure to your senses or to your mind ▶ *The orchestra played the most **beautiful** music I have ever heard. I saw a **beautiful** peacock at the park.*

LOVELY pretty in a graceful or delicate way ▶ *I got a **lovely** thank-you card from Alexa.*

HANDSOME pleasing in appearance, especially in an impressive or dignified way ▶ *Jason bought a **handsome** set of leather-bound books of poetry for his father.*

GORGEOUS very pleasing to look at, especially in a brilliant or magnificent way ▶ *We saw a **gorgeous** sunset as we drove across the desert.*

ATTRACTIVE pleasing to look at ▶ *She wore an **attractive** silk blouse with a dark plaid skirt.*

EXQUISITE strikingly beautiful, especially in an elaborate and delicate way; perfect in appearance ▶ *The archaeologist discovered an **exquisite** Roman brooch made of gold and covered with an intricate design.*

I will admit that I have a **partiality** for chocolate cake.

n = noun vb = verb adj = adjective adv = adverb prep = preposition conj = conjunction **155**

PREVENT vb to keep from happening
▸ *We must do everything we can to* **prevent** *war.*

HINDER to delay or make progress difficult; to interfere with ▸ *Our first attempt to climb the mountain was* **hindered** *by rain and fog.*

BLOCK to put something in the way of; to prevent the progress of ▸ *The mayor tried to* **block** *our plans to march in the parade.*

STOP to bring to an end; to keep from carrying out an action ▸ *The dog was digging in the garden, but I* **stopped** *him before he did any real damage.*

CHECK to slow down or bring to an end ▸ *I* **checked** *the impulse to jump up and cheer when I won the final game in the chess match.*

RESTRAIN to hold back; to prevent from doing ▸ *Amy* **restrained** *the little boy from running into the street.*

see **STOP**

PRIDE n a sense of your own importance or worth; a feeling of satisfaction in something someone has done
▸ *George felt a sense of* **pride** *when he finished the job by himself. Leah should take great* **pride** *in her science project.*

VANITY a feeling of extreme pride and conceit and a desire to be admired by others ▸ *His* **vanity** *was wounded when I criticized his necktie.*

SELF-RESPECT pride in yourself and your abilities ▸ *He has too much* **self-respect** *to do anything that would embarrass his friends.*

SELF-ESTEEM a feeling of pride and belief in yourself and your abilities ▸ *Joel's dignity and* **self-esteem** *were helpful in getting through the interview successfully.*

PRIZE n something won in a game or competition ▸ *There is a* **prize** *of fifty dollars for the best essay on protecting the environment.*

AWARD something given as official recognition of an accomplishment
▸ *Marcia was given an* **award** *by the mayor for her bravery in rescuing three children from a burning building.*

REWARD something that you receive for doing something good or useful ▸ *They offered a* **reward** *of twenty-five dollars to anyone finding their lost cat. You've worked so hard we will go out to dinner as a* **reward***.*

HONOR something done or given to show respect for a person; a special privilege
▸ *One wall of her office is covered with the* **honors** *she has received from all over the world. It is an* **honor** *to be here today.*

PROBLEM n a question or difficulty to be solved or answered
▸ *I can't fix the engine because I can't figure out what the* **problem** *is.*

MYSTERY something beyond understanding or not understood ▸ *The origin of life is a great* **mystery***. It's a* **mystery** *where the hair dryer went; I just used it yesterday!*

PUZZLE a question or problem that can be solved by careful thinking ▸ *How birds evolved from dinosaurs is a* **puzzle** *that may take scientists many years to figure out.*

RIDDLE a question that has a surprising or humorous answer ▶ *My favorite **riddle** is "Who is buried in Grant's Tomb?"*

DILEMMA a problem that involves a difficult choice ▶ *We were faced with a **dilemma**—either walk home in the rain or stay dry in the cave with no dinner.*

see **TROUBLE**

▶ **PROMISE** n an agreement given to do or not do something ▶ *I made a **promise** to be home by dinnertime.*

OATH a formal promise ▶ *The president took an **oath** of office at the inauguration ceremony.*

VOW a serious and binding promise ▶ *Some monks and nuns take a **vow** of silence and speak only during worship services.*

WORD a promise to do something ▶ *I gave my **word** that I would pay him back.*

PLEDGE a sincere promise or agreement ▶ *We **pledged** to be friends forever.*

▶ **PROOF** n facts or other information showing that something is true ▶ *The lawyer claimed to have **proof** that her client was innocent. Do you have any **proof** of your age?*

EVIDENCE facts or information that help to demonstrate that something is true, especially when presented in court ▶ *All the **evidence** points to the fact that the crime was committed by a left-handed person with red hair and size twelve shoes.*

TESTIMONY a statement given by a witness who is under oath in a court of law ▶ *In his **testimony** the detective said he discovered a broken window where someone broke into the house.*

▶ **PROTECT** vb to keep safe from harm, attack, or injury ▶ *Skaters wear helmets to **protect** their heads. Troops were sent to **protect** the refugees leaving the city.*

DEFEND to drive away danger or attack ▶ *The government raised a large army to **defend** the country's borders when war was declared.*

GUARD to protect from attack or escape, especially by keeping a careful watch ▶ *He bought a dog to **guard** the warehouse at night. The prisoners were **guarded** night and day.*

SHIELD to protect with armor or as if with a protective barrier ▶ *He wore sunglasses to **shield** his eyes from the sun.*

SHELTER to provide safe housing or a protective covering for ▶ *During the storm, hundreds of people were **sheltered** in the school building.*

tip

The differences in meaning among **defend**, **protect**, and **guard** can be seen in the following sentence: *The fortress was **defended** by cannon on all sides, **protected** by a high wall, and **guarded** by sentries on the watchtowers.*

PROUD adj 1 pleased and satisfied with what you or someone else has achieved; having a sense of your own importance or worth ▶ Byron's parents were **proud** of his performance in the orchestra.

DIGNIFIED having or showing the proper dignity and pride ▶ Alison behaved in a very **dignified** manner after she won the contest.

DISTINGUISHED having qualities or abilities that are worthy of recognition ▶ He has a reputation as a **distinguished** flutist.

SELF-RESPECTING having a proper respect for oneself ▶ No **self-respecting** person would allow a small child to be mistreated.

PROUD adj 2 having too much pride or too high an opinion of your own importance ▶ Mark was too **proud** to ask for help.

EGOTISTIC having an exaggerated sense of your own importance or worth ▶ Robert strikes me as an **egotistic** snob.

CONCEITED having an exaggerated opinion of yourself or your abilities ▶ Daniel is so **conceited** he never passes the ball to anyone else.

VAIN too proud of yourself, especially of the way you look ▶ He is so **vain** he is always looking at himself in the mirror to make sure his hair is combed.

ARROGANT too proud of yourself, especially in an aggressive or overbearing way ▶ The **arrogant** general refused to listen to the advice of his officers.

PSEUDONYM n a false name, especially one used by someone instead of his or her real name ▶ George Eliot is the **pseudonym** of the English novelist Mary Ann Evans.

PEN NAME a false name used by an author ▶ Mark Twain is the **pen name** of Samuel Langhorne Clemens.

ALIAS a false name, especially one used by a criminal or to keep someone's identity secret ▶ The witness is testifying under the **alias** John Doe.

STAGE NAME a false name used by an actor or performer ▶ Ringo Starr is the **stage name** of Richard Starkey.

PULL vb to apply force to something so that it moves toward you ▶ If you **pull** the rope, the bell will ring. André caught a fish so big he couldn't **pull** it out of the water.

TOW to pull along behind you; to pull with a rope, chain, or cable ▶ Sam put the boat on a trailer and **towed** it to the lake. We had to **tow** the car out of the mud.

DRAG to pull along the ground or floor ▶ The first settlers had to **drag** these huge stones out of the field before they could plow.

HAUL to pull steadily, especially on something heavy ▶ The two small boys managed to **haul** the canoe out of the water and on to shore.

DRAW to pull continuously toward
▶ *A magnet will **draw** iron filings into a pattern. **Draw** a chair up to the table and sit down.*

TUG to pull hard ▶ *Sarah **tugged** so hard on her shoelace it broke.*

YANK to give a quick, strong pull
▶ *I **yanked** on my loose tooth and it came right out.*

▶ **PUNISH** vb to cause someone to suffer for committing a crime or behaving badly
▶ *I was **punished** for hitting my brother.*

DISCIPLINE to punish in order to train, control, or correct bad behavior
▶ *The class got too noisy, so the teacher **disciplined** us by giving a test.*

SCOLD to tell someone in an angry way that he or she has done something wrong or done a bad job ▶ *Tom was **scolded** by his mother for not doing his chores.*

CHASTISE to scold sharply; to punish by beating or whipping ▶ *We were **chastised** for not obeying the rules.*

▶ **PUSH** vb to apply force to something so that it moves away from you
▶ *Dorothy **pushed** the door lightly and it swung open. Kate **pushed** the shopping cart for her mother.*

PRESS to push steadily
▶ *Both of us had to **press** down on the top of the suitcase to get it closed.*

SHOVE to push roughly or suddenly
▶ *He was so angry he just **shoved** me out the door and slammed it in my face!*

NUDGE to push gently
▶ *I **nudged** Thomas with my elbow to wake him up during the principal's speech.*

THRUST to push hard and quickly
▶ *Emily **thrust** her feet into her boots and ran out to play in the puddles.*

POKE to push with a finger, a knife, or another pointed object
▶ *Will **poked** a hole in the cloth with a sharp stick.*

I was **punished** for hitting my brother.

n = noun vb = verb adj = adjective adv = adverb prep = preposition conj = conjunction **159**

▶ **PUT** vb to cause to be in a certain place or position ▶ *Will you **put** your bicycle in the garage, please? If you have a question, **put** your hand up.*

PLACE to put in a particular place, position, or relationship ▶ ***Place** these books on the shelf in alphabetical order.*

SET to put in a certain place or in a stable or steady position ▶ *We unpacked all of Grandmother's china dishes and **set** them carefully on the table. Andrea **set** up the tent on a level patch of grass.*

LAY to put down or set down, especially in a flat or lying-down position ▶ *When the test was over, Jason **laid** his pen on the desk and breathed a sigh of relief. **Lay** down your weapons and surrender!*

Andrea **set** up the tent on a level patch of grass.

QUALITY n a special feature that helps to make something what it is
▶ *Heather is intelligent, patient, hardworking, and understanding—all **qualities** necessary for being a successful doctor.*

PROPERTY a basic quality
▶ *Two of the **properties** of a liquid are that it will flow downward and that it has no shape of its own.*

CHARACTERISTIC a typical quality or feature that helps to identify something
▶ *Curly hair is a **characteristic** of our family. Large loops on her p's and g's are a **characteristic** of her handwriting.*

CHARACTER the main or essential nature
▶ *The rapid growth of the population has greatly changed the **character** of the town.*

TRAIT a quality or characteristic that helps to distinguish one thing from another
▶ *Loyalty is an important **trait** for a friend to have.*

QUESTION n a sentence that asks something; doubt or uncertainty
▶ *"Does anyone have a **question**?" is a **question**. Bernardo has a **question** about his homework.*

QUERY a question or doubt about something
▶ *The editor had several **queries** for the author.*

INQUIRY a request for information; a study or an investigation, especially an official or scientific one
▶ *Let me make some **inquiries** about when the trains leave. The police are making **inquiries** about the crime.*

QUIET adj not loud; free from noise or disturbance ▶ *There was **quiet** music playing in the background. We spent a **quiet** afternoon reading and playing chess.*

SILENT completely or absolutely quiet; without any noise or sound
▶ *Everyone has to remain **silent** in the library. Rachel likes to watch old **silent** movies.*

STILL quiet and calm, without sound
▶ *The forest grew **still** as darkness settled over the mountains.*

NOISELESS without noise; producing very little or no noise
▶ *I want to get a **noiseless** electric fan to keep me cool at night.*

see **CALM**

▶ **QUOTE** vb to use the same words that were spoken or written by someone else
▶ *Kim **quoted** Dr. Martin Luther King, Jr., in her speech.*

CITE to quote from a written work
▶ *My essay **cited** lines from the book Black Beauty.*

REPEAT to say or do again
▶ *Jane **repeated** the message word for word. I'll never **repeat** that mistake!*

Kim **quoted** Dr. Martin Luther King, Jr., in her speech.

r

▶ **RAIN** n water that falls in drops from clouds ▶ *Rain fell for two hours and cooled everything down. The game was delayed because of rain.*

PRECIPITATION water falling from the sky in the form of rain, snow, sleet, or hail ▶ *We will be getting some form of precipitation tomorrow, probably as either freezing rain or wet snow.*

SHOWER a brief or light rainfall ▶ *There was a shower but it didn't ruin our picnic.*

DOWNPOUR a very heavy rain ▶ *We got drenched in a downpour yesterday.*

▶ **READY** adj in a state or condition to do something or to be used ▶ *The car has been repaired and is ready to go back on the road again.*

PREPARED made ready, especially for a particular purpose ▶ *I've cleaned the house and done the shopping, so now I am prepared for my grandmother's visit.*

SET ready to begin doing something ▶ *We are all packed and set to leave as soon as the taxi gets here. On your mark; get set; go!*

AVAILABLE ready to be used or bought; not busy, and therefore free to talk to people ▶ *The new toys will be available in stores next week. One of our sales staff will be available to help you in a moment.*

QUALIFIED having met the requirements or conditions necessary for doing something ▶ *After finishing college, Sandra will be qualified to teach science.*

RIPE ready to be picked or eaten; ready for some purpose ▶ *Cecile gave me a bag of ripe fruit. After three days of rain, the children were ripe for some excitement.*

▶ **REAL** adj true and not imaginary; not artificial ▶ *The real story of what happened is not quite so exciting. These silk flowers are pretty, but I prefer real ones.*

GENUINE real and not fake; honest or true ▶ *This is a genuine Navajo blanket. She has a genuine love of modern painting.*

ACTUAL existing in fact or in reality and not just possible ▶ *A fire drill prepares you for an actual fire. Do you mean that this is the actual skull of a dinosaur?*

▶ **REASON** n an idea that causes you to do or believe something; a statement that explains or justifies why you did something ▶ *I hope you had a good **reason** for jumping into the lake with all your clothes on.* *Can you give me a **reason** why you're late?*

PURPOSE a goal or aim; the reason why something is made or done, or an object's function ▶ *My **purpose** in getting a job is to save money for college. What is the **purpose** of this button on the TV?*

CAUSE something that produces an effect or result ▶ *Last week's ice storm was the **cause** of many car accidents.*

MOTIVE a desire, impulse, or need that causes you to do something ▶ *Pat's **motive** for getting good grades was his desire to go to college.*

EXPLANATION a statement that explains something ▶ *Her **explanation** of the phases of the moon was very clear.*

▶ **REFUSE** vb to say that you will not do something or accept something ▶ *Alec **refused** to go on the roller coaster by himself.*

REJECT to refuse to accept ▶ *Julio **rejected** all offers of help.*

DECLINE to turn down or refuse, especially politely ▶ *Joyce **declined** our offer of a ride home, saying she enjoyed walking. He **declined** the reward for finding my wallet.*

▶ **RELIABLE** adj suitable to be relied on or counted on to do what is expected ▶ *Steve is a **reliable** worker and has never been late. This is a **reliable** refrigerator that should last for years.*

DEPENDABLE able to be depended on ▶ *Bridget is a **dependable** ally who will stick with you no matter what happens.*

TRUSTWORTHY able to be trusted completely ▶ *Ryan has been a **trustworthy** friend for many years.*

see FAITHFUL

▶ **RELIGION** n belief in God or gods; a specific system of belief, faith, and worship ▶ *Anthropologists study the **religions** and cultures of different peoples. What **religion** were you raised in?*

FAITH belief and trust in God; a religion; complete trust or confidence ▶ *Because of his **faith** in God, Mark decided to become a priest. I was brought up in the Muslim **faith**. I have **faith** that we will find my lost book.*

MYTHOLOGY the myths dealing with the gods and legendary heroes of a people or culture ▶ *We are studying Greek **mythology**. A culture's **mythology** tries to explain how the world was created.*

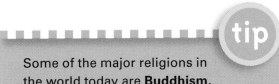

tip

Some of the major religions in the world today are **Buddhism, Christianity, Hinduism, Islam, Judaism,** and **Shintoism.**

see BELIEF

▶ **RELIGIOUS** adj believing in and following the beliefs and rules of a religion; concerned with religion
▶ *She was brought up in a **religious** family. That bookstore sells only **religious** books.*

DEVOUT deeply religious
▶ *They were very **devout** and went to the synagogue every Sabbath.*

PIOUS practicing a religion faithfully and seriously ▶ *His mother was a **pious** woman who prayed regularly every day.*

▶ **REMAINDER** n the amount or number left over ▶ *I'll put the **remainder** of my money in the bank. If you subtract 7 from 15, the **remainder** is 8.*

REST the others; the remaining part
▶ *We arrived early but the **rest** of the class was late. I'll do six problems now and leave the **rest** until tomorrow.*

REMNANT a piece or part that is left over
▶ *After I made a skirt for myself, I made some doll clothes out of the **remnants** of material.*

RESIDUE what is left after something burns up or evaporates; anything that remains after the main part has been taken away
▶ *There was a **residue** of soap and dirt left in the tub. Rinse off the food **residue** before you put the dishes in the dishwasher.*

BALANCE something left over *(used especially in reference to money)*
▶ *Out of the $100, I spent $34 and left the **balance** in the bank. After paying our bills, we have a **balance** of $400.*

SURPLUS an amount greater than what is used or needed ▶ *U.S. farmers produced a **surplus** of wheat and corn last year.*

She was brought up in a **religious** family.

n = noun   vb = verb   adj = adjective   adv = adverb   prep = preposition   conj = conjunction   **165**

Judd made a nasty **remark** about my haircut.

▶ **REMARK** n something said briefly, especially an expression of opinion ▶ *Fiona just made a few remarks at the beginning of the meeting. Judd made a nasty remark about my haircut.*

COMMENT a remark or note that expresses your opinion or gives an explanation ▶ *My teacher wrote a brief comment at the end of my essay to say that she liked it. Does anyone have any comments?*

STATEMENT something that is said or stated in words ▶ *The president read a statement about his proposed plan before answering questions from reporters.*

OBSERVATION a remark made after observing or thinking about something carefully ▶ *Mr. Anderson made the observation that no one had been able to answer all the questions correctly.*

see SAYING

▶ **REMEMBER** vb to bring back to mind; to keep in your mind ▶ *I will always remember Marco, even though he has moved away. Remember that you have a test today.*

RECALL to bring back to mind ▶ *I recall your saying that you would help me today.*

RECOLLECT to bring back to a level of awareness, especially with some effort ▶ *I am trying to recollect the details of the accident.*

REMINISCE to think or talk about the past and things that you remember ▶ *She loved to reminisce about her first trip to Africa many years ago.*

REMIND to make someone remember ▶ *Please remind me to lock the door.*

▶ **RESPECT** n a feeling of admiration and serious appreciation ▶ *My respect for Sarah has grown ever since she started doing volunteer work with the elderly. I left him alone after the funeral out of respect for his feelings.*

HONOR a good reputation and the respect that it inspires ▶ *Tom would never risk losing his honor by telling a lie. The city erected a monument in honor of those who died in the disaster.*

REVERENCE great respect and love, especially for something considered sacred or very dear ▶ *They held the memory of their deceased grandparents in* **reverence**. *She treats her antique books with great* **reverence**.

ESTEEM the high opinion that you have of a person or of a person's actions ▶ *We hold her in great* **esteem**. *I have great* **esteem** *for your work.*

REGARD consideration or concern; the good opinion and respect you have for someone ▶ *You should have some* **regard** *for the safety of others. I have a high* **regard** *for volunteer workers.*

▶ **RESPECT** vb to have a high opinion of; to treat with politeness and deference ▶ *We all* **respect** *your decision to find another job. In our family, children are taught to* **respect** *their elders.*

ESTEEM to prize highly or set a high value on ▶ *She is greatly* **esteemed** *by her friends because of her loyalty, generosity, and cheerfulness.*

ADMIRE to like and respect ▶ *You have to* **admire** *his courage.*

see **APPRECIATE**

▶ **REVEAL** vb to uncover, show, or tell something hidden or unknown ▶ *Moving the picture* **revealed** *a secret hiding place in the wall. I didn't want to* **reveal** *my name.*

DISCLOSE to make known or make public ▶ *The reporter refused to* **disclose** *the source of her information.*

DIVULGE to make known, especially something secret or that shouldn't be told ▶ *My grandmother would never* **divulge** *her true age.*

EXPOSE to uncover something so it can be seen; to reveal the truth about someone or something ▶ *He took off his shirt and* **exposed** *his muscles. I didn't want to* **expose** *my ignorance by asking a foolish question.*

see **DISCOVER, SHOW**

▶ **RICH** adj having lots of money or possessions; having a lot of a particular thing or quality ▶ *Bernie grew* **rich** *selling handcrafted furniture at low prices. Milk is* **rich** *in calcium. She sings in a full,* **rich** *voice.*

WEALTHY having lots of money or possessions, especially over a long period of time ▶ *He comes from a* **wealthy** *family. She became moderately* **wealthy** *as a writer of children's books.*

AFFLUENT having plenty of money, especially an increasing amount ▶ *Before being elected mayor, Charles was an* **affluent** *businessman who made his fortune from a chain of grocery stores.*

PROSPEROUS successful or thriving ▶ *Her father was a* **prosperous** *farmer until several years of drought drove them to the city.*

▶ **RIGHT** n something that the law says you can have or do ▶ *In this country, everyone eighteen and older has the* **right** *to vote.*

POWER the authority or right to command, control, or make decisions ▶ *The president has the* **power** *to veto a bill passed by Congress.*

PRIVILEGE a special right or advantage given to a person or a group of people ▶ *Our school band is so good it won the* **privilege** *of leading the Fourth of July parade.*

PREROGATIVE a special right or privilege held by someone because of their position or job ▶ *Only the head of the school board has the* **prerogative** *of closing schools on account of the weather.*

▶ **RIVER** n a large natural body of flowing water that flows into a lake, an ocean, or another river ▶ *Most of the boats on the* **river** *now are pleasure boats.*

STREAM a body of flowing water; a small river ▶ *I love to fish in the* **stream** *that runs past my grandmother's house.*

CREEK a very small river ▶ *When the snow melts in the spring, the* **creek** *sometimes overflows its banks.*

BROOK a very small body of running water, often smaller than a creek ▶ *A pleasant* **brook** *meanders among the trees and fields.*

RIVULET a very small stream, often a temporary one ▶ *After the rainstorm there were* **rivulets** *of water running down the hill.*

TRIBUTARY a body of flowing water that flows into a larger river or stream ▶ *The Platte River is a* **tributary** *of the Missouri.*

ESTUARY the wide part of a river where it joins a sea ▶ *An important shipping port grew up along the* **estuary** *of the river.*

I love to fish in the **stream** that runs past my grandmother's house.

Both **creek** and **brook** are widely used terms for a small stream. **Brook** is more commonly used in the northeastern U.S., especially in New England, and **creek** is much more frequently used in the rest of the country. Thus, they may both refer to streams of the same size, although some people specifically use **brook** to refer to a stream smaller than one they would call a **creek**.

▶ **ROUGH** adj not smooth or even, but with dents or bumps on the surface; not gentle or polite, and perhaps violent; not finished ▶ *Diane smoothed off the* **rough** *spots with sandpaper. The bullies gave him* **rough** *treatment. I've written a* **rough** *draft.*

COARSE having a rough texture or surface; having large particles; rude and having bad manners ▶ *First she used* **coarse** *sandpaper. I like to cook with* **coarse** *salt. Her* **coarse** *behavior began to annoy everyone.*

UNEVEN not flat, smooth, or level ▶ *It was hard to walk very far on the* **uneven** *ground.*

RUGGED rough or having a jagged outline; harsh or difficult ▶ *The horses slowly picked their way across the* **rugged** *mountains. Settlers of the frontier led very* **rugged** *lives.*

BUMPY very uneven ▶ *Our bikes bounced along the* **bumpy** *trail.*

see **RUDE**

▶ **ROUND** adj shaped like a ball or a circle ▶ *Peaches are a* **round** *fruit covered with fuzz. He has a* **round** *face. Chris cut the cookie dough into* **round** *shapes.*

CIRCULAR having the shape of a circle ▶ *He waved his hands in a* **circular** *motion.*

SPHERICAL having the three-dimensional shape of a sphere or globe ▶ *Josh made a* **spherical** *model of the planet Mars.*

Josh made a **spherical** model of the planet Mars.

▶ **RUDE** adj not polite, courteous, or well-mannered ▶ *Our teacher does not allow **rude** behavior in class. The salesperson was very **rude** to me so I left without buying anything.*

IMPOLITE not polite; behaving in a rude manner ▶ *It was very **impolite** to close the door in his face.*

INSOLENT insulting, disrespectful, or defiant in speech or behavior ▶ *Sometimes teenagers are **insolent** to adults.*

DISCOURTEOUS not courteous or polite ▶ *It was rather **discourteous** of him not to apologize for bumping into you.*

IMPERTINENT not showing the proper respect ▶ *I was annoyed by his **impertinent** replies to all my questions.*

IMPUDENT rude, bold, and outspoken ▶ *She was punished for her **impudent** remarks about her father's driving.*

SASSY not respectful; rude and outspoken (also spelled **saucy**) ▶ *The teacher will not tolerate any **sassy** behavior.*

see **VULGAR**

▶ **RULE** n an official instruction that tells you what you must or must not do; a statement that explains something ▶ *It is against school **rules** to run in the hall. The **rules** of grammar explain the order of words in a sentence.*

LAW one or all of the rules of conduct enforced by a government; an explanation of a scientific truth ▶ *There is a **law** against riding in a car without a seat belt. The **law** of gravity explains why things fall to the ground.*

REGULATION a rule or law that controls conduct ▶ *We made a list of **regulations** for the members of our club.*

CUSTOM a usual or traditional way of doing something ▶ *It is a polite **custom** to open the door for others. It is the **custom** in India to eat with your fingers.*

PRINCIPLE a general rule of behavior; a general truth or scientific law ▶ *She always sticks to her **principles**. An airplane designer needs to know the **principles** of flight.*

▶ **RUMOR** n something said by many people although it may not be true ▶ *It was just a **rumor** that Ted ran away from home; he was visiting his grandparents.*

GOSSIP baseless or unfounded talk about other people's personal lives or business ▶ *I refuse to believe all the **gossip** I hear about our new neighbors.*

HEARSAY things that you are told but have not actually seen or experienced and that may not be true ▶ *The jury was instructed to ignore any evidence based only on **hearsay**.*

SCANDAL harmful or mean-spirited talk ▶ *Eloise was the victim of malicious **scandal**.*

▶ **RUN** vb to move along steadily at a speed faster than a walk, with springing steps so that both feet leave the ground
▶ *Rob can walk a mile in 20 minutes, but he can **run** a mile in less than 8 minutes.*

JOG to run at a slow but steady pace
▶ *My dog loves to prance around me as I **jog**.*

TROT to go at a pace between a walk and a run *(used especially of four-legged animals)*
▶ *The winning horse **trotted** around the track for a victory lap. Will you **trot** down to the store and get a loaf of bread?*

DASH to move with sudden speed
▶ *When the rain began, we **dashed** into the nearest store.*

RACE to run with great speed
▶ *The nurse **raced** over to help the man who had fallen.*

SPRINT to run at top speed for a short distance ▶ *Toward the end of the one-mile race, the runners put on a burst of speed and **sprinted** across the finish line.*

My dog loves to prance around me as I **jog**.

SAD adj feeling sorrow, grief, or unhappiness ▶ *Miriam felt **sad** when her guinea pig died.*

UNHAPPY without joy or happiness ▶ *He had an **unhappy** childhood in one foster home after another.*

MISERABLE feeling great sorrow, sadness, or discomfort; causing great discomfort or misery ▶ *Aaron was **miserable** for the whole first week of camp. I can't sing at all with this **miserable** cold.*

GLOOMY very sad, dejected, or pessimistic ▶ *Janice was feeling very **gloomy** at the prospect of spending a week by herself.*

DEPRESSED very sad or low in spirits ▶ *We became **depressed** when it rained for the ninth day in a row during our vacation.*

MELANCHOLY very sad; thoughtful and serious ▶ *I've been feeling **melancholy** since my best friend moved away last week.*

BLUE feeling sad or marked by sadness ▶ *Gray winter days make me **blue**. I've been in a **blue** mood all day.*

see **LONELY**

SAFE adj not in danger of being harmed or stolen; not dangerous or risky ▶ *We will be **safe** in this cave for tonight. Is it **safe** to lean on this railing?*

SECURE free from danger; free from worry, fear, or doubt ▶ *She kept her jewelry secure in the hotel safe. Rob felt **secure** in the knowledge that his mother was home that evening.*

PROTECTED guarded or kept safe from harm ▶ *Thank goodness my head was **protected** by my bicycle helmet when I fell!*

HARMLESS not able to cause injury or damage ▶ *All the ingredients in this chemistry set are **harmless**. She liked to play **harmless** jokes on her big brother.*

SNUG protected from the weather; safe, warm, and comfortable ▶ *We felt much better when we were finally **snug** in our beds.*

SAME adj resembling or matching in every way; the specific one and not another *(always used with* the *or with* this, that, these, *or* those*)* ▶ *The books on the lawyer's shelves all look the **same**. This is the **same** seat I had yesterday.*

IDENTICAL being exactly the same ▶ *My grandmother wore this **identical** dress at her wedding. Peter and Paul are **identical** twins.*

ALIKE having a close resemblance without being exactly the same ▶ *The two kittens look **alike**, but this one has a white paw.*

EQUAL the same in size, value, or amount; the same for each member of a group ▶ *Two pints are **equal** to one quart. Everyone is entitled to **equal** treatment under the law.*

EQUIVALENT the same in amount, value, or importance ▶ *Mr. Lee said that swimming a mile was* **equivalent** *to running five miles.*

see SIMILAR

▶ **SAVE** vb 1 to take out of danger; to make safe ▶ *Ted was given an award for* **saving** *his brother from drowning.*

RESCUE to save someone who is in danger or is trapped somewhere ▶ *Tanya* **rescued** *three children from the burning building before the fire department arrived.*

DELIVER to save or set free ▶ *At the end of the war, many people were* **delivered** *from enemy prison camps.*

▶ **SAVE** vb 2 to set aside safely to be used in the future ▶ *Denise has managed to* **save** *over $300. I* **save** *my good trousers to wear on special occasions.*

KEEP to hold and not get rid of ▶ *Martin* **kept** *the interesting pieces of driftwood he found on the beach.*

PRESERVE to protect something so that it stays in its original state ▶ *The best way to* **preserve** *these drawings is to have them framed. The library* **preserves** *its rare books in a special room.*

HOARD to gather and store or hide ▶ *Squirrels* **hoard** *nuts for the winter. Shelley is still* **hoarding** *the candy she got last Halloween.*

see FREE *vb,* GATHER

▶ **SAY** vb to express out loud using words ▶ *My mom* **says** *it is too late to go swimming. "Okay,"* **said** *Ellen, "let's go tomorrow."*

STATE to announce or declare something in very straightforward terms ▶ *The lawyer asked the witness to* **state** *her name, address, and occupation.*

REMARK to point out or offer a comment or an opinion on something ▶ *After reading the article, Jed* **remarked** *that he thought the author didn't know what he was talking about.*

EXCLAIM to cry out or say with sudden emotion ▶ *"I can't believe you ate that entire cake!"* **exclaimed** *Cheryl.*

see TALK, TELL

"I can't believe you ate that entire cake!" **exclaimed** Cheryl.

▸ **SAYING** n a well-known phrase or sentence, especially one that repeats some wisdom or truth ▸ *My father often repeats the **saying** "It takes money to make money." "You should look before you leap," as the **saying** goes.*

EXPRESSION a phrase that has a particular meaning ▸ *"Lock, stock, and barrel" is an **expression** that means "completely."*

MOTTO a phrase or sentence that is meant to guide behavior, state a belief, or express an ideal ▸ *The **motto** of the District of Columbia is "Justitia Omnibus," which means "Justice for all." My **motto** is "Be prepared."*

PROVERB a wise old saying that tells a common truth ▸ *Her favorite **proverb** is "A stitch in time saves nine."*

MAXIM a statement of a general truth based on observation or experience ▸ *I try to live according to the **maxim** "Honesty is the best policy."*

ADAGE an old saying that people generally believe is true ▸ *I know you feel disappointed now, but remember the **adage** "Time heals all wounds."*

see REMARK

▸ **SCARE** vb to fill with fear, especially suddenly ▸ *My brother tried to **scare** me by jumping out from behind the door.*

FRIGHTEN to cause to feel fright or fear ▸ *Dan was **frightened** by a raccoon scratching at the garbage can.*

ALARM to make afraid that something bad might happen ▸ *I don't want to **alarm** you, but I can smell smoke.*

STARTLE to surprise or scare someone and make the person jump ▸ *I was **startled** by a loud knock on the door.*

TERRIFY to scare greatly; to fill with terror ▸ *I must admit that the roller coaster **terrified** me!*

▸ **SEIZE** vb to take possession of, especially quickly and by using force; to arrest ▸ *Rebel soldiers **seized** the town in a surprise attack at dawn. The police **seized** the suspect as she stepped off the plane.*

TAKE to get, catch, or capture with the hands ▸ *Ken is trying to **take** my pen. The rebels **took** control of the government without firing a shot.*

GRAB to seize suddenly and roughly ▸ *Miranda **grabbed** the ball out of Jane's hand.*

Ken is trying to **take** my pen.

SNATCH to seize very quickly
▸ Mitch **snatched** the letter out of my hand before I had a chance to read any of it.

see CATCH, GET

▸ **SERIOUS** adj concerned with earnest or important matters; needing careful thought; not humorous or trivial
▸ Mr. Thompson is a **serious** man who never allows fooling around in class. The flu epidemic is a **serious** problem.

SOLEMN very serious and formal
▸ The memorial service was a **solemn** occasion. She made a **solemn** promise to stay with the children over the holiday.

GRAVE important and requiring serious thought; likely to produce great danger
▸ I have **grave** doubts about your ability to keep this job. The boat was in **grave** danger during the storm.

SOMBER very sad or depressed; dark and gloomy ▸ Many disappointments put Carl in a **somber** mood. Yesterday was a rainy, cold, **somber** day.

SOBER earnest, thoughtful, and objective
▸ We need to take a **sober** look at our financial situation before buying a new car.

see IMPORTANT

n = noun   vb = verb   adj = adjective   adv = adverb   prep = preposition   conj = conjunction   **175**

▶ **SHAKE** vb to move quickly up and down or back and forth ▶ *Shake the bottle before you open it. The trees shook in the wind.*

VIBRATE to move back and forth very rapidly over a very short distance
▶ *If you pluck the string of a guitar, it begins to vibrate and make a sound. The house vibrates every time a train goes by.*

TREMBLE to shake rapidly, especially from cold, fear, or excitement
▶ *Carla's hands were trembling as she accepted the award. The earth trembled as the volcano erupted.*

SHUDDER to shake violently and suddenly from cold, fear, or disgust
▶ *Barbara shuddered when she thought of all the people who had been hurt in the train wreck.*

SHIVER to shake from the cold or from fear
▶ *He shivered as the cold wind blew through the broken window.*

QUIVER to shake slightly and rapidly
▶ *The wind was so slight the leaves were only quivering on the trees. Her lip quivered as she tried not to cry.*

QUAKE to shake violently ▶ *I quaked with fear when the monster appeared on the screen. Buildings shook and toppled as the earth quaked.*

▶ **SHARP** adj having an edge or point that cuts or pierces easily; sudden and intense; able to think or notice things quickly
▶ *It is easier to cut tomatoes with a sharp knife than a dull one. I felt a sharp jab in my rib. Liz has a sharp mind.*

KEEN having a very sharp edge or point; able to notice things easily; quick and alert
▶ *This sword has a keen blade. Alan has keen eyesight. It takes a keen mind to become a chess champion.*

ACUTE shrewd and quick of mind; sharp or severe; able to detect things easily
▶ *Scott has an acute wit. I suddenly felt an acute pain in my foot. Jackie has an acute sense of smell.*

see SMART

▶ **SHORT** adj less than the average length, height, distance, or time
▶ *Alison is short for her age. I read a short book over the weekend. We had a short wait at the dentist's office.*

BRIEF lasting only a short time; using only a few words ▶ *We made a brief visit to the city. Be as brief as you can.*

SLIGHT small or not very important; small and slender ▶ *There will be a slight delay. The jockey has a slight build.*

▶ **SHOW** vb to let see or be seen; to make known or clear ▶ *Show me the picture. He showed his happiness by whistling on the way home from school.*

DISPLAY to show in a careful way so that others can see ▶ *The store displays all the new books on a table near the front.*

EXHIBIT to show in public in a way that is easy for people to see
▶ *After the judges choose the winners, we will exhibit all of the students' paintings in the library.*

The store **displays** all the new books on a table near the front.

PRESENT to offer for view
▶ *My class is going to **present** a play about the experiences of immigrant children.*

▶ **SHRINK** vb to become smaller
▶ *Our savings are **shrinking** faster than we had hoped.*

CONTRACT to make or become smaller, especially by drawing the parts closer together ▶ *The heart pumps blood by **contracting** and expanding. Bridges are designed to **contract** in cold weather without damage.*

SHRIVEL to shrink and become wrinkled, especially after drying in heat or sunlight
▶ *Raisins are dried and **shriveled** grapes.*

CONDENSE to make thicker by boiling away liquid; to make a piece of writing shorter by taking out unnecessary parts
▶ *We fed the lamb **condensed** milk. Ms. Thornton told me to **condense** my paper by cutting out the repetition.*

▶ **SHY** adj easily frightened or startled; not comfortable around people or with strangers
▶ *Most wild deer are too **shy** to get close to people. Will is a **shy** boy who almost never talks to others.*

BASHFUL shy and easily embarrassed around others ▶ *The little girl was too **bashful** to go onstage in front of such a large audience.*

TIMID shy and easily frightened
▶ *Rita was too **timid** to raise her hand in class.*

MEEK quiet, patient, and obedient
▶ *Arthur was so **meek** that he never even complained when they forgot to send him the money they owed him.*

RESERVED tending not to draw attention by talking or actions
▶ *Margaret became **reserved** when her older cousins were visiting.*

DIFFIDENT lacking in self-confidence
▶ *Even though she is very smart, Marsha is very **diffident** toward all her teachers.*

▶ **SICK** adj suffering from an illness; nauseated, or feeling as though you are going to vomit ▶ *Yolanda has been **sick** for a week now. Ramon began to feel **sick** during his ride on the roller coaster.*

ILL suffering from a disease or illness; in poor health ▶ *I was **ill** with the flu for the entire vacation.*

AILING in poor health, especially over a long period of time ▶ *She may be **ailing** and old, but she can still make me laugh with her stories.*

SICKLY weak and often ill or in poor condition ▶ *My grandfather is **sickly** and rests in bed most of the day. You should water this plant; it looks pretty **sickly**.*

▶ **SICKNESS** n the condition of being sick or ill; ill health ▶ *There has been a lot of **sickness** in our family this winter.*

ILLNESS an unhealthy condition of your body or mind ▶ *Is there a history of mental **illness** in his family?*

DISEASE a specific illness ▶ *Measles is an infectious **disease**.*

AILMENT an illness, usually an annoying one that continues for a long time but is not serious ▶ *My grandfather was complaining about the **ailments** suffered by the elderly.*

MALADY an illness that continues for a long time and is often serious or fatal ▶ *Justin suffered for years from a **malady** that his doctors could not identify.*

▶ **SIGN** n a gesture, mark, or action that stands for something; a trace or piece of evidence ▶ *Don't forget to put in a dollar **sign**. We saw several **signs** that deer had been in the orchard. There was no **sign** of foul play.*

SYMBOL a design or an object that represents something else ▶ *On many maps, a small green pine tree is the **symbol** for a forest.*

SIGNAL anything agreed on to send a message or warning ▶ *The railroad **signal** warns cars to stay off the tracks. A baseball catcher gives hand **signals** to the pitcher.*

A baseball catcher gives hand **signals** to the pitcher.

TOKEN a visible sign
▶ *A ring is the **token** of a bishop's authority. This gift is just a small **token** of my gratitude.*

OMEN a sign or warning about something that will happen in the future
▶ *Those massive clouds are an **omen** of a coming storm.*

▶ **SIMILAR** adj having some features or characteristics in common ▶ *Phil and I have **similar** ideas about how to train the puppy.*

ALIKE looking or acting the same
▶ *The twins are **alike** in the way they look and how they dress, but not in how they behave!*

LIKE the same or almost the same
▶ *Tina and Amy were of **like** minds and opinions and thus they became close friends.*

> **tip**
>
> **Alike** is also frequently used as an adverb meaning "in the same manner": *All the students in her class were treated **alike**.*

see **SAME**

▶ **SIMILARITY** n the state of being similar or alike ▶ *Do you see any **similarities** between Francine and her sister? Yes, there is a **similarity** in the way they walk.*

LIKENESS a very close similarity; a copy or portrait ▶ *There is a remarkable **likeness** between him and his father. This photo is not a very good **likeness** of Ann.*

RESEMBLANCE a similarity in appearance or form, but not in detail ▶ *I can see a slight **resemblance** between them, but I never would have guessed they are in the same family.*

▶ **SLANT** vb to be at an angle that is neither vertical nor horizontal ▶ *The roof **slants** up at a steep angle. Left-handed people often have handwriting that **slants** to the left.*

TILT to move or be moved so as to slant to one side ▶ *The picture was **tilted** at a weird angle.*

LEAN to bend toward or over something
▶ *The mother **leaned** over her baby. Have you seen pictures of the **Leaning** Tower of Pisa?*

LIST to slant to one side (used especially of a boat or ship) ▶ *The damaged ship was **listing** to starboard, but managed to make it safely into the harbor.*

INCLINE to be in or move to a position that is neither vertical nor horizontal; to cause to tilt or bend ▶ *The road **inclines** steeply. He **inclined** his head to the side so he could see around the column in front of his seat.*

SLOPE to slant, especially gradually
▶ *The path **slopes** down to the river in a broad curve.*

▶ **SLOW** adj not fast; moving without great speed ▶ *The dancer used **slow** movements of his arms to suggest tiredness. Traffic was very **slow** on the way home this afternoon.*

LEISURELY not hurried or rushed ▶ *We enjoyed a long, **leisurely** breakfast.*

GRADUAL taking place slowly but steadily ▶ *There has been a **gradual** improvement in my grades this year.*

SLUGGISH moving very slowly and lacking in energy ▶ *The water in the pool was so warm that the entire swimming team was very **sluggish** during practice today.*

▶ **SLY** adj skillful, clever, and secretive ▶ *He is always making **sly** remarks about the people he doesn't like. She is too **sly** to be completely trustworthy.*

CRAFTY skillful at tricking other people ▶ *She turned out to be a **crafty** chess player, often making subtle, unexpected moves.*

CUNNING skillful in using your intelligence to trick someone or avoid something ▶ *They came up with a **cunning** lie to fool the police. The **cunning** fox managed to escape from the hounds.*

TRICKY likely to use tricks; requiring skill or caution ▶ *He is a very **tricky** basketball player. We suddenly found ourselves in a **tricky** situation.*

SNEAKY behaving or done in a secretive, underhanded way ▶ *He is so **sneaky** I'm never sure what to expect from him. That was a **sneaky** trick to get the ball from me.*

▶ **SMALL** adj not large or big; not much in number, quantity, or value ▶ *We live in a **small** old house. A **small** number of fans came to the game in the rain. Ann gets only a **small** allowance.*

LITTLE not big in size; smaller than usual; not great in amount ▶ *I would rather drive a **little** car than a big one. Tom is a **little** man with a generous heart. I like a **little** sugar on my cereal.*

TINY very small ▶ *Your baby brother is the **tiniest** person I've ever seen. The plane was just a **tiny** speck in the distance.*

MINIATURE very small in scale ▶ *When she was three she started playing on a **miniature** violin.*

MINUTE extremely small ▶ *It is important to have a **minute** amount of zinc in your diet.*

▶ **SMART** adj mentally alert and quick in thinking ▶ *Oscar is probably the **smartest** student in the class; he always gets A's.*

INTELLIGENT able to learn and understand easily ▶ *Andrea is an **intelligent** girl who wants to become a writer or an archaeologist.*

CLEVER able to understand things quickly ▶ *Paulo must have been very **clever** to figure out how to put that clock back together.*

BRIGHT smart in a lively and eager way ▶ *He was a **bright** boy who enjoyed winning a good argument.*

WISE having or showing great understanding and judgment ▶ *A **wise** old man gave me some excellent advice. You have made a **wise** decision.*

LEARNED having much knowledge or education ▶ *Eleanor is a **learned** scholar who has written several history books.*

tip

Smart, clever, and bright, which all suggest quickness in learning, are more often applied to young people than are intelligent, wise, and learned, which suggest the wisdom that comes from experience, education, and age.

see **SHARP**

▶ **SMELL** n the property of something that makes it possible for you to sense it with your nose ▶ *I love the **smell** of pine needles. Bananas have a very distinctive **smell**. What is that terrible **smell**?*

SCENT a particular smell, especially a pleasant one ▶ *The **scent** of roses filled the room. The dog started barking when it caught the **scent** of a rabbit.*

ODOR a smell, particularly a strong or long-lasting one ▶ *The gym was filled with the **odor** of sweat. Wonderful **odors** drifted out from the kitchen.*

AROMA a smell that is usually pleasant ▶ *I could suddenly smell the **aroma** of freshly baked blueberry pie.*

FRAGRANCE a sweet or delicate smell ▶ *The **fragrance** of fresh flowers was carried to us by the breeze.*

STENCH a strong, unpleasant smell ▶ *There is a constant **stench** of garbage at the dump.*

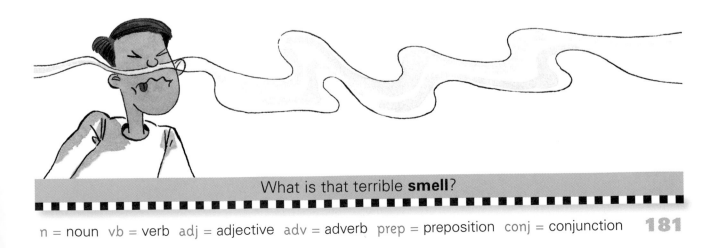

What is that terrible **smell**?

n = noun   vb = verb   adj = adjective   adv = adverb   prep = preposition   conj = conjunction

► **SMILE** vb to widen your mouth and turn it up at the corners to show that you are happy or amused ► *Alice **smiled** when the audience began to applaud.*

GRIN to give a large, cheerful smile ► *Josh was so happy he was **grinning** from ear to ear.*

SMIRK to smile in a smug, knowing, or annoying way ► *Even though he apologized, I could tell by the **smirk** on his face that he wasn't really sorry.*

SNEER to smile in a hateful or mocking way ► *The boxer **sneered** at his opponent.*

tip

All of these words may also be used as nouns: *She had a big **smile** on her face when she won the prize. I could tell that Ian was teasing by the **grin** he was wearing. Wipe that **smirk** off your face or you'll be in real trouble! The bully's **sneer** alone was enough to scare the small children.*

► **SOUL** n the bodiless part of a person that many people believe gives life and controls the ability to think, feel, and act ► *Many people believe the **soul** lives after the body dies.*

SPIRIT the bodiless part of a person, especially when considered in contrast to the body or the physical world ► *I will be there in **spirit**, if not in body. In many religions, people pray to the **spirits** of their ancestors.*

GHOST the soul of a dead person believed by some people to be able to haunt people or places, and sometimes to become visible ► *After dark, Ellen told us a frightening **ghost** story.*

see MIND

► **SOUR** adj having a sharp, acid taste ► *This lemonade is too **sour**; you should add some sugar to it.*

TART slightly sharp or sour to the taste, but not unpleasantly so ► *I like this cherry pie; it's nice and **tart**.*

After dark, Ellen told us a frightening **ghost** story.

BITTER having a harsh, unpleasant taste
▶ *The aspirin left a **bitter** taste in my mouth.*

RANCID having the sharp bad taste or smell of stale fat or oil ▶ *This butter is so old it has gone **rancid**.*

▶ **SPECIAL** adj unusual or easily distinguished from others of the same kind
▶ *Today is **special** because it is my birthday. I only wear this dress on **special** occasions.*

PARTICULAR different from any other; unusual or out of the ordinary
▶ *I want to paint my room this **particular** shade of blue. I want you to pay **particular** attention to these instructions.*

SPECIFIC of a special kind, usually stated very clearly ▶ *Rhoda insists on having this **specific** brand of cereal every morning. The lawyer named three **specific** cases just like ours.*

UNIQUE being the only one of its kind
▶ *Each one of these pottery bowls is handmade and **unique**.*

NOTEWORTHY deserving attention, especially because of excellence
▶ *The peacock is **noteworthy** for its beautiful tail feathers.*

▶ **SPEECH** n an address spoken to an audience; the ability to speak
▶ *Peter gave a **speech** about bicycle safety. As far as we know, only humans have the power of **speech**.*

LECTURE a formal speech given to a class or an audience in order to teach
▶ *We went to hear a **lecture** about the inventions of Leonardo da Vinci.*

TALK an informal speech; a conversation
▶ *My mom is giving a **talk** to the class about her work as a lawyer. We need to have a **talk** about what happened.*

SERMON a speech during a religious service; a serious speech, especially one dealing with morals or correct behavior
▶ *The rabbi gave a **sermon** about trust and faith. My parents gave me a **sermon** about the importance of studying.*

▶ **SPEED** n the rate at which something moves; the rate of any action
▶ *Jessie may be small, but she can run with amazing **speed**. I am taking a class to improve my reading **speed**.*

VELOCITY a more formal or scientific term for speed ▶ *Earth moves around the sun at a **velocity** of more than 66,000 miles per hour.*

HASTE speed or quickness in moving or acting
▶ *We ate breakfast in great **haste** so we could get to school on time.*

HURRY a state of excited haste or eagerness
▶ *In my **hurry** to answer the phone, I knocked over a pot on the stove. I can't talk now; I'm in a **hurry** to catch the bus.*

SWIFTNESS the state or fact of being swift or fast; the ability to move with great speed
▶ *The package was delivered with the **swiftness** of a jet plane. Because of its **swiftness**, a hawk can catch birds in flight.*

▶ **SPOT** n a small area that is different in color or feel from the area around it
▶ *Ladybugs have little black or red* **spots** *on their backs. A Dalmatian is white with black* **spots**.

SPECK a very small spot; a tiny particle or bit ▶ *You have a* **speck** *of paint on your nose! I watched the plane fly away until it was just a* **speck** *in the sky. She had a* **speck** *of sand in her eye.*

DOT a small, usually round spot
▶ *Phyllis wore a red skirt with green* **dots** *on it. Don't forget to put the* **dot** *over the i.*

MARK a line, spot, or other shape that you can see on something
▶ *The farmer puts a red* **mark** *on the left ear of each of his sheep. I polished my shoes to get off the scuff* **marks**.

STAIN a spot of dirt or some other substance that makes something dirty or discolored ▶ *I have a gravy* **stain** *on my shirt.*

BLOT a stain, especially of ink or paint
▶ *My pen leaked and left a big* **blot** *of ink on my homework.*

BLEMISH a spot or slightly damaged area that makes something less than perfect
▶ *We bought this canoe for half price because there is a small* **blemish** *in the paint.*

see ATOM

▶ **START** vb to set out from a particular point; to take the first step in a process or course of action
▶ *We will* **start** *at this line and run around the track twice. You may* **start** *writing when the bell rings and stop when it rings again.*

BEGIN to set something going or in progress; to take the first step in a process or course of action
▶ *She* **begins** *her day with a good breakfast. The movie* **begins** *at 7:00 and ends at 9:00.*

COMMENCE a more formal word for begin
▶ *The court proceedings will* **commence** *when the judge enters the room. Church services* **commence** *at 8:30.*

▶ **STATE** n the way someone or something is at a certain time ▶ *Bryan was in a* **state** *of excitement the night before school started, and he couldn't get to sleep.*

CONDITION a state of being that affects or is affected by something else; a state of health
▶ *Under the right weather* **conditions** *these plants can grow up to four feet high. Rachel is in very good physical* **condition**.

CIRCUMSTANCE a fact or event that affects something else ▶ *Whether or not we go to the beach depends on the* **circumstances**; *we need clear weather and you have to finish your work.*

SITUATION the combination of circumstances at a particular time
▶ *Simon was in a difficult* **situation**; *his bike had a flat tire, he was six miles from home, and it was starting to rain.*

Rachel is in very good physical **condition**.

▶ **STOP** vb to come to an end; to put an end to; to bring some motion to an end
▶ *Everyone clapped when the music* **stopped***. She asked us to* **stop** *shouting. He* **stopped** *the car at the corner.*

FINISH to end or complete
▶ *I'm not allowed to watch television until I* **finish** *my homework. Sally* **finished** *the race in record time.*

HALT to stop marching or traveling; to stop with force or authority ▶ *After hiking for an hour, we* **halted** *for a brief rest. The bus was* **halted** *by guards at the border.*

CEASE to come to an end (*used of a state of being or a condition*) ▶ *The noise* **ceased** *as soon as the train stopped. When you stand up, your lap* **ceases** *to exist.*

TERMINATE to end or bring to an end
▶ *The railway line* **terminates** *at the harbor. We decided to* **terminate** *our agreement.*

tip

Notice how these words are used to describe different sorts of situations. For example, a moving train can **stop**, but it does not **cease** or **finish**. However, you can say that when the motion of the train **ceased**, your journey was **finished**. If you say *The train* **stops** *at this station*, you might mean either "The train pauses at this station to let passengers get on and off" or "The journey of the train ends at this station; it doesn't go any farther." But if you say *The train* **terminates** *here*, you mean only "The journey of the train ends here; this train doesn't go any farther."

see FINISH

▶ **STORY** n a description of real or imaginary events ▶ *He likes to read* **stories** *about animals.*

NARRATIVE an account of events ▶ *She wrote a long* **narrative** *of her years in Paris.*

ACCOUNT a description, report, or explanation ▶ *Paul gave us an* **account** *of his trip to Peru.*

HISTORY a record of past events ▶ *The doctor has a file of my medical* **history***.*

SAGA a long story of heroic events ▶ *This book is the* **saga** *of a family of pioneers for three generations.*

CHRONICLE a record of events in the order they happened ▶ *The senator kept a* **chronicle** *of her years in office.*

TALE a story of true or imaginary events ▶ *She told a long* **tale** *about living on a Mississippi riverboat.*

see MYTH

▶ **STRANGE** adj different from the usual; not known, heard, or seen before; unfamiliar

▶ *We saw a* **strange** *sight last night—three elephants in the middle of town. I knocked and a* **strange** *man answered the door.*

ODD different from the usual; difficult to explain or understand ▶ *She has an* **odd** *sense of humor. It is* **odd** *that he hasn't called me yet.*

PECULIAR different in a puzzling way; different from all others ▶ *What do you make of the cat's* **peculiar** *behavior? Skunks have a* **peculiar** *smell that is easy to recognize.*

UNUSUAL not usual, common, or ordinary ▶ *She has an* **unusual** *name. We've been having some* **unusual** *weather lately.*

FUNNY strange or out of the ordinary ▶ *What is that* **funny** *smell in the kitchen?*

WEIRD very strange or mysterious ▶ *Arthur has a rather* **weird** *hairdo. We heard some* **weird** *noises during the night.*

▶ **STRENGTH** n the quality of being strong; the ability to resist or hold up under strain or stress ▶ *I am building up my* **strength** *by lifting weights. Test the* **strength** *of the rope before you climb it.*

I pushed the piano with all my **might** and it began to move.

POWER physical, mental, or moral strength or ability ▶ *It takes immense **power** to put a spacecraft into orbit. Politicians should never underestimate the **power** of the press.*

FORCE strength or energy, especially causing motion or change ▶ *The wind blew with terrific **force**. The **force** of gravity draws things to the earth. We had to use **force** to break into the box.*

MIGHT great physical or bodily strength ▶ *I pushed the piano with all my **might** and it began to move.*

see ENERGY

▶ **STRONG** adj having great force or power; hard to break ▶ *These **strong** winds make sailing dangerous. She has very **strong** arms.*

POWERFUL having great power, strength, or authority ▶ *Willie hit a home run with a **powerful** swing of the bat. He was a **powerful** king. She has a **powerful** influence on her students.*

HARDY tough and able to survive under difficult conditions ▶ *These little plants are **hardy** enough to survive the long arctic winter.*

MUSCULAR having strong, well-developed muscles ▶ *A gymnast must be both supple and **muscular**.*

VIGOROUS energetic, lively, or forceful ▶ *She engages in **vigorous** exercise three times a week. We made a **vigorous** protest against the new rules.*

see TOUGH

▶ **STUBBORN** adj not willing to give in or change; set on having your own way ▶ *Sam is too **stubborn** to admit that he made a mistake.*

OBSTINATE stubborn and not willing to give in to argument, reason, or persuasion ▶ *Irene was **obstinate** in her belief that her sister was innocent.*

WILLFUL not yielding to the wishes of others ▶ *He persisted in his **willful** refusal to ask for directions, and we ended up hopelessly lost.*

HEADSTRONG determined to have your own way ▶ *Jennifer was a **headstrong** girl, and she was determined to join the all-boy basketball team, even against the rules.*

▶ **STUDY** vb to look at closely or think about carefully ▶ *We **studied** the problem of air pollution.*

ANALYZE to separate into parts in order to understand ▶ *After **analyzing** our situation we realized that it would be a good idea to make some money.*

EXAMINE to look at or look into closely and carefully ▶ *The security officer **examined** our suitcases. The doctor **examined** her new patient.*

INVESTIGATE to search into carefully ▶ *The detective was **investigating** a series of robberies.*

EVALUATE to find out the worth or quality of ▶ *After **evaluating** my work the boss gave me a raise.*

see CONSIDER

▶ **STUPID** adj slow to learn or understand; lacking common sense
▶ *I felt **stupid** in math class because I hadn't studied. It was **stupid** of him to run out into the street after his ball.*

IGNORANT not educated, or not knowing about many things; not aware of
▶ *She often felt **ignorant** because she never finished school. I was completely **ignorant** of Ben's intentions.*

UNINTELLIGENT not very intelligent or smart
▶ *He was too **unintelligent** to understand the simple directions I gave him.*

DULL not very perceptive
▶ *There were several **dull** students in the class who slowed down our lessons.*

DUMB not very smart
▶ *You won't believe the **dumb** thing I did—I put my shoes in the freezer! She is the **dumbest** person I know.*

tip

Dumb, when used to mean "not very smart," is usually informal in use. Some people consider it rude to use **dumb** in reference to people. When you are writing, it might be better to use one of the other more precise synonyms, depending on what you want to say.

see **FOOLISH**

▶ **SUBJECT** n the person or thing studied, discussed, or thought about in a book, newspaper article, speech, or conversation
▶ *English is his favorite **subject** in school. Tony wrote an essay on the **subject** of money.*

THEME the main subject or idea developed in a piece of writing or a talk ▶ *The **theme** of this book is that good triumphs over evil.*

Cooking is her favorite **topic** of conversation.

TOPIC the subject of a discussion, study, lesson, speech, or piece of writing ▶ *Cooking is her favorite* **topic** *of conversation. I have to pick a* **topic** *for my history essay.*

▶ **SUDDEN** adj happening without warning; quick or hasty ▶ *Jane was caught in a* **sudden** *rainstorm. The train came to a* **sudden** *stop.*

ABRUPT happening quickly, without preparation or warning ▶ *I bumped my head when the car made an* **abrupt** *right turn. Paul made an* **abrupt** *decision to quit his job.*

IMPETUOUS doing things suddenly, eagerly, or impatiently, without thinking first ▶ *He is so* **impetuous** *he rushed into the room without knocking. She made an* **impetuous** *decision to go to France.*

▶ **SUGGEST** vb 1 to put forward as an idea or a possibility ▶ *I* **suggested** *going to the mountains for our next vacation.*

RECOMMEND to suggest as being good or worthy; to give counsel or suggestions ▶ *My dentist* **recommended** *this toothpaste. I* **recommend** *that you have a doctor look at your sore ankle.*

PROPOSE to suggest a plan or idea ▶ *Carla* **proposed** *that we all go swimming.*

ADVISE to give advice, information, or suggestions ▶ *Tom* **advised** *me to stay at home until rush hour was over.*

▶ **SUGGEST** vb 2 to bring or call to mind; to show indirectly ▶ *Those fluffy clouds* **suggest** *sheep to me. This painter uses different colors to* **suggest** *her feelings.*

IMPLY to suggest or mean without actually saying ▶ *The look on Van's face* **implied** *that he was sorry. Are you* **implying** *that I'm not telling the truth?*

HINT to suggest or bring to mind by giving just a little information ▶ *Ramona* **hinted** *that she would like to come to the movies with us.*

INSINUATE to introduce or suggest in an indirect or secretive way ▶ *Diane* **insinuated** *that Brian had stolen the money.*

Those fluffy clouds **suggest** sheep to me.

▶ **SUPPORT** vb to hold something up in order to keep it from falling; to help and encourage; to believe in ▶ *These rafters **support** the roof. We all **supported** Carmen when she got into trouble. I **support** recycling.*

UPHOLD to support something that you believe to be right ▶ *The jury's verdict in the first trial was **upheld** by the court of appeals.*

SUSTAIN to keep something going; to give someone the energy and strength to keep going ▶ *Jeremy **sustained** a conversation with his cousin for two hours. The hot soup **sustained** the hikers for miles.*

MAINTAIN to continue to say that something is so; to continue something and not let it come to an end ▶ *The suspect **maintains** that he is innocent. We have always **maintained** a close friendship.*

see **BEAR, HELP**

▶ **SURE** adj having little or no doubt ▶ *I am pretty **sure** my brother will be there to meet us at the bus station when we arrive.*

CERTAIN without doubt or question; very sure ▶ *Tanya is **certain** she will win the tennis tournament because she hasn't lost a match in three weeks.*

POSITIVE very sure ▶ *I was **positive** I saw you at the mall on Wednesday, but you were out of town.*

CONFIDENT full of confidence, especially about something that is expected to happen ▶ *Alfredo was **confident** that he would do well on all his exams.*

DEFINITE beyond doubt or question; already determined or decided ▶ *It is **definite** that the hurricane will hit the coast by tomorrow morning. The date for the party is **definite** and can't be changed.*

▶ **SURPRISE** vb to cause to feel wonder, pleasure, or fear by doing or saying something unexpected ▶ *Ben's success in school this year **surprised** the whole family.*

STARTLE to surprise or frighten someone and make them jump ▶ *Maria was so **startled** when Ken walked through the door that she dropped the eggs she was holding.*

AMAZE to cause to feel very surprised or confused ▶ *We were **amazed** by the magician's tricks.*

ASTONISH to cause to feel very surprised by something that seems unbelievable ▶ *Kelly **astonished** me with her kindness.*

SHOCK to surprise, horrify, or disgust ▶ *The news of the murder **shocked** us all.*

▶ **SURRENDER** vb to give up ▶ *The troops **surrendered** when they realized they were greatly outnumbered.*

SUBMIT to agree to obey ▶ *I **submitted** to the judge's decision.*

YIELD to give up or surrender under pressure of force or persuasion ▶ *The band **yielded** to the enthusiastic cheers of the crowd and played an encore.*

CONCEDE to admit unwillingly;
to admit as certain or right
▶ Natalie finally **conceded** that she
was wrong. The candidate **conceded**
victory to his opponent.

RESIGN to give up a job, a position,
or an office voluntarily ▶ After 10 years in
office, the senator **resigned** so that he could
spend more time with his family.

RELINQUISH to give up out of necessity or
weakness; to let go ▶ Thea **relinquished**
her lead in the chess tournament.

QUIT to give up an activity; to leave
▶ My mother **quit** smoking 10 years ago.
Andrei **quit** his job at the restaurant.

▶ **SWING** vb to move back and forth,
especially when hanging from a support; to
pivot ▶ I love to **swing** on a rope and jump
into the river. The door **swung** open and
there was George, home at last!

SWAY to move or swing from side to side
▶ The branches were **swaying** in the wind.

ROCK to move gently backward
and forward or from side to side
▶ The mother **rocked** the baby's cradle.
I like to sit in this chair and **rock**.

see **TURN**

t

▶ **TALENT** n a natural ability or skill
▶ *Bill has a real **talent** for playing the oboe.*

GIFT a special ability, especially one that you have by nature
▶ *Lori has a **gift** for growing flowers.*

APTITUDE a natural ability or tendency
▶ *You should take advantage of your **aptitude** for math. Steve seems to have an **aptitude** for getting into trouble!*

GENIUS great intellectual talent
▶ *Ethan is a **genius** at repairing electrical equipment. It takes a lot of **genius** to be a successful inventor.*

▶ **TALK** vb to say words; to use your voice to produce language ▶ *Rebecca loves to **talk** about almost anything. Will you **talk** to Michele about going to the party tomorrow?*

SPEAK to say words; to express your thoughts, feelings, or ideas ▶ *Could you **speak** louder, please? The principal **spoke***

for 15 minutes about treating each other with respect.

CONVERSE to talk with someone; to exchange thoughts, feelings, or ideas
▶ *We sat **conversing** about our hopes for peace for over an hour.*

DISCUSS to talk back and forth, especially to come to a decision or deeper understanding
▶ *We will have to **discuss** our plans for the summer. The doctors **discussed** the case for hours, but couldn't reach an agreement.*

CHAT to talk in a friendly and informal way
▶ *Nan and I **chatted** about school as we waited for the bus.*

see **ARGUE, CHATTER, SAY, TELL**

▶ **TEACH** vb to give a lesson, or show how to do something ▶ *Today Ms. Cooney **taught** us about plant cells. Joel is going to **teach** me how to swim.*

The doctors **discussed** the case for hours, but couldn't reach an agreement.

INSTRUCT to teach in a systematic way
▶ *Ginger* **instructed** *me in the basics of tap dancing.*

EDUCATE to give knowledge or a skill
▶ *I want to be a teacher and* **educate** *young children. He was* **educated** *in Italy and Brazil.*

TRAIN to give instructions or drills to a person or an animal to teach them how to do something ▶ *She was* **trained** *as a pilot. We* **trained** *our dog to do tricks.*

▶ **TELL** vb to put into words
▶ *Please* **tell** *the truth. Can you* **tell** *us exactly what happened?*

REPORT to give a detailed account of something that has happened
▶ *My mom* **reported** *every word of her conversation with my teacher.*

DECLARE to say something formally or officially ▶ *The mayor* **declared** *that next week will be Be Kind to Animals Week in our town.*

INFORM to give knowledge or information to someone ▶ *The police are required to* **inform** *suspects of their rights.*

DISCLOSE to reveal ▶ *André promised not to* **disclose** *where his parents hid his brother's birthday present.*

NOTIFY to tell someone about something officially or formally ▶ *The hospital* **notified** *us about the test results.*

CONVEY to tell or communicate by speech or action ▶ *She* **conveyed** *the good news about her grades. His slumping posture* **conveyed** *his disappointment.*

see **SAY, TALK, WARN**

▶ **THEFT** n the act of stealing
▶ *Keith is being punished for* **theft**.

ROBBERY the act of stealing, especially directly from a person or in their presence, often using threats or violence
▶ *They committed a bank* **robbery** *in broad daylight.*

BURGLARY the act of stealing, especially by breaking into a house to take something
▶ **Burglary** *is most often committed at night.*

She **conveyed** the good news about her grades.

▶ **THEORY** n an idea or statement that explains how something happens; an idea or opinion based on some evidence but not proved ▶ *The theory of evolution explains the development of life on earth. The police have a theory about who robbed the store.*

HYPOTHESIS a temporary prediction that can be tested about how a scientific investigation or experiment will turn out ▶ *Before doing the experiment, each student wrote down a hypothesis about what would happen.*

CONJECTURE a conclusion reached by guessing ▶ *Your idea that I took your book is pure conjecture; you have no real evidence, because I didn't take it!*

SPECULATION a guess or decision based on incomplete evidence ▶ *Our first speculation was that the disease was caused by a virus, but we were wrong.*

see **IDEA, REASON**

▶ **THEREFORE** adv as a result; for that reason ▶ *Byron did not finish his homework, therefore he will have to stay after school to finish it.*

CONSEQUENTLY as a consequence or result; in view of what has been said before ▶ *Dolores spent all her money at the store and consequently she didn't have enough for the bus ride home.*

HENCE because of something already stated ▶ *The children were playing in the rain and mud all day; hence the large load of laundry!*

ACCORDINGLY in a proper or fitting way; in due course ▶ *This is a serious occasion and I expect you to act accordingly.*

THUS in this way; because of this ▶ *You should hold the blade away from you thus.*

▶ **THICK** adj growing, being, or having parts that are close together; great in width or depth ▶ *Polar bears have thick fur. The castle has very thick walls. How thick is the earth's mantle?*

DENSE having the parts very close or crowded together; difficult to move, see, or get through ▶ *The population is very dense in this part of the city. A dense fog settled into the valley. We came to a dense forest.*

COMPACT packed or put together very closely, especially in a neat or orderly way; designed to take up little space ▶ *The molecules of a solid are more compact than those of a liquid or gas. All the tools fit into a compact carrying case.*

▶ **THIN** adj small in width or depth; not fat or not having much flesh or muscle ▶ *The wall is so thin you can hear everything through it. John has been thin his whole life.*

SLENDER long and thin; thin and well proportioned ▶ *I like to write with a slender pencil. Rose is a slender girl, but she is a very fast runner.*

SLIM very thin ▶ *Brian is a slim and graceful ice-skater.*

LEAN thin and muscular ▶ *A good gymnast must be lean and agile.*

SLIGHT small and thin ▶ *Aaron is a slight boy who plays the cello wonderfully.*

SKINNY extremely thin and without much muscle ▶ *Ted was skinny as a boy but now he is muscular and well built.*

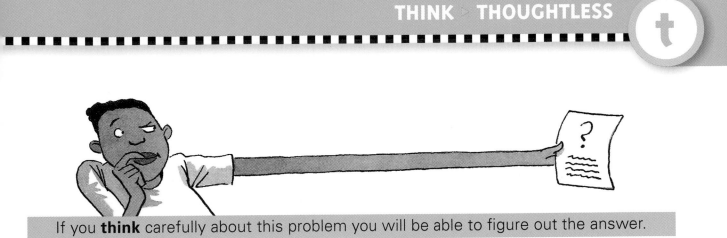

If you **think** carefully about this problem you will be able to figure out the answer.

▶ **THINK** vb to use your mind; to form ideas or make decisions
▶ *Think before you speak. If you think carefully about this problem you will be able to figure out the answer.*

REASON to think in a logical way
▶ *Isaac reasoned that it would be quicker to walk than to wait for the bus.*

PONDER to think about things carefully, often for a long time ▶ *As a philosopher she has pondered the meaning of life for most of her career.*

CONTEMPLATE to think seriously about
▶ *Matthew contemplated leaving school, but his friends convinced him to stay.*

▶ **THOUGHTFUL** adj serious and involving a lot of thought; thinking about other people's feelings and needs
▶ *I got an A because my teacher said I wrote a thoughtful essay. It was very thoughtful of you to send me flowers.*

CONSIDERATE considering the feelings and needs of others when you do something
▶ *It was very considerate of you to turn down the radio while I was on the phone.*

SYMPATHETIC able to understand how someone else is feeling
▶ *I felt very sympathetic toward Sean when his dog was hurt in an accident.*

see FRIENDLY, NICE

▶ **THOUGHTLESS** adj not thinking about other people's feelings and needs; done without thinking ▶ *It was thoughtless of the company to lay off people right before the holidays. It was thoughtless of me to leave the oven on.*

INCONSIDERATE not considering the feelings and needs of others when you do something ▶ *It was inconsiderate of you to invite everyone but me to the party.*

CARELESS not paying enough attention or thinking before you do something; done without being careful ▶ *I was careless and almost got hit by a car when I crossed the street. He made several careless mistakes on the test.*

RECKLESS not careful about your own or other people's safety
▶ *He is a very reckless driver.*

▶ **THROW** vb to send through the air with a swift motion of the arm and hand
▶ *Dean **threw** the ball. **Throw** me a towel, please.*

PITCH to throw in a definite direction or with a definite aim
▶ *Megan **pitched** the baseball over the plate. Sam likes to **pitch** horseshoes.*

TOSS to throw with little force
▶ ***Toss** me that pencil, will you?*

HURL to throw with great force
▶ *Rob **hurled** the football sixty yards.*

FLING to throw with force but not precision
▶ *Marcia **flung** herself off the diving board and into the air. Just **fling** that suitcase into the back of the car.*

CAST to throw quickly, as a fishing line; to get rid of ▶ *Jennifer **cast** her line under the trees and immediately caught a fish.*

▶ **TIRED** adj weak or unable to continue because of a lack of rest
▶ *We began to get **tired** as the hill got steeper. Ellen was too **tired** to cook, so we all went out to eat.*

EXHAUSTED extremely tired
▶ *After canoeing all day, Sam came home too **exhausted** to eat her dinner.*

WEARY very tired, especially from doing or putting up with something for a long time
▶ *Mom was **weary** of cleaning the house, so we all pitched in and helped her finish in 20 minutes.*

WORN OUT completely out of energy, especially after a long period of activity
▶ *He was **worn out** after seven years of trying to make the farm successful.*

SLEEPY ready for sleep
▶ *Reading for two hours made me tired and **sleepy**.*

▶ **TOOL** n a piece of equipment that you use to do a particular job
▶ *You will need several **tools** to fix this—a hammer, a screwdriver, a wrench, and a drill.*

INSTRUMENT a tool or apparatus for delicate or scientific work
▶ *The dental **instruments** are carefully sterilized before each use.*

UTENSIL a tool or container, often used in the kitchen, that has a special purpose
▶ *The pots, pans, and **utensils** hang on a rack over the counter. What **utensils** will you need to make a cake?*

MACHINE a piece of equipment made up of moving parts that is used to do a job
▶ *A vise is a simple **machine** used to hold things tightly. Leo likes to work with large **machines**.*

APPLIANCE a piece of equipment designed to do a particular job and that usually runs on electricity or gas
▶ *We have several electric kitchen **appliances**, including a toaster, a blender, and a food processor.*

GADGET a small tool, often held in the hand, that does a particular job
▶ *We have a **gadget** for slicing hard-boiled eggs.*

IMPLEMENT any device or tool used for some task ▶ *The sculptor gathered her **implements** before beginning her work.*

▶ **TOP** n the highest point or part of something ▶ *We climbed to the **top** of the hill. A catbird sang at the **top** of a tree. What's that on the **top** of your head?*

PEAK the pointed top of a high mountain ▶ *Clouds surrounded the snow-capped **peaks** as the sun rose.*

SUMMIT the highest point or elevation of a hill or mountain ▶ *There is an old hotel at the **summit** of the trail.*

PINNACLE a sharply pointed peak; the highest point or level ▶ *The climbers planted a flag on the **pinnacle** of the mountain. Katy has reached the **pinnacle** of her profession.*

The climbers planted a flag on the **pinnacle** of the mountain.

n = noun   vb = verb   adj = adjective   adv = adverb   prep = preposition   conj = conjunction   **197**

▶ **TOTAL** n the entire quantity or amount
▶ *Count up all this money and tell me the **total**.*

SUM the number that you get by adding two or more numbers together; the whole or final amount ▶ *What is the **sum** of these six numbers? She has saved a considerable **sum** of money in the last three months.*

WHOLE the entire thing; all the parts ▶ *The **whole** of her fortune was given to charity. Two halves make a **whole**.*

▶ **TOUGH** adj strong and difficult to damage
▶ *The elephant has a **tough** hide.*

STURDY strong and firm; solidly made or built ▶ *I stood on a **sturdy** ladder to paint the ceiling. The weight lifter has a **sturdy** build.*

DURABLE tough and lasting for a long time ▶ *I got some **durable** boots for hiking.*

RUGGED strongly built or made; having a strong character ▶ *You will need a **rugged** pair of boots for climbing these mountains. The original settlers here were **rugged** farmers.*

STOUT able to endure great stress or hard use ▶ *We used **stout** poles to build a raft.*

see **STRONG**

▶ **TOWN** n a place that has houses, stores, offices, schools, and other buildings
▶ *We live in a **town** that has a population of about 15,000.*

VILLAGE a group of houses, stores, and other buildings that make up a community smaller than a town
▶ *We live in a small **village** about four miles outside of town.*

CITY a very large or important town; a large town that has a charter from a state, outlining its government and boundaries
▶ *Anchorage is the largest **city** in Alaska. We moved from the country to the **city** when I was seven years old.*

SUBURB an area or district close to the outer edge of a city, made up mostly of homes, with few businesses or factories
▶ *Ruth lives in a **suburb** of Montreal.*

METROPOLIS a very large, important city ▶ *Mexico City is a large, sprawling **metropolis**.*

MEGALOPOLIS a very large, heavily populated area that includes several cities
▶ *The East Coast of the U.S. is one great **megalopolis** from Washington, D.C., to Boston, Massachusetts.*

▶ **TRADE** vb to give one thing in order to get another ▶ *My friends and I like to **trade** baseball cards.*

EXCHANGE to give one thing and receive another ▶ *Sarah and Ruth always **exchange** gifts on New Year's Day. My tent mates at camp all **exchanged** addresses.*

SWAP to give in trade
▶ *I'll **swap** you my CD for a video game.*

SWITCH to change one for another
▶ Laura and Cheryl **switched** seats so that Cheryl could row the boat.

BARTER to get something by exchanging food or other goods or services, rather than by using money
▶ The explorers **bartered** clothing and trinkets for fresh food from the island natives.

tip

Swap is more often used in speech than in writing. For your serious writing, choose one of the other synonyms.

▶ **TRAP** n a device used for capturing an animal; anything used to trick someone
▶ We used a **trap** to catch the skunk that was living under our porch. The police set a **trap** at the store and caught the burglar.

PITFALL a hidden, covered pit for capturing animals; a hidden danger or difficulty
▶ Large game can be caught in a **pitfall**. You can avoid the **pitfalls** of poor spelling by carefully proofreading your work.

SNARE a trap with a noose that jerks tight to catch birds and animals; something dangerous or risky that tempts you
▶ We set **snares** to catch the rabbits in the garden. He was caught helplessly in a **snare** of lies.

We used a **trap** to catch the skunk that was living under our porch.

n = noun vb = verb adj = adjective adv = adverb prep = preposition conj = conjunction **199**

▶ **TRASH** n things that you have thrown away because they are worthless ▶ *We fill up a 30-gallon can with **trash** every week at our house alone.*

GARBAGE food waste or other things thrown away ▶ *On Saturdays we take our **garbage** to the dump.*

RUBBISH something worthless ▶ *The basement is full of **rubbish** that we should just throw away.*

REFUSE things or materials that are useless and thrown away ▶ *Several tons of **refuse** are carted away from the factory every month.*

WASTE something left over and not needed ▶ *Chemical **wastes** from the paint factory used to be poured right into the river.*

DEBRIS the scattered pieces of something that has been broken or destroyed ▶ *The **debris** from the plane crash was all over the field.*

RUBBLE broken fragments, as of bricks and stones ▶ *All that was left of their house was a pile of **rubble**.*

tip

In the Middle Ages **garbage** meant the heads, feet, and innards of chickens and other birds that were eaten. Several recipes from the fifteenth century tell how to cook these parts into a stew that was also called *garbage*. Here is an example: *"Take the garbage of young geese — heads, necks, wings, feet, gizzard, heart, and the liver — and boil them well and cut the wings, the feet, and the gizzards, the heart, the liver, and the lungs, and fry them in clean grease."* Sound good? Today we no longer eat all of these parts; instead we throw them away, and thus **garbage** primarily refers to food waste that we throw away.

▶ **TRAVEL** vb to go from one place to another; to take a trip ▶ *We **traveled** from Maryland to Florida by car last summer. I like to **travel** by plane.*

On Saturdays we take our **garbage** to the dump.

JOURNEY to take a trip, especially a long one on land ▶ *Early settlers **journeyed** across the plains on foot and horseback and by wagon.*

VOYAGE to take a long trip, especially by water ▶ *The yacht stopped at many islands while **voyaging** around the South Pacific.*

TOUR to take a trip visiting several places ▶ *The band **toured** through seven states in three weeks.*

CRUISE to travel smoothly and easily ▶ *We **cruised** to the Greek islands last year.*

TREK to make a slow, difficult journey ▶ *The hikers **trekked** up the mountain.*

COMMUTE to travel a relatively long distance to work or school each day, usually by car, bus, or train ▶ *I have to **commute** 45 minutes each way to get to school and back every day.*

EXPLORE to travel in order to discover what a place is like ▶ *For three weeks we **explored** the Canadian lakes and woods in our canoe.*

see **GO**

▶ **TRIP** n an instance of going from one place to another ▶ *We took a **trip** to see an exhibit at the art museum. It is a short **trip** from here to the beach.*

JOURNEY a long trip, especially on land ▶ *The **journey** across the desert was very dangerous a hundred years ago.*

VOYAGE a long trip, especially by water ▶ *We took a long ocean **voyage** from Baltimore to Singapore.*

TOUR a trip in which several places are visited ▶ *This past summer we made a **tour** of six states in the Southwest.*

EXCURSION a short trip, especially to a place of interest ▶ *We made an **excursion** from our hotel to the shops along the riverfront.*

EXPEDITION a long trip for a special purpose, such as exploring ▶ *Admiral Peary led the first **expedition** to reach the North Pole.*

CRUISE a trip, especially a vacation trip, on a ship that docks at several places ▶ *Alex and Pam went on a honeymoon **cruise** in the Caribbean.*

▶ **TROOP** n a group of people or animals, especially an organized group of soldiers or scouts ▶ *Enemy **troops** surrounded the city. A great **troop** of tourists crowded into the exhibit.*

TROUPE a group of actors or performers ▶ *Martha joined a dance **troupe** that toured the country.*

COMPANY a group of people connected in some way; one or more guests; a group of performers ▶ *We have **company** for dinner. He joined the local theater **company**.*

see **BAND, GROUP, BUSINESS**

▶ **TROUBLE** n a difficult, dangerous, or upsetting situation ▶ *We knew we were in* **trouble** *when the wind began to blow the canoe away from shore.*

DIFFICULTY trouble or distress, especially trouble that is hard to deal with ▶ *We had great* **difficulty** *getting the tent set up in the storm.*

PREDICAMENT an awkward, embarrassing, or difficult situation ▶ *Sam was in a real* **predicament**—*the dog really had eaten his homework, but he knew no one would believe him!*

see PROBLEM

▶ **TRY** vb to make an effort; to do the best you can ▶ *I would like to* **try** *hang gliding someday. Maybe you can't jump over this, but why don't you* **try**?

ATTEMPT to make an effort ▶ *I will* **attempt** *to do a flip off the diving board. He* **attempted** *to fly, but of course he landed flat on his face.*

STRIVE to make a great effort ▶ *Bryn is* **striving** *to get all A's on her next report card.*

STRUGGLE to try very hard, especially in the face of difficulties ▶ *Maria* **struggled** *to climb the rope. He has been* **struggling** *to overcome his illness.*

▶ **TURN** vb to change direction; to move in a circular direction ▶ **Turn** *left at the corner.* **Turn** *to the right until you are facing east. To tune in the radio you have to* **turn** *this knob.*

SPIN to turn rapidly in a circular motion ▶ *The wheels were* **spinning** *so fast you couldn't see the spokes. Brett* **spun** *around to see what had happened.*

REVOLVE to keep turning in a circle or orbit around a central point or object; to move in a repeating circular motion ▶ *The moon* **revolves** *around the earth. Some hotels have* **revolving** *doors to save energy.*

A light breeze set the child's pinwheel **twirling**.

ROTATE to turn around and around an axis or center ▶ *The earth **rotates** on its axis once a day. Friction will stop the wheel from **rotating**.*

TWIRL to turn or spin around quickly and smoothly or gracefully ▶ *A light breeze set the child's pinwheel **twirling**. The dancers **twirled** in a shifting pattern of colors.*

SWIVEL to turn or rotate on a spot ▶ *Sharon **swiveled** in her seat. The needle of the compass **swivels** on a pin.*

PIVOT to turn on a pin or shaft; to turn suddenly, as if on a pin ▶ *Each gear **pivots** on an axle. Janice **pivoted** on her heel and left the room.*

WIND to turn or rotate in a circular motion ▶ *You have to **wind** the key to make this toy car go.*

see BEND, SWING

▶ **TYPE** n a group of objects or people similar to each other in a particular way ▶ *This **type** of rock formation is found only in deep canyons. Jan is a rather nervous **type** of person.*

KIND a group of the same or similar things ▶ *The beagle is my favorite **kind** of dog. What **kind** of pie do you want?*

SORT a type or kind ▶ *This is the **sort** of behavior that makes me mad! What **sort** of fool do you think I am?*

CLASS a group of people who are taught together; a group or set of similar things or people ▶ *Our **class** took a trip to the museum. Vowels and consonants are two different **classes** of speech sounds.*

CATEGORY one of several different classes to which something belongs ▶ *I arranged my books according to the **categories** fiction, nonfiction, and reference.*

tip

Type, **kind**, and **sort** are close synonyms and are usually interchangeable. They are used in very general ways in ordinary speech, although **sort** is more often used in negative or critical contexts than **type** and **kind**, as suggested by the examples above. **Class** and **category** are more precise in suggesting the nature of the group referred to.

What **sort** of fool do you think I am?

u

UGLY adj offensive or very unpleasant to look at ▶ *The accident left an **ugly** scar across his cheek.*

UNATTRACTIVE not pleasant or pretty to look at ▶ *That coat is much too big and **unattractive**.*

UNSIGHTLY not pleasing to look at ▶ *This ointment should help you get rid of those **unsightly** blemishes on your arm.*

HIDEOUS horrible or very ugly ▶ *I dreamed about a **hideous** giant insect.*

UNDER prep in or moving into a position so as to be covered, concealed, or overhung by something ▶ *Your shoes are **under** the table. I stepped **under** his umbrella when it began to rain.*

BELOW lower in position or value than ▶ *We looked across the valley far **below** us. The temperature dropped **below** freezing.*

BENEATH in or to a lower position than; directly under ▶ *Fish were swimming happily **beneath** the waves. We sat **beneath** a tree.*

UNDERNEATH directly under; hidden under ▶ *Write the date **underneath** your name. Miles of tunnels run **underneath** the city.*

UNION n the joining of two or more things to form a larger group; a group of workers organized to improve work conditions ▶ *The U.S. is a **union** of 50 states. Labor **unions** allow workers to bargain as a group for better wages and conditions.*

ASSOCIATION an organization, a club, or a society ▶ *The merchants in town form an **association** to make the downtown area cleaner and more beautiful.*

ALLIANCE a friendly agreement to work together; the group formed by such an agreement ▶ *The free trade **alliance** was signed by six nations in the region. The three islands formed an **alliance** to protect each other.*

FEDERATION a union of states, nations, or other groups joined together by an agreement ▶ *The International Ski **Federation** sets the rules for international and Olympic skiing competitions.*

UPSET vb to tip, turn, or knock over ▶ *Mary **upset** the glass of milk. I **upset** a lamp trying to walk through the room in the dark.*

OVERTURN to turn upside down or on the side ▶ *The trailer of a truck was **overturned** in the accident.*

CAPSIZE to turn over in the water (used of boats, ships, or rafts) ▶ *It is not as easy to **capsize** a canoe as you might think, but you still need to be careful.*

▸ **URGE** vb to try to persuade, to recommend, or to present strongly
▸ *Joni's father **urged** her to work a little harder.*

COAX to influence, urge, or persuade gently
▸ *We had to **coax** the parakeet back into its cage with its favorite treat. We've **coaxed** Jacqui into staying for supper.*

ENCOURAGE to give confidence by praise or support ▸ *We like to **encourage** the team by going to all the games. The teacher **encouraged** us to do our best.*

GOAD to tease or urge into doing something
▸ *Will was **goaded** into fighting by the constant taunts of the bully.*

PROD to push or urge into action
▸ *My parents had to **prod** me all week to study for my test.*

SPUR to urge or stimulate into action
▸ *I was **spurred** to run faster by the cheering of the crowd.*

tip

Goad, **prod**, and **spur** all derive from the use of a sharp or pointed rod or spur to make animals, such as cattle or horses, move where you want them to go. Thus, these words have stronger connotations than the others in this list. More than **spur**, **goad** and **prod** suggest an unwillingness on the part of the person being urged.

see **PERSUADE**

▸ **USE** vb 1 to do a job with
▸ *I **used** a penknife to cut through the wrapping. May I **use** your skis? I could really **use** some advice.*

EMPLOY to pay to work for you; to use, especially for a particular purpose
▸ *Mrs. Scott **employs** me to cut her grass in the summer. You will have to **employ** all your math skills to complete this project.*

UTILIZE to make use of; to turn to good or practical use ▸ *They discovered several ways to **utilize** the waste materials they had been throwing away for years.*

▸ **USE** vb 2 to spend or make use of until gone or made less *(often used with **up**)*
▸ *This truck **uses** far too much gasoline. Who **used** up all the soap?*

CONSUME to use up completely; to eat or drink; to destroy *(used especially of fire)*
▸ *Many trees are **consumed** to make paper. We **consumed** a quart of ice cream. The barn was **consumed** by the fire.*

DEPLETE to empty or to use up almost completely ▸ *The long strike **depleted** our savings.*

EXHAUST to use up entirely
▸ *By the end of the week our funds were **exhausted**. We have **exhausted** the supply of pencils.*

▶ **USEFUL** adj able to be used a lot for a good purpose ▶ *This is a very* **useful** *knife; it has a knife blade, a saw, scissors, and a can opener. Your advice proved very* **useful** *to me.*

HELPFUL being of help, service, or assistance; friendly and willing to help ▶ *The loan of your bike was very* **helpful** *for getting my paper route finished on time. She is a* **helpful** *friend.*

PRACTICAL able to be put to use ▶ *Her knowledge of Spanish turned out to be quite* **practical** *on our trip.*

HANDY easy to use ▶ *A small iron is a* **handy** *thing to take on vacation. This is a* **handy** *little gadget for unclogging drains.*

▶ **USELESS** adj having no use, function, purpose, or value; not capable of producing any result ▶ *What shall we do with all these* **useless** *broken tools? It's* **useless** *to ring that broken doorbell.*

FUTILE serving no useful purpose; absolutely without effect ▶ *It is* **futile** *to try raking the leaves on such a windy day.*

VAIN unsuccessful or without effect ▶ *Ben made a* **vain** *attempt to stop the bus.*

FRUITLESS without result ▶ *Weeks of effort to protect the town from the flood were* **fruitless***; the water washed right over the sandbags.*

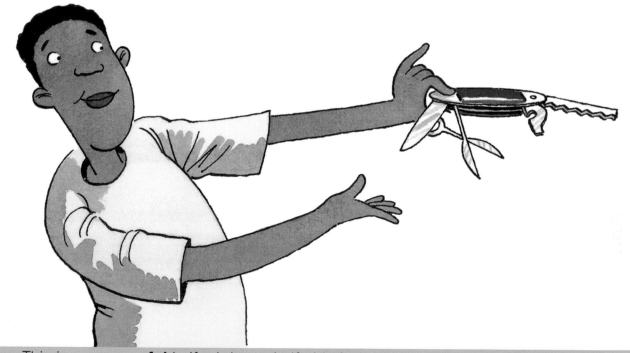

This is a very **useful** knife; it has a knife blade, a saw, scissors, and a can opener.

▶ **USUAL** adj normal, common, or expected
▶ *The baby is tired because she missed her* **usual** *nap today. Most of our friends will be at the party—all the* **usual** *crowd.*

REGULAR following a pattern or rule; according to habit or usual behavior
▶ *This is my* **regular** *route home. He is one of our* **regular** *customers; he buys a newspaper here every day.*

CUSTOMARY according to the usual customs or practices of a person or group

▶ *It is* **customary** *for me to sleep late on Saturdays. It is* **customary** *to leave a tip after eating at a restaurant.*

HABITUAL following a usual practice that is the result of habit; done over and over again
▶ *Kelly's father took his* **habitual** *seat at the head of the table. His* **habitual** *lies are upsetting his friends.*

see **COMMON, NORMAL**

It is **customary** for me to sleep late on Saturdays.

V

▶ **VALID** adj based on facts, evidence, or good sense; acceptable and supported by the proper authority or force
▶ *You can leave early if you have a valid reason. Do you have a valid passport?*

SOUND based on facts, logic, or evidence and free from mistakes
▶ *He presented a sound argument in favor of completing our project early. Molly usually gives sound advice.*

CONVINCING having the power to convince or overcome doubt
▶ *Your excuse for being late is not very convincing.*

see LEGAL

▶ **VEHICLE** n something in which people or goods are carried from one place to another
▶ *There were more than 70 vehicles of all sorts and sizes in the parade.*

AUTOMOBILE a passenger vehicle that usually has four wheels and is powered by an engine ▶ *Henry Ford was the first to produce automobiles on a large scale.*

TRUCK a large motor vehicle used for carrying goods by road
▶ *We had to rent a truck to move the piano from my grandmother's house to our house.*

see AIRPLANE, BOAT

▶ **VERIFY** vb to establish the truth or accuracy of ▶ *You will need to verify all your facts before you print this story in the school paper.*

PROVE to establish the truth or existence of, especially by using logic or evidence; to test the truth or genuineness of
▶ *We were never able to prove that she took the money. The trial proved his guilt in the robbery. The exception proves the rule.*

CONFIRM to remove doubt about the truth of ▶ *The rumors about the damage caused by the storm were confirmed by the news report.*

SUBSTANTIATE to verify with proof or evidence ▶ *Philip could not substantiate his claim that the wallet we found belonged to him.*

CORROBORATE to support or make more certain with evidence
▶ *Her story was corroborated by several witnesses to the accident.*

▶ **VERY** adv to a great extent; much, or most ▶ *I am very pleased to see you. This is a very happy occasion.*

EXTREMELY to a very great extent
▶ *It is extremely important that you get to the doctor's office on time. The weather is extremely cold today.*

UNUSUALLY to a greater extent than is usual ▸ *She is an **unusually** gifted musician. There was an **unusually** long line at the theater.*

GREATLY to a greater extent; very much ▸ *This revision of your essay is **greatly** improved. Your prompt reply would be **greatly** appreciated.*

ABSOLUTELY completely or totally ▸ *This afternoon is **absolutely** gorgeous. I was **absolutely** flabbergasted by this surprise party!*

▸ **VICTORY** n a win in a battle or contest ▸ *Our team had a party to celebrate our **victory** in the soccer tournament.*

TRIUMPH a great victory, success, or achievement ▸ *It was a **triumph** for Richard to win a full scholarship to college. Eliminating smallpox was a medical **triumph**.*

CONQUEST the act of conquering; something that is won, such as land, valuables, or buildings ▸ *The Roman **conquest** of Britain took many years. The **conquests** of Alexander the Great stretched from the eastern Mediterranean to India.*

▸ **VIEW** n the act of looking or seeing; what you can see from a certain place ▸ *Their first **view** of the mountains was from an airplane. The **view** from my window is lovely.*

SIGHT the ability to see; the act of seeing; the range or distance you can see; a view or something you can see

▸ *She lost her **sight** in an accident. It was love at first **sight**. Keep your suitcase in **sight**. The harbor is a beautiful **sight**.*

GLIMPSE a very brief or quick look at something ▸ *I just got a **glimpse** of his face as he walked past the door.*

SCENE a view or a picture; the place where something happens ▸ *Outside the window was a splendid **scene**. Sheila painted a wedding **scene**. The police rushed to the **scene** of the crime.*

VISION the power of seeing; a lovely or beautiful sight; something you imagine or dream about ▸ *Eagles have superb **vision**. In her youth, my mother was a **vision** of loveliness. He has **visions** of being famous.*

▸ **VIOLENT** adj showing or caused by great physical force; showing or caused by strong feeling or emotion ▸ ***Violent** thunderstorms ruined our camping trip. Ben has a **violent** temper.*

VEHEMENT marked by intense emotion; expressed very strongly ▸ *Roger had a **vehement** dislike of large dogs. Martha and Dennis launched into a **vehement** debate about the movie.*

INTENSE very strong; showing strong feeling ▸ *The fire gave off **intense** heat. When Jill concentrates, she gets an **intense** look on her face.*

DESTRUCTIVE causing lots of damage ▸ *Waves crashed into the pier with **destructive** force.*

see **WILD**

▸ **VOLUNTARY** adj done by your own free choice; controlled by your will
▸ *Jim made a voluntary decision to clean the garage. You move your arms and legs with voluntary muscles.*

INTENTIONAL done on purpose for a reason; not accidental ▸ *I'm sorry I stepped on your toe; it wasn't intentional.*

DELIBERATE planned and done on purpose, with an awareness of the consequences
▸ *She told a deliberate lie in order to avoid punishment.*

WILLFUL done by your own will, especially in an obstinate or stubborn way
▸ *Your willful refusal to help is making me upset.*

▸ **VOTE** n an expression of opinion, especially to approve or disapprove in a group decision or election

▸ *My vote is that we go biking. Marnie received most of the votes for class president.*

BALLOT a sheet of paper used to cast a secret vote or the record of a vote in a machine
▸ *It took several hours to count all the ballots cast in the election. I cast my ballot for president and vice president.*

ELECTION the act or process of choosing or deciding by voting
▸ *She won the election by only 15 votes.*

REFERENDUM a vote by the people on a public measure
▸ *The ballot included a referendum on building a new firehouse.*

I'm sorry I stepped on your toe; it wasn't **intentional**.

POLL a survey of opinions or beliefs
▶ *We took a **poll** to find out what people thought about closing the public swimming pool.*

▶ **VULGAR** adj in bad taste
▶ *We were told not to use **vulgar** language. There was an ornate and rather **vulgar** vase on the table, containing a few withered vines.*

TASTELESS not having or showing good taste
▶ *It was **tasteless** of her to ask about the will even before her uncle's funeral.*

INDECENT offensive to good morals or manners ▶ *He got in trouble for making **indecent** remarks to people passing by on the street.*

OBSCENE extremely offensive to good morals or manners
▶ *The film was rated R because it contains **obscene** language unsuitable for children.*

see **RUDE**

There was an ornate and rather **vulgar** vase on the table, containing a few withered vines.

W

WAIT vb to stay in a place or do nothing for a period of time until someone comes or something happens
▶ We **waited** an hour for the train.

REMAIN to stay in a place after others leave or are removed
▶ While we rode our bikes, my sister **remained** in the house. Six oranges **remain** in the bowl.

LINGER to stay, especially because you do not want to leave
▶ We **lingered** around the stage door, hoping to see the members of the band when they left.

LOITER to stand around, usually because you have nothing to do
▶ We just **loitered** around the house until the rain stopped. No **loitering** in the bus station.

WALK vb to move along by placing one foot on the ground before lifting the other
▶ I **walk** to school every morning. **Walk** down the stairs; don't run!

STROLL to walk in a slow, relaxed way
▶ Saadja and I **strolled** around the park for an hour.

MARCH to walk somewhere quickly and in a determined way; to walk together taking steps at the same time
▶ Elaine **marched** straight into her boss's office and demanded a raise. A column of soldiers **marched** down the street.

HIKE to walk vigorously, especially for a long distance through the countryside
▶ We **hiked** for six miles and camped by the river.

STRIDE to walk with long steps, especially in an active manner
▶ The team **strode** proudly across the field after winning the game.

TRUDGE to walk slowly and with effort
▶ The losing team **trudged** wearily into the locker room. I was so tired I could barely **trudge** upstairs to bed.

SHUFFLE to walk slowly, hardly raising your feet from the floor or ground
▶ Angela **shuffled** into the kitchen in her slippers to get a glass of milk.

STRUT to walk with a swagger or in an arrogant manner
▶ The bully **strutted** across the playground.

WANDER vb to move about without a particular purpose
▶ Marcia and Ron **wandered** around the mall for an hour until the shops opened.

ROAM to move about slowly or with no definite direction or destination
▶ All afternoon she **roamed** through the fields collecting wildflowers.

RAMBLE to move from place to place without purpose; to explore at leisure; to speak without sticking to the point
▶ *Todd **rambled** through the park. We **rambled** through the old mansion. The conversation **rambled** on meaninglessly.*

MEANDER to move slowly along a winding course or path
▶ *The river **meanders** across the open plain. His stories seemed to **meander** without end.*

STRAY to wander away or get lost
▶ *We **strayed** from the path and soon lost all sense of direction.*

DEVIATE to go in a different direction; to do differently from the usual or recommended way
▶ *The mail carrier **deviated** from her usual route. If you **deviate** from these instructions, the machine will not work.*

▶ **WANT** vb to feel that you would like to have, do, or get something; to need or require
▶ *I **want** an apple. She **wants** to go on vacation. What this story **wants** is some suspense.*

DESIRE to have a strong wish or need for
▶ *Do you **desire** another glass of milk? Margaret simply **desired** an afternoon of quiet.*

CRAVE to want desperately
▶ *Tonight I **crave** some seafood for dinner. After three weeks of solid rain, I absolutely **crave** some sunshine.*

see ENVY, NEED

▶ **WARN** vb to tell about a serious danger or bad thing that might happen
▶ *The weather report **warned** us that a hurricane was coming toward us.*

CAUTION to urge to be cautious or careful
▶ *The police officer didn't give me a ticket, but she **cautioned** me to stop driving so fast.*

ALERT to warn that there might be danger; to make aware of
▶ *They **alerted** the fire department that the storm was likely to knock down some electrical lines.*

see SCARE, TELL

▶ **WARNING** n something that tells you of possible danger or harm
▶ *The label included a **warning** not to take the medicine on an empty stomach. **Warning**: Smoking is bad for your health.*

ALARM a sound, noise, or flashing light that wakes people or warns them of danger; a device that produces this
▶ *I didn't hear the **alarm** this morning. When the fire **alarm** goes off, leave the building by the nearest exit.*

SIGNAL anything agreed upon to send a message or warning
▶ *When I wave my hand, it will be a **signal** to start the race. Always obey the traffic **signals**.*

ADMONITION a gentle or friendly warning or rebuke
▶ *The principal gave us a final **admonition** about making too much noise.*

▶ **WASTE** vb to use or spend something carelessly or foolishly
▶ *Don't **waste** your time. Martha's dad thinks she **wastes** her money on magazines.*

SQUANDER to spend something recklessly or wastefully
▶ *Ezra **squandered** his entire fortune gambling and had to sell his house and car to pay his debts.*

▶ **WEAK** adj having little strength, force, or power
▶ *David's leg muscles grew **weak** after being in a cast for so long. Janice's argument was very **weak** and she lost the debate.*

FEEBLE very weak
▶ *The patient had become so **feeble** he couldn't even feed himself. The baby bird gave a **feeble** little cry.*

Martha's dad thinks she **wastes** her money on magazines.

HELPLESS not able to care for or look after yourself
▶ *A human child is virtually **helpless** for the first few years of life.*

PUNY small and weak or underdeveloped
▶ *Randy was a **puny** child, but now he's over six feet tall. Sam was the **puniest** puppy in the litter, but also the cutest.*

DELICATE finely made and easily hurt or damaged; not very strong and becoming ill easily
▶ *Don't touch that crystal bowl; it is very **delicate**. Ted was a **delicate** boy who was often in the hospital.*

FRAGILE weak and delicate and liable to break easily
▶ *Please pack the good china very carefully because it is quite **fragile**.*

FLIMSY thin and easily broken; not well made; not believable
▶ *Some people live in **flimsy** shacks made of cardboard. The **flimsy** TV antenna blew down in the storm. What a **flimsy** excuse!*

▶ **WELL** adv in a good or skillful way
▶ *Jenna did **well** on her science test.*

PROPERLY in a correct, appropriate, or suitable way ▶ *Can he do the job **properly**? We are all **properly** equipped for our camping trip.*

THOROUGHLY carefully and completely
▶ *Be sure to wash your hands **thoroughly** when you are finished gardening.*

COMPETENTLY in a way that meets all the necessary requirements
▶ *She does her work **competently** and efficiently.*

SATISFACTORILY in a way that is good enough, but not outstanding
▶ *She answered the questions **satisfactorily**, but she would have gotten a better grade if she had written more.*

ADEQUATELY in a way that is just enough or just good enough
▶ *He has been doing his job **adequately**, but not well enough to get a pay raise this month.*

▶ **WET** adj covered with or containing water or other liquid
▶ *Be careful; the floor is slippery when it is **wet**. Everything on my desk got **wet** when the roof started leaking again.*

SOAKED completely wet
▶ *We both got **soaked** when a car drove through the puddle. It was very hot, and my shirt was soon **soaked** with sweat.*

DRENCHED extremely wet
▶ *By the time we got back to the cabin we were **drenched** to the skin.*

SATURATED having absorbed as much liquid, moisture, or odor as possible
▶ *The rags quickly became **saturated** with oil as Jill cleaned the engine. The room was **saturated** with the smell of her perfume.*

SODDEN heavy with water or moisture
▶ *After three days of rain it was hard to dig in the **sodden** ground.*

see DAMP

▶ **WILD** adj natural and not controlled or tamed by humans; not controllable
▶ *A flock of **wild** geese flew over. This little flower grows **wild** all around here. What can I do about their **wild** behavior?*

UNTAMED not tamed or domesticated; not gentle or easy to control
▶ *We have two **untamed** horses that have never been ridden.*

FIERCE having a violent or cruel nature; violent and uncontrolled
▶ *The tiger is a **fierce** hunter. I'm afraid I have a **fierce** temper. A **fierce** storm blew down several trees last night.*

FEROCIOUS extremely violent or brutal
▶ *We were chased through the field by a **ferocious** bull.*

SAVAGE not tamed; dangerous or violent
▶ *Michael was making a film about the **savage** beasts of the African plains. The enemy made a **savage** attack on the city.*

see **VIOLENT**

▶ **WILL** n the power to choose what you do and do not do; a strong sense of purpose
▶ *Eli decided to rake the garden of his own free **will**. Cicely has an amazing **will** to succeed.*

WILLPOWER strength of mind and purpose
▶ *It takes a lot of **willpower** to stay on a strict diet.*

DETERMINATION the power of deciding firmly to do or try something
▶ *He has a strong **determination** to do well at his new job.*

RESOLUTION firmness of mind and purpose, along with the will to overcome difficulties or opposition
▶ *Susannah approached the difficult task with great **resolution**.*

▶ **WIN** vb to come in first in a contest; to gain or deserve ▶ *Rebecca **won** first prize for her poem. Alex worked hard to **win** the respect of his teachers.*

TRIUMPH to obtain victory ▶ *The basketball team **triumphed** over their opponents in the last few seconds of the game.*

PREVAIL to succeed in spite of difficulties; to be common or usual ▶ *Justice **prevailed** when the innocent woman was acquitted. Poverty and crime **prevail** in many cities.*

SUCCEED to manage to do; to do well or get what you want ▶ *Bill **succeeded** in fixing the car. Carlotta **succeeds** at everything she does.*

The tiger is a **fierce** hunter.

▶ **WIND** n moving air ▶ *This steady **wind** should be good for flying our kites.*

BREEZE a gentle wind
▶ *The **breeze** along the seashore was very refreshing after a hot week in the city.*

GALE a strong wind, especially one ranging from 32 to 63 miles per hour
▶ *It was hard to walk upright against such a strong **gale**. **Gale** force winds knocked down trees and power lines.*

TEMPEST a violent storm with strong winds
▶ *The ship was tossed about on the waves by a fierce **tempest**.*

GUST a sudden strong blast of wind
▶ *An unexpected **gust** of wind blew away her umbrella.*

▶ **WISDOM** n the quality of being wise; the ability to use your intelligence and experience wisely ▶ *There is a certain **wisdom** that grows with age. I rely on my grandfather's **wisdom** to help me make important decisions.*

JUDGMENT the ability to decide or to form opinions wisely
▶ *They showed good **judgment** in deciding not to drink and drive.*

KNOWLEDGE the things that someone knows; awareness or a clear idea
▶ *The quiz tested our **knowledge**. The **knowledge** that he would be punished stopped the boy from misbehaving.*

REASON the ability to think logically and clearly and to make sound decisions
▶ *It is better to be guided by **reason** than by desire, greed, and envy.*

UNDERSTANDING the ability to know what something means or how something works; the ability to have sympathy
▶ *Risa has enough **understanding** and intelligence to do well this year. Don has a good **understanding** of young children.*

Don has a good **understanding** of young children.

▶ **WOMAN** n an adult female person
▶ *Who is that **woman** in the gray coat? She is a very successful **woman** who owns her own company.*

LADY a woman; a girl or woman who has good manners ▶ *Good evening, **ladies** and gentlemen. She is a charming **lady** with a smile for everyone.*

GIRL a female child or young woman
▶ *There are 11 **girls** in my class.*

WIFE a married woman, especially when referred to in relation to her husband
▶ *His **wife** is a famous writer.*

FEMALE a person or an animal of the sex that gives birth to young animals or lays eggs
▶ *The police have arrested a **female** suspect. Many male birds are brightly colored, while the **females** are duller for camouflage.*

---

tip

Woman comes from the Anglo-Saxon word *wifman*, which literally meant "a person who is a woman."

Wife is from Anglo-Saxon *wif*, which originally meant simply "a woman," whether married or not.

Lady is derived from the Anglo-Saxon *hlœfdige*, "the one who kneads bread."

Girl first appeared in the thirteenth century, spelled *gurle* or *girle*, and originally meant "a child of either sex."

Female does not come from the word *male*, but from the Latin *femella* "a young woman."

see HUMAN BEING, HUMANITY, MAN

▶ **WORK** n physical or mental effort to make or achieve something ▶ *My **work** as a volunteer is very rewarding. How much **work** will it take to build this fence?*

LABOR hard work ▶ *It took immense amounts of **labor** to build the pyramids.*

TOIL long, continuous hard work
▶ *Writing this book required long hours of **toil** for over a year.*

EFFORT the energy necessary to do something; something hard to do
▶ *The **effort** of running all the way home made me tired and hungry. It was quite an **effort** to climb all those stairs.*

DRUDGERY boring, tiring work
▶ *The company is trying to take the **drudgery** out of working on the assembly line.*

see JOB

▶ **WORRY** n a feeling of being troubled, especially about some problem ▶ *His greatest **worry** was that he would not wake up in time to catch the plane.*

CONCERN a feeling of being troubled about something you have affection for or interest in ▶ *The speeding traffic caused great **concern** about the safety of children crossing the road on the way to school.*

CARE a feeling of worry, especially caused by responsibility ▶ *Jake is always happy and acts like he doesn't have a **care** in the world.*

ANXIETY a feeling of fear or worry about something that might happen ▶ *For no good reason, Martha felt a sense of **anxiety** that something would ruin her vacation.*

▶ **WORTH** n the quality that makes something valuable or important; the amount of something you can get for a certain sum
▶ *Do you know the* **worth** *of a good education? I asked for five dollars'* **worth** *of stamps.*

VALUE the fair equivalent in money or goods for something sold or traded
▶ *What is the* **value** *of this watch?*

IMPORTANCE the quality of being important or of having great worth or significance
▶ *The development of the arch was of great* **importance** *in the history of architecture.*

BENEFIT something that provides help or gives an advantage
▶ *The smallpox vaccine was a great* **benefit** *to humanity. The donation of these books will be a* **benefit** *to our library.*

MERIT a good point or quality in a person or a thing
▶ *What are the* **merits** *of your invention?*

VIRTUE a desirable or beneficial quality or trait
▶ *One of the* **virtues** *of this umbrella is that it folds up very small.*

▶ **WRITER** n a person who writes, especially one whose job is to write
▶ *It is not easy to make a living as a* **writer**.

AUTHOR the writer of a book, play, article, or poem ▶ *Their mother is the* **author** *of two books of poetry and a novel.*

REPORTER someone who gathers, writes, and reports the news for radio, television, a newspaper, or a magazine
▶ *A* **reporter** *from the local newspaper came to interview us about our new school.*

JOURNALIST someone who collects information and writes articles for radio, television, a newspaper, or a magazine
▶ *Danny is a* **journalist** *who writes about new developments in science for a national newspaper.*

> **tip**
>
> Some synonyms for **writer** indicate a particular kind of writing: **novelist, poet, playwright, historian, biographer, screenwriter, essayist.**

What are the **merits** of your invention?

▶ **WRONG** adj not correct or not true; bad or immoral
▶ *There were three **wrong** answers on my test. It is **wrong** to steal.*

INCORRECT not correct, accurate, or true; improper
▶ *We were given **incorrect** information about when the plane would arrive. Henry was punished for his **incorrect** behavior.*

FALSE not genuine; not true or correct, sometimes intentionally
▶ *My grandmother has **false** teeth. The witness gave **false** testimony at the trial.*

MISTAKEN having an incorrect understanding of something; misunderstood
▶ *You are **mistaken** if you think I will drive you to the mall. My brother was blamed, but it was just a case of **mistaken** identity.*

INACCURATE not very precise or correct
▶ *This cheap clock seems to be **inaccurate** more often than it is correct.*

ERRONEOUS containing errors
▶ *The suspect gave **erroneous** information to the police about where he had been that night.*

▶ **XYLOPHONE** n a musical instrument with bars of different lengths that are struck with small hammers to give different notes
▶ *The notes on a **xylophone** are arranged like those on a piano.*

MARIMBA a type of xylophone with long, hollow resonators beneath the bars to increase the sound
▶ *The **marimba** originated in Africa.*

VIBRAPHONE a type of marimba with electrically operated valves in the resonators to make the sound vibrate
▶ *The **vibraphone** is a popular jazz instrument.*

GLOCKENSPIEL a portable instrument like a xylophone, with metal bars in a frame
▶ *Many marching bands include a **glockenspiel** because of the clear, bell-like sound it makes.*

The **vibraphone** is a popular jazz instrument.

y

▶ **YELL** vb to cry out in a loud voice, as in surprise, anger, or to attract attention ▶ *Mother **yelled** at us for tracking mud through the house. The crowd **yelled** excitedly when the team scored again.*

SHOUT to cry out in a loud voice, especially to be heard a long distance or above other sounds ▶ *Mason **shouted**, "Timber!" as the tree began to fall.*

SCREAM to cry out loudly in a high voice, especially out of fear, horror, or pain ▶ *Billy **screamed** when he saw a large spider walking up his arm.*

SHRIEK to cry out in a shrill, piercing way ▶ *The whole audience **shrieked** when the monster suddenly appeared on the screen.*

SCREECH to make a high, unpleasant sound ▶ *I could hear two cats fighting and **screeching** in the darkness. The car **screeched** to a halt.*

BELLOW to roar or cry out loudly with a powerful sound ▶ *We heard a bull moose **bellow** across the lake. Fred **bellowed** in pain when the rock fell on his foot.*

tip

All of these words are also used as nouns: *Give a **yell** if you need help. Phil heard a **shout** coming from the barn. I gave a **scream** when the wind blew the door shut. There were **shrieks** of laughter coming from the children's bedroom. The car came to a stop with a **screech** of brakes. We could hear the coach's **bellow** from the other end of the field. Was that the **call** of an owl?*

see CALL

▶ **YOUNG** adj having lived or existed for only a short time ▶ *Sammy is too **young** to ride the bus by himself.*

YOUTHFUL not yet mature or old; having the energy or freshness of youth ▶ *We had a **youthful** audience of schoolchildren from several towns. He stays **youthful** by exercising every day.*

IMMATURE young and not fully developed; acting in a silly or childish way ▶ *The **immature** ducks all have brown feathers for camouflage. Peggy got into trouble for acting so **immature** in class.*

JUVENILE childish or immature; suitable for young people ▶ *His **juvenile** behavior began to annoy his sister. The library has a special section for **juvenile** books.*

see CHILDISH

▶ **ZONE** n a space that is separate from others and used for a special purpose
▶ *Dad got a ticket for parking in a No Parking zone. The quarterback carried the ball into the end zone and scored a touchdown.*

AREA a space on a surface, especially one that is marked by boundaries or is in some way different from others around it
▶ *This whole area of the state is covered with forests. They live in a very poor area of town.*

REGION a large area, especially one characterized by some specific feature

▶ *This hardy little flower is found in many mountainous regions. What region of the brain controls your eyesight?*

DISTRICT a locality with known boundaries or with some clearly defined feature
▶ *We live in the Twelfth Congressional District. We went to see a show in the theater district of the city.*

BELT an area or strip that is marked by some particular feature ▶ *Our family has farmed in the corn belt for four generations. There is a wide belt of parkland surrounding the city.*

Dad got a ticket for parking in a No Parking **zone**.

Index

All headwords (in capital letters) and synonyms are listed here in alphabetical order. The headword for the entry in which a word will be found is listed immediately after the word *see*. Many of the headwords in this index are followed by a *see also* cross-reference listing other entries with closely related synonyms. Antonyms to many of the headwords are shown in *ITALIC CAPITALS*.

FOG . . . . *see* FOG
FOLLOW . . . . *see* FOLLOW *LEAD*
fond, be fond of *see* LIKE
fondle . . . . *see* PET
fondness . . . . . *see* LOVE n
fool . . . . *see* CHEAT
FOOLISH . . . . *see* FOOLISH
. . . . *see also* FUNNY,
STUPID *SMART*
FORBID . . . . *see* FORBID
FORCE vb . . . . . *see* FORCE
force n . . . . *see* STRENGTH
forecast . . . . . . *see* PREDICT
FOREIGN . . . . . . *see* FOREIGN
FOREIGNER . . . . *see* FOREIGNER
foretell . . . . . . *see* PREDICT
forfeit . . . . *see* LOSE 2
FORGET . . . . *see* FORGET
REMEMBER
FORGIVE . . . . . . *see* FORGIVE
FORM . . . . *see* FORM
see also BUILD,
INVENT, MAKE
formerly . . . . . . *see* ONCE
fort . . . . *see* CASTLE
fortitude . . . . . *see* COURAGE
fraction . . . . . . *see* PART
fracture . . . . . . *see* BREAK
fragile . . . . *see* WEAK
fragment . . . . . *see* PART
fragrance . . . . . *see* SMELL
FREE . . . . *see* FREE
FREEDOM . . . . . . *see* FREEDOM
freezing . . . . . . *see* COLD
frequently . . . . *see* OFTEN
fresh . . . . *see* NEW
FRIEND . . . . *see* FRIEND *ENEMY*
FRIENDLY . . . . . . *see* FRIENDLY
see also NICE
fright . . . . *see* FEAR
frighten . . . . . . *see* SCARE
frightened . . . . *see* AFRAID
frigid . . . . *see* COLD
FROG . . . . *see* FROG
frosty . . . . *see* COLD
frugal . . . . *see* CHEAP 2
fruitless . . . . . . *see* USELESS
FULL . . . . *see* FULL, COMPLETE
EMPTY
full-grown . . . . *see* ADULT
fun . . . . *see* PLEASURE

FUNCTION n . . . . *see* FUNCTION
see also DUTY, JOB
function vb . . . *see* ACT
FUNNY . . . . *see* FUNNY, STRANGE
see also FOOLISH
furious . . . . *see* ANGRY
fury . . . . *see* ANGER
fussy . . . . *see* CROSS
futile . . . . *see* USELESS

g

gadget . . . . *see* TOOL
gag . . . . *see* JOKE
gain . . . . *see* GET
gale . . . . *see* WIND
GAME . . . . *see* GAME
gang . . . . *see* GROUP
garbage . . . . . . *see* TRASH
garment . . . . . . *see* CLOTHES
gateway . . . . . . *see* DOOR
GATHER . . . . *see* GATHER
see also SAVE 2
gathering . . . . . *see* PARTY
gaze . . . . *see* LOOK
genius . . . . *see* TALENT
GENTLE . . . . *see* GENTLE
gentleman . . . . *see* MAN
genuine . . . . . . *see* REAL
GET . . . . *see* GET
see also CATCH, SEIZE
ghost . . . . *see* SOUL
gibber . . . . *see* CHATTER
GIFT . . . . *see* GIFT
gift . . . . *see* TALENT
giggle . . . . *see* LAUGH
girl . . . . *see* WOMAN
girlfriend . . . . . *see* FRIEND
GIVE . . . . *see* GIVE
glad . . . . *see* HAPPY
glance . . . . *see* LOOK
glaring . . . . *see* BRIGHT
GLASS . . . . *see* GLASS
glide . . . . *see* FLY
glimpse . . . . . . *see* VIEW
gloat . . . . *see* BOAST
glockenspiel . . *see* XYLOPHONE
gloomy . . . . *see* DARK, SAD
glow . . . . *see* BURN
glowing . . . . . . *see* BRIGHT

GO . . . . *see* GO
see also LEAVE, MOVE,
TRAVEL *COME*
goad . . . . *see* URGE
GOOD . . . . *see* GOOD
see also FAIR, GREAT,
NICE *BAD*
good-natured . *see* NICE
gorgeous . . . . . *see* PRETTY
gossip . . . . *see* RUMOR
GOVERN . . . . *see* GOVERN
see also CONTROL
G.P. . . . . *see* DOCTOR
grab . . . . *see* SEIZE
gracious . . . . . . *see* POLITE
gradual . . . . . . *see* SLOW
grain . . . . *see* ATOM 2
GRAND . . . . *see* GRAND
grant n . . . . *see* GIFT
grant vb . . . . . . *see* GIVE
GRATEFUL . . . . . . *see* GRATEFUL
gratify . . . . *see* PLEASE
grave adj . . . . . *see* SERIOUS
graze . . . . *see* EAT
GREAT . . . . *see* GREAT
see also GOOD,
GRAND, NICE
greatly . . . . *see* VERY
GREEDY . . . . *see* GREEDY,
JEALOUS
grimy . . . . *see* DIRTY
grin . . . . *see* SMILE
gripe . . . . *see* COMPLAIN
grouchy . . . . . . *see* CROSS
GROUP . . . . *see* GROUP
see also BAND, TROOP
GROW . . . . *see* GROW
grown-up . . . . *see* ADULT
grumble . . . . . . *see* COMPLAIN
guard . . . . *see* PROTECT
GUESS . . . . *see* GUESS
guffaw . . . . *see* LAUGH
guide . . . . *see* LEAD 1
gust . . . . *see* WIND
guts . . . . *see* COURAGE
guy . . . . *see* MAN

HABIT . . . . *see* HABIT

habitual. . . . . . *see* USUAL
hallowed . . . . . *see* HOLY
halt. . . . . *see* STOP
handsome . . . . *see* PRETTY
handy. . . . . *see* USEFUL
HAPPEN . . . . . . *see* HAPPEN
HAPPY . . . . *see* HAPPY *SAD*
HARD . . . . *see* HARD, FIRM *EASY*
hardly. . . . . *see* ONLY
hardy . . . . *see* STRONG
harmless. . . . . . *see* SAFE
haste. . . . . *see* SPEED
hasten. . . . . . . *see* HURRY
HATE. . . . . *see* HATE *LOVE*
haul. . . . . *see* CARRY, PULL
hazard . . . . . . *see* DANGER
haze . . . . *see* FOG
head . . . . *see* BOSS
headstrong . . . *see* STUBBORN
HEAL. . . . . *see* HEAL
hearsay. . . . . . *see* RUMOR
heart. . . . . *see* MIDDLE
HEAVY . . . . *see* HEAVY
heed . . . . *see* OBEY
hefty. . . . . *see* HEAVY 1
HEIGHT. . . . . . . *see* HEIGHT
HELP. . . . . *see* HELP
helpful . . . . . . *see* USEFUL
helpless . . . . . *see* WEAK
hence . . . . *see* THEREFORE
heroic. . . . . . . *see* BRAVE
HIDE. . . . . *see* HIDE *REVEAL*
hideous . . . . . *see* UGLY
HIGH. . . . . *see* HIGH
hike. . . . . *see* WALK
hilarious. . . . . . *see* FUNNY
hinder. . . . . . . *see* PREVENT
hint. . . . . *see* SUGGEST 2
HIRE . . . . *see* HIRE
history . . . . . . *see* STORY
HIT . . . . *see* HIT
        see also KNOCK

hoard . . . . *see* SAVE 2
hoist . . . . *see* LIFT
hold . . . . *see* CONTAIN, OWN
HOLE. . . . . *see* HOLE
hollow adj . . . . *see* EMPTY
hollow n . . . . . *see* HOLE
HOLY. . . . . *see* HOLY
home. . . . . *see* HOUSE
homesick . . . . . *see* LONELY

homograph. . . *see* HOMONYM
HOMONYM. . . . . *see* HOMONYM
homophone. . . *see* HOMONYM
honor . . . . *see* PRIZE, RESPECT n
hoodwink. . . . . *see* CHEAT
hop . . . . *see* JUMP
HOPE . . . . *see* HOPE
horde . . . . *see* CROWD
horrible . . . . . *see* AWFUL
horror. . . . . . . *see* FEAR
HORSE. . . . . . . *see* HORSE
host. . . . . *see* CROWD
HOT . . . . *see* HOT *COLD*
hound. . . . . . . *see* DOG
HOUSE . . . . . . *see* HOUSE
however. . . . . . *see* BUT conj
hub. . . . . *see* MIDDLE
hubbub . . . . . . *see* NOISE
huge. . . . . *see* BIG
human . . . . . . *see* HUMAN BEING
HUMAN BEING . . *see* HUMAN BEING
        see also HUMANITY,
        MAN, WOMAN
HUMANITY. . . . . *see* HUMANITY
        see also HUMAN
        BEING, MAN, WOMAN
humankind . . . *see* HUMANITY
HUMBLE . . . . . . *see* HUMBLE *PROUD*
humid. . . . . . . *see* DAMP
humor. . . . . . . *see* PAMPER
humorous. . . . . *see* FUNNY
HUNT . . . . *see* HUNT
hurl. . . . . *see* THROW
hurry n . . . . . . *see* SPEED
HURRY vb . . . . . *see* HURRY
husband. . . . . . *see* MAN
hustle . . . . *see* HURRY
hut . . . . *see* HOUSE
hypothesis. . . . *see* THEORY

icy. . . . . *see* COLD
IDEA. . . . . *see* IDEA
        see also THEORY
ideal. . . . . *see* PERFECT
identical. . . . . . *see* SAME
ignorant. . . . . . *see* STUPID
ill. . . . . *see* SICK
illness. . . . . . . *see* SICKNESS

imagine. . . . . . *see* GUESS
IMITATE . . . . . . *see* IMITATE
imitation . . . . . *see* FAKE
immature. . . . . *see* YOUNG
immigrant. . . . . *see* FOREIGNER
impartial . . . . . *see* FAIR
impeccable. . . *see* PERFECT
impertinent. . . *see* RUDE
impetuous. . . . *see* SUDDEN
implement. . . . *see* TOOL
imply . . . . *see* SUGGEST 2
impolite. . . . . . *see* RUDE
importance. . . . *see* WORTH
IMPORTANT . . . *see* IMPORTANT
        see also NECESSARY

imported . . . . . *see* FOREIGN
impress. . . . . . *see* AFFECT
impression. . . . *see* IDEA
impudent. . . . . *see* RUDE
inaccurate . . . . *see* WRONG
incessant . . . . . *see* CONTINUAL
incident. . . . . . *see* EVENT
incinerate . . . . *see* BURN
incline . . . . . . *see* SLANT
include. . . . . . . *see* CONTAIN
inconsiderate . *see* THOUGHTLESS
incorrect . . . . . *see* WRONG
increase . . . . . *see* GROW
indebted . . . . . *see* GRATEFUL
indecent. . . . . . *see* VULGAR
independence. *see* FREEDOM
indignation. . . *see* ANGER
indispensable. *see* NECESSARY
indistinct. . . . . *see* DIM
individual . . . . *see* HUMAN BEING
indoor. . . . . . . *see* INSIDE
indulge. . . . . . . *see* PAMPER
industry. . . . . . *see* BUSINESS 1
inexpensive. . . *see* CHEAP 1
infant. . . . . *see* CHILD
influence. . . . . *see* AFFECT, PERSUADE
inform . . . . *see* TELL
INFORMATION. . . *see* INFORMATION
inner. . . . . *see* INSIDE
inquire. . . . . . . *see* ASK
inquiry. . . . . . . *see* QUESTION
inquisitive. . . . *see* CURIOUS
insect . . . . *see* BUG
INSIDE . . . . *see* INSIDE
insinuate . . . . . *see* SUGGEST 2
insolent . . . . . *see* RUDE

pledge . . . . *see* PROMISE
plot . . . . *see* PLAN
plunge . . . . . . *see* FALL
poke . . . . *see* PUSH
POLITE . . . . *see* POLITE
        see also FRIENDLY,
        THOUGHTFUL *RUDE*

poll . . . . *see* VOTE
ponder . . . . . . *see* CONSIDER, THINK
ponderous . . . . *see* HEAVY 1, 2
pony . . . . *see* HORSE
POOR . . . . *see* POOR *RICH*
portion . . . . . . *see* PART
positive . . . . . *see* SURE
possess . . . . . . *see* OWN
possessive . . . . *see* GREEDY
POSSIBLE . . . . . . *see* POSSIBLE
possibly . . . . . *see* MAYBE
postpone . . . . . *see* DELAY
pound . . . . *see* HIT
power . . . . *see* STRENGTH, RIGHT
powerful . . . . *see* STRONG
practical . . . . . *see* USEFUL, POSSIBLE
practical joke . *see* JOKE
practice . . . . . *see* HABIT
prank . . . . *see* JOKE
prattle . . . . . . *see* CHATTER
precipitation . . *see* RAIN
precise . . . . . . *see* CORRECT
predicament . . *see* TROUBLE
PREDICT . . . . . . *see* PREDICT
PREJUDICE . . . . . . *see* PREJUDICE
prepared . . . . . *see* READY
prerogative . . . *see* RIGHT
present n . . . . *see* GIFT
present vb . . . . *see* GIVE, OFFER,
        SHOW

preserve . . . . . *see* SAVE 2
press . . . . *see* PUSH
presume . . . . . . *see* GUESS
PRETTY . . . . *see* PRETTY *UGLY*
prevail . . . . . . *see* WIN
PREVENT . . . . *see* PREVENT
        see also STOP

previously . . . . *see* ONCE
PRIDE . . . . *see* PRIDE
priest . . . . *see* MINISTER
principal . . . . . *see* IMPORTANT
principle . . . . . *see* RULE
prison . . . . *see* JAIL

privilege . . . . . *see* RIGHT
PRIZE n . . . . *see* PRIZE
prize vb . . . . . *see* APPRECIATE
probable . . . . . *see* POSSIBLE
PROBLEM . . . . . . *see* PROBLEM
        see also TROUBLE
proceed . . . . . . *see* GO
prod . . . . *see* URGE
produce . . . . . . *see* MAKE
profession . . . . *see* BUSINESS 2
program . . . . . . *see* LIST
progress . . . . . *see* GO
prohibit . . . . . *see* FORBID
project . . . . . . *see* PLAN
prolong . . . . . . *see* LENGTHEN
prominent . . . . *see* FAMOUS
PROMISE . . . . . . *see* PROMISE
PROOF . . . . *see* PROOF
proper . . . . . . *see* FIT
properly . . . . . *see* WELL
property . . . . . *see* MONEY,
        QUALITY
prophesy . . . . . *see* PREDICT
propose . . . . . . *see* INTEND, SUGGEST 1
prosperous . . . . *see* RICH
PROTECT . . . . . . *see* PROTECT
        ATTACK
protected . . . . *see* SAFE
protest . . . . . . *see* COMPLAIN,
        OBJECT vb
PROUD . . . . *see* PROUD *HUMBLE*
prove . . . . *see* VERIFY
proverb . . . . . . *see* SAYING
prying . . . . . . *see* CURIOUS
PSEUDONYM . . . . *see* PSEUDONYM
PULL . . . . *see* PULL *PUSH*
punch . . . . *see* HIT
PUNISH . . . . *see* PUNISH
puny . . . . *see* WEAK
puppy . . . . *see* DOG
purpose . . . . . . *see* REASON
pursue . . . . . . *see* FOLLOW 2
PUSH . . . . *see* PUSH *PULL*
PUT . . . . *see* PUT
puzzle n . . . . . *see* PROBLEM
puzzle vb . . . . . *see* CONFUSE

q

quake . . . . *see* SHAKE

qualified . . . . . *see* ABLE, READY
QUALITY . . . . . . *see* QUALITY
quantity . . . . . *see* NUMBER 2
quarrel n . . . . *see* ARGUMENT
quarrel vb . . . . *see* ARGUE
queen . . . . *see* KING
query . . . . *see* QUESTION
QUESTION n . . . . *see* QUESTION
question vb . . . *see* ASK, DOUBT vb
questionable . . *see* DOUBTFUL
quick . . . . *see* FAST
QUIET . . . . *see* QUIET
        see also CALM *LOUD*
quit . . . . *see* SURRENDER
quiver . . . . *see* SHAKE
QUOTE . . . . *see* QUOTE

r

rabbi . . . . *see* MINISTER
race . . . . *see* RUN
racket . . . . *see* NOISE
radiant . . . . . . *see* BRIGHT
rage . . . . *see* ANGER
RAIN . . . . *see* RAIN
raise . . . . *see* LIFT
ramble . . . . . . *see* WANDER
rancid . . . . *see* SOUR
rap . . . . *see* KNOCK
rapid . . . . *see* FAST
reach . . . . *see* COME
READY . . . . *see* READY
REAL . . . . *see* REAL
        see also FAKE
realize . . . . . . *see* DISCOVER 2,
        KNOW
REASON n . . . . . *see* REASON, WISDOM
reason vb . . . . . *see* THINK
reasonable . . . . *see* CHEAP 1
recall . . . . *see* REMEMBER
receive . . . . . . *see* GET
recent . . . . *see* NEW
reception . . . . *see* PARTY
reckless . . . . . *see* THOUGHTLESS
recognize . . . . *see* KNOW
recollect . . . . . *see* REMEMBER
recommend . . . *see* SUGGEST 1
recreation . . . . *see* GAME
referee . . . . . . *see* JUDGE
referendum . . . *see* VOTE